Barter, exchange and value

This book concerns barter, a transaction in which objects are exchanged directly for one another without the use of money. Economists treat barter as an inefficient alternative to market exchange, and assume that it is normal only in 'primitive' economies or marks the breakdown of more developed exchange mechanisms. For their part, anthropologists have been more interested in the social and moral complexities of the 'gift', and treat barter dismissively as mere haggling.

The authors in this collection do not accept that barter occupies a residual space between monetary and gift economies. Using accounts from different parts of the world, they aim to demonstrate that it is more than a simple and self-evident economic institution. Barter may constitute a mode of exchange with its own social characteristics occupying a specific moral space. This novel treatment of barter represents an original and topical addition to the literature on economic anthropology.

Inter-ethnic barter in the early nineteenth century from Louis Claude de Saules de Freycinet, *Voyages Autour du Monde*, plates vol., Paris, 1824–6. (By permission of the Syndics of Cambridge University Library.)

Barter, exchange and value

An anthropological approach

Edited by

Caroline Humphrey

University Lecturer in Social Anthropology, University of Cambridge

and

Stephen Hugh-Jones

University Lecturer in Social Anthropology, University of Cambridge

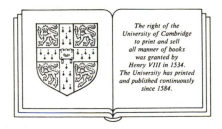

The right of the
University of Cambridge
to print and sell
all manner of books
was granted by
Henry VIII in 1534.
The University has printed
and published continuously
since 1584.

Cambridge University Press

Cambridge
New York   Port Chester
Melbourne   Sydney

Published by the Press Syndicate of the University of Cambridge
The Pitt Building, Trumpington Street, Cambridge CB2 1RP
40 West 20th Street, New York, NY 10011, USA
10 Stamford Road, Oakleigh, Victoria 3166, Australia

First published 1992

Printed in Great Britain at the University Press, Cambridge

A catalogue record for this book is available from the British Library

Library of Congress cataloguing in publication data

Barter, exchange, and value : an anthropological approach / edited by
  Caroline Humphrey and Stephen Hugh–Jones.
      p.   cm.
  Includes index.
  ISBN 0–521–40493–2 (hard). –– ISBN 0–521–40682–X (pbk.)
  1. Barter.   2. Ceremonial exchange.   I. Humphrey, Caroline.
II. Hugh–Jones, Stephen, 1945–
GN450.4.B37   1992
306.3′4––dc20   91–19013
                                                                    CIP

ISBN 0 521 40493 2 hardback
ISBN 0 521 40682 X paperback

Contents

Figures

Contributors

LUCA ANDERLINI is a fellow of St John's College, Cambridge.

ALFRED GELL is reader in social anthropology at the London School of Economics and is author of *Metamorphosis of the Cassowaries* (1975).

STEPHEN HUGH-JONES is a lecturer in social anthropology at the University of Cambridge. He is the author of *The Palm and the Pleiades* (1979).

CAROLINE HUMPHREY lectures in social anthropology at the University of Cambridge. She is the author of *Karl Marx collective* (1983).

HAMID SABOURIAN is a lecturer in the faculty of economics, University of Cambridge. His book, *Essays on non-Walrasian Economics* will be published shortly.

MARILYN STRATHERN is professor of social anthropology at Manchester University. Her books include *The Gender of the Gift* (1988) and *After Nature* (1992).

NICHOLAS THOMAS holds a research fellowship in the department of prehistory and anthropology at the Australian National University. He is the author of *Out of Time* (1990) and *Marquesan Societies* (1990).

1   Introduction: Barter, exchange and value

Caroline Humphrey and Stephen Hugh-Jones

At a dinner-party last year a Rumanian dealer in primitive art, based in Paris, described his delightful trip to the depths of the Celebes. 'I often have to trade', he said. 'Just a month ago, for example, I discovered a wonderful carving of a god but the owner wouldn't sell it to me. I had to have it. He wouldn't take money at any price I offered him. He wanted a pair of two-year-old oxen, nothing more and nothing less.' 'So what did you do?' 'Oh, there was a market round the corner and I sent a man down there to buy the oxen. I couldn't go myself, of course, or the price would have shot up. I took the oxen round and got the carving.'

What the dealer called 'trade' is an example of barter which displays some of a range of features often associated with this kind of exchange. (a) The focus is on demand for particular things which are different in kind; in other cases it may be for services exchanged for goods or other services. (b) The protagonists are essentially free and equal, either can pull out of the deal and at the end of it they are quits. (c) There is no criterion by which, from the outside, it can be judged that the oxen are equal in value to the carving. Some kind of bargaining is taking place, but not with reference to some abstract measure of value or numeraire; each simply wants the object held by the other. (d) In the case above, the two parts of the transaction occur simultaneously; sometimes the two may be separated in time. (e) Finally the act is transformative; it moves objects between the 'regimes of value' (Appadurai, 1986) sustained by the two actors. Here, these are identified with two distinct cultures, the Celeban village where the oxen are used to plough and the carving is 'a god', and the Parisian art world where the oxen are mere substitutes of money and the carving becomes a 'primitive statue' whose equivocal value the dealer will push to its highest in the circle of his buyers. This too is a common, but not a necessary, feature of barter exchanges.

We would emphasise that this is not meant to be a check-list for a definition of barter. Attempts to produce a universal definition or model of barter usually involve stripping it from its social context and result in imaginary abstractions that have little or no correspondence to reality. In our view barter is better understood when seen in the light of its social context; as this context varies so will the features of barter itself. This introduction and the papers that follow it will show that some of the features mentioned above may be absent from transactions that we or others call barter, and yet others may be present. Like many other phenomena studied cross-culturally by anthropologists such as 'marriage', 'shamanism', 'the gift', barter involves a constellation of features not all of which are necessarily present in any particular instance. Thus we provide no definition of barter. Instead we treat it as what Needham (1975) has called a 'polythetic category'.

Although we see barter as separable from other types of exchange – gift exchange, credit, formalised trade and monetised commodity exchange – there are not always hard and fast boundaries between them: barter in one or another of its varied forms coexists with these other forms of exchange, is often linked in sequence with them and shares some of their characteristics. In some cases too, like that of our Celeban native and Parisian art dealer, the parties involved may see one and the same transaction from different perspectives, one as 'barter' pure and simple, the other as a disguised or surrogate form of monetary exchange (see the papers by Thomas and Hugh-Jones in this volume). This is a further reason against isolating off barter as a bounded type and giving it a tidy definition.

The papers in this volume provide ethnographic descriptions of a variety of barter transactions examined in relation to other forms of exchange and to their social context. In addition, we include one chapter from two economists, Anderlini and Sabourian, who provide a formal, theoretical discussion of the organisation of different types of exchange. By producing new ethnographic evidence and setting these different examples together, we hope to raise new questions and to stimulate a rethinking both of barter itself and of gift and commodity exchange which are usually given pride of place in the theoretical literature and between which barter so uncomfortably lies.

In our view barter is an important phenomenon which has been both misunderstood and underestimated in anthropology. It has been misconstrued largely because of the persistence of the creation-myth in classical and neo-classical economics that in barter lie the origins of money and hence of modern capitalism. In this perspective money originates as a solution to the problems of barter. We disagree with this, and the paper by Anderlini and Sabourian in this volume provides a lucid counter-argument from within contemporary economics. The underestimation of barter in anthropology is also linked with this idea, perhaps because of its identification in Western thought with something necessary, but base, in human nature.

Adam Smith expressed this as follows: 'This division of labour, from which so many advantages are derived, is not originally the effect of any human wisdom. It is the necessary, though very slow and gradual, consequence of a certain propensity in human nature which has in view no extensive utility: the propensity to truck, barter and exchange one thing for another' (Smith, 1776, vol. I: 17). Here barter appears as the engine for the evolution of economies, but at the same time as something self-oriented or even selfish, an apt target for the Christian tradition which has at its heart the doctrine of original sin, but no clear delineation of what that sin is.

The very vocabulary – 'higgling', 'haggling', 'swapping', 'dickering', 'truck', and 'barter' itself – is disparaging. Tarred with the brush of 'negative reciprocity' (see Sahlins, 1972: 195), barter is too easily elided with selfish profiteering, on the dark side of Gell's formula: gift/reciprocity = Good; market-exchange = Bad (see this volume). Had there been one in the English language we, as editors of this volume, would have used another word than 'barter'.

Recently writers such as Bourdieu (1977) and Tambiah (1984) have challenged the more stereotyped views of the spirit of gift exchange often accredited to Mauss. Drawing on certain underplayed aspects of Mauss' original analysis, they have re-emphasised the elements of strategy, calculation and self-interest which are common to both gift and commodity exchange (see also Appadurai, 1986). In exploring the cultural dimensions of barter, so often represented simply as the primitive essence of economic self-interest, the papers in this volume represent a complementary endeavour, a move away from a discrete stereotype towards the characterisation of a complex phenomenon which, like the gift, includes ideas, values and visions of the transacting other.

Barter is important partly because of its ubiquity. Not just the rare and perhaps dubious instances of silent trade (Woodburn, n.d.) or a few petty exchanges on the fringes of groups, but whole trade systems have been based on barter as their major mode of exchange (see Wolf 1982; Helms, 1988: 119–30). Such systems criss-cross Australia, link the Andes with the forest, the Amazon and Orinoco, and are documented in native north America, in pre-Columbian Mexico, in Central Asia, Siberia and many other places. Anthropology's earlier preoccupation with 'societies' as bounded units has led to a disastrous undervaluation of the socioeconomic relations between groups which are actually essential to the reproduction of cultures. Bartered objects in such regional trade systems are not simply items of humble everyday use. In fact they were rarely such. Cultural distance itself and the exceptional significance attributed to objects from mysterious places, made these items pivotal in the legitimation of religious and political power internal to the receiving group (see Thomas this volume and also Servet, 1981–2 and Helms, 1988).

What is essential as far as barter is concerned is not so much the mystery as the fact of difference: the existence of a realm where there are objects of desire, that is, objects one has not got and for which one is prepared to sacrifice what one has. In those regions such as the Andes or Himalayas where, for ecological or social reasons, many different economic niches have been established, this 'realm' may be just down the trail. Or it may be continents away in remote and dangerous places inhabited by beings who hover between the divine and the demonic. In any case, as the papers by Thomas and Hugh-Jones both show, the source of such desired objects is not unthought about but has its place in a geography of the world, indeed in a cosmology, which sometimes preserves mystery, as European cultures have always done with regard to 'the Orient'.

If it is not the case that the problems of barter led inevitably to the development of money, nor is it the case that, in the contemporary world, money has destroyed barter. In international trade, Colombian coffee was once bartered for Polish bricks and these for American cars to import back into Colombia, and, on a more domestic level, American suburbanites now consult special handbooks on the procedures and etiquette of barter as they swap goods and services with their neighbours (see Matison and Mack, 1984). Barter occurs in the absence of money and where there is no over-arching monetary system, but also where a common currency exists but where people prefer not to use it, or where there is not enough money to go round. Barter may even serve as a solution to the problems of money.

An example of the deliberate rejection of money is the Lhomi of North-East Nepal, where a marginal political position between the states of Nepal, Sikkim and Tibet has enabled them to operate a predominantly barter economy and maintain an, admittedly flimsy, independence by being 'unable' to pay money taxes to anyone (Humphrey, 1985). Another example is the pastoralists of the West-African savannah zone, who reject the market, and barter for what they want from agriculturalists. Refusing to sell their cattle keeps the value of livestock high, whereas on the occasions when drought has forced sales the prices go down (Hart, 1987).

Perhaps more common than rejection of monetary exchange is a simple lack of money leading to barter: people may be so poor, may need things so much in order to carry on daily life, that they cannot afford to hold any of their assets in money. States as well as individuals may find themselves in such a situation, as the meat for grain trade in West-African countries shows (Hart, 1987). Clearly, these two situations, a decision to use barter and a lack of money, may coincide and reinforce one another. In such situations, money may become so unpervasive and so patchily present that it itself becomes yet another object to be bartered. Currency thus may cease to measure the value of commodities in general, i.e. cease to act as a numeraire (Humphrey, 1985). Even in more or less fully monetised economies, cultures may conceive of money not as a whole, but as different species, as it were, which are not inter-changeable (see, for example, the 'devil's money' in Taussig, 1980).

In short, barter is not just a historical institution or one peculiar to archaic or 'primitive' economies; it is a contemporary phenomenon which covers both large and small-scale transactions and occurs within and between many different types of society. This book itself deals mainly with barter in peasant and tribal societies living on the fringes of the capitalist world in historical Polynesia, and in contemporary Melanesia, Latin America and the Himalayas. Although its aim is not to analyse barter in industrial society or in contemporary world trade between sovereign states, the continued existence of barter in advanced, complex societies with fully monetised economies shows parallels with barter elsewhere and throws light on some key issues. It may be worth mentioning them briefly for this reason.

Up to now much of the international trade between the West and the socialist bloc countries has taken the form of barter. This is because money itself has had a different function in the economies of capitalist and socialist countries, and therefore is not strictly commensurable (Neale, 1976). We see this as the result of the existence of separate 'regimes of value'. In socialist countries workers pay a tiny proportion of their wages for housing and transport, and more for clothing and consumer items, for example, but in the West the reverse is the case. The money prices indicating 'more' or 'less' in these separate regimes are not a universal measure of value. It is a political decision to organise an economy in a particular way, just as it is to establish separate currency zones. The surface reason why East–West trade usually takes the form of barter is the lack of hard currency reserves in the East. But an underlying cause is the existence of different cultural conceptions as regards the values in each economic system, and the maintenance of boundaries between them. Large-scale money transactions threaten the boundaries between such regimes in a way that barter does not, because the regulation of money is perhaps the major way in which governments attempt to control their economies. The link between barter and separate regimes of value, a theme of the papers by Humphrey, Thomas and Hugh-Jones on Nepal, Polynesia and Amazonia, is thus also found in the case of barter between advanced, industrialized nation states.

Another common feature emerges at the other end of the scale, in barter deals between individuals in the contemporary United States, the home of rampant commercialism. Here, barter is culturally located as non-commercial, as the following instruction from a recent American barter handbook shows:

Do not ask for money. You are supposed to trade your skill in repairing the sink for eggs from someone else's chickens. Such behaviour (asking for money instead) injures the non-commercial image of the exchange or co-op and undermines people's faith in its integrity ... Whether you join a barter club, swap with a cousin, or use a network, most of your trades will be part of an ongoing relationship. In effect, this is what separates bartering from cash sales. Since mixing business and friendship is a delicate matter at best, you may need some general guidelines. Remember you want to keep the door open for the next swap. Besides you may meet your barter partner at the pool, or be invited to the same party. (Matison and Mack, 1984: 99).

As our papers show, this 'sociable' or non-commercial aspect is a prominent feature of many non-Western barter exchanges too and one which goes against the popular anthropological stereotype.

There are few if any whole economies of any sizeable scale which are known to have operated by barter alone. This is the case even, for example, in the Ancient Near East before the emergence of coinage. Here, it seems, state taxes in grain and centralised and priestly redistributive systems were the major organising features of the economy, and barter probably operated only at the micro-level (Polanyi, 1957). So barter should be seen as one mode of exchange amongst others, not as the single means of running an economy. As our papers show, it is not only the case that barter coexists with gift exchange, money transactions, formalised trading, etc. so that strategies and obligations in one sphere will spill across into others, but also that objects enter and leave systems of any one of these economic institutions by means of the others. These include various types of exchange such as those just mentioned and also, of course, specific forms of production and consumption. For these reasons it is not useful to analyse barter as an isolated phenomenon.

An anthropological perspective provides a new understanding of the implications of the 'disutility' of barter. In the standard view, the famous 'coincidence of wants', whereby each partner must not only know from whom to obtain what he wants but these wants must be simultaneous, is so inconvenient that it leads inevitably to the emergence of money. But, as Anderlini and Sabourian show in this volume, what is necessary to allow barter to happen is information. In the real world there are many kinds of social relationships where sufficient information is present. Barter occurs mostly in local face-to-face situations, where people and the paths of goods are known. Trading partnerships, which are frequently ritualised, are another means to this end, as are regular seasonal marts and fairs. From the formal point of view, it is information, not any particular social context, which is essential. In the post-industrial West there are computerised barter networks which link firms across the United States (the aim here is to trade without having to pay tax), and most towns and regions have barter cooperatives and other organisations which operate by means of newspapers, computer print-outs, etc. It is noteworthy that even with such computerised networks the actual bargaining is carried out face-to-face and requires personal assessment of the partner. To sum up, there can be very few, if any, economies which operate without barter.

But it is not simply the pervasiveness of barter which makes us think its place should be re-assessed. For anthropology, barter should be an important theoretical concept. The literature has been dominated by a model of ceremonial exchange ('the gift') and to a lesser extent by those of sharing and hierarchical redistribution. The other major category is market-exchange (the 'commodity transaction'), which has a long history in economic anthropology (Polanyi, 1957; Sahlins, 1972; Dalton, 1961; Gregory, 1982). What is missing here is a concept of barter in its own right.

The polar contrast between 'the gift' and 'commodity exchange' is exemplified by Gregory (also discussed by Gell in this volume). Each neatly opposes the other in a number of ways: in gift exchange, inalienable objects, of the same kind, pass between people already bound together by social ties whilst in commodity exchange, alienable objects, of different kinds, pass between people acting as free agents. Gift exchange underwrites social relations and is concerned with social reproduction; commodity exchange establishes relations between things and ensures their reproduction (Gregory, 1980, 1982). The 'commodity transaction' in this analysis is abstracted from Marx's analysis of capitalism, but it is left to stand as a catch-all for any exchange in which objects are alienated and in which the aim is accumulation, in other words, implicitly including barter. This seems to us wrong for several reasons, chief of which is that the abstraction of a typical transaction-type from nineteenth-century capitalism simply does not correspond to what we know about how barter works.

Whereas Gregory counterposes gift and commodity as a binary pair, Sahlins places them at opposite ends of a continuum: from the positive altruism of what he confusingly calls 'generalized reciprocity' to the 'unsociable extreme' of 'negative reciprocity'. The latter is exemplified by barter, chicanery, haggling, etc. By using phrases such as 'the mentality of the market place', Sahlins (1972: 200) appears to link this to proto-capitalist thinking. In their different ways, Gregory and Sahlins thus come to much the same conclusion. But we maintain that barter is not an archaic prototype of capitalism, any more than is gift exchange. It is a mode of exchange in its own right.

Essentially the exchange in barter is determined by the interest which each side has in the object of the other, an interest which is satisfied by the transaction. The objects exchanged have direct consumption values for the participants. Monetary exchange is different: here the value of one exchange object (money) has no direct use, but is merely a claim on other definite values. The realisation of such a claim depends on its acknowledgement by the economic community as a whole, or on a government as the representative of the community (Simmel, 1978: 177). In barter, on the other hand, the transactors are on their own: if they decide that one object is worth another one that is all that matters. In other words, the objects are not measured against one another by some external criterion, but substituted for one another by an internal balance. This implies a lack of integration of exchange ratios, the possibility of not having socially defined pervasive values, and it is why barter tends to occur between communities or within economically weakly articulated ones. But it does not mean that barter implies an absence of social relations. As Simmel forcefully argues, it is not that society, as an 'absolute entity', exists and creates exchange, but that exchange itself creates the bonds of society. Society does not 'allow' relations of cohesion, a division of labour, or any other institution, to develop within its framework, but is itself the synthesis in a general form of these relations (ibid: 174–5). Barter, in this perspective, is one kind of exchange which creates social relations in its own mode.

What are these social relations? Perhaps four can be singled out as most important. One: because a barter exchange consists of mutual payment, i.e. it requires no further transaction (as would be the case with money) to satisfy the wants of the actors, the relationships created by simultaneous barter are in themselves discontinuous and unstable. It is possible to call quits and turn aside never to see the partner again. This fitful incoherence, however, should be immediately qualified by the other three factors, which interact in a tense and unstable way with it.

Two: it is comparatively rare for opportunities for barter to happen quite spontaneously and by pure chance and then never occur again. People may often wish, or need, to repeat a transaction at a later date. Given the necessity of information about what is to be traded, where, when, and by whom, if barter is to occur at all efficiently, the result is what we may call barter systems. Goods tend to be exchanged with known people at particular times and places. There is therefore an in-built tendency to act fairly, that is, in a way which will satisfy the other partner such that the exchange may be repeated in the future. This is all the more likely in that barter is more functional if it includes the possibility of delay, or credit. Thus, where barter is simultaneous people will aim to acquire a reputation for fair-dealing, and, when a time element enters, their aim will be that of trustworthiness. These points are taken up at a theoretical level in the paper by Anderlini and Sabourian in this volume. It is perhaps worth stressing here that when Anderlini and Sabourian state that 'barter is the extreme case in which no trust is present in the system' (p. 100) they have in mind that, in both logic and in real life, a *system* of simultaneous barter (which alone does not require such trust) is a virtual impossibility. The paper by Humphrey shows clearly that, for the Lhomi, issues of trust may be of paramount importance in the workings of real barter networks.

Not only is it logically the case that credit increases the range of opportunities for barter, but in the real world products from subsistence activities each have their own particular seasonalities, whilst supplies of exotic and foreign goods are often sporadic and unpredictable, with the result that exchange on credit may be unavoidable. Credit implies trust. So, although simultaneous barter is perhaps that economic transaction which can best dispense with trust, because barter is very rarely a one-off transaction, its actual operation in social life must work to create both fair-play and trust (see Humphrey, this volume). For this reason we disagree with the point made by Sahlins and repeated by Hart (1986) that barter, being little short of chicanery, therefore requires the existence of over-arching peace-enforcing structures to prevent 'the economic friction from kindling a dangerous situation' (Sahlins, 1972: 201). Our view would be that barter creates its own social relations which can exist in a wide range of political situations.

Three: in barter, unlike certain forms of 'the gift' where it is enjoined, for example, that pigs be repaid by other pigs, the objects which are exchanged are dissimilar. I want to give up something I have got because I want something else more. Not only are the goods unlike, they are also frequently incomparable. Even if some notion of monetary value hovers in the background, as was perhaps the case with the Parisian art merchant and the peasant from the Celebes, it would be a mistake to think that the consumption or use values of the objects are measurable by some common, abstract standard held in the heads of the two parties.

This important point was made by the economist Marshall, whose argument we briefly summarise here. He said, 'The real distinction between the theory of buying and selling and that of barter is that in the former it generally is, and in the latter it generally is not, right to assume that the stock of one of the things which is in the market and ready to be exchanged for the other (i.e. money) is very large and in many hands; therefore its marginal utility is practically constant' (Marshall, 1920: 793). What Marshall is saying here is that if we barter say potatoes for shoes, both of these items will have diminishing marginal utility for us, i.e. the more we have of them the less useful to us will be each additional amount. This is not the case with money in general, even though for individual people the marginal utility of money will not be constant (for a poor person the benefit measured by £1 is greater that it is to the rich man: for example the latter may take the tube 100 times before he feels that he has spent enough on fares, a poor man only 10 times).

In commodity markets the value of money is steadied as a whole by the presence of wealthy dealers and institutions, such as banks, which can always afford to buy large quantities and thus maintain the rate at which money exchanges for other things. This means that in any particular commodity market, for example buying and selling corn for money, the price in the end will reach what Marshall calls the true equilibrium, i.e. that which, if fixed at the beginning of trading and adhered to throughout, would exactly equate supply and demand. This is not the case with barter. The marginal utility of all commodities in barter varies and there is no single item which can exert a steadying influence. Although an equilibrium price of, say, apples for nuts may be reached, it will not be the true equilibrium, but an accidental one. In practice, the price or exchange ratio reached will depend on many extraneous factors, one, but not necessarily the only one, of which is often skill in bargaining. The ratio is therefore better seen as the outcome of the exchange rather than as its precondition. It is an expression of the fact that 'those two people, on that particular occasion, saw those things as substitutable for each other'.

Thus it makes no sense to ask, in the abstract, how many oxen a statue is worth. The 'many extraneous factors' which influence the accident of an exchange ratio actually reached are in fact the sum of economic, political, social and psychological pressures on either side brought to bear in a particular instance. Therefore, the values which bartered objects represent are indicative of the confrontation between ways of life, or, as Strathern puts it in her chapter in this volume, of the regard in which the other is held. If 'the gift' is in Mauss' term 'total prestation', then barter is equally total exchange, whereby people are identified with the products of their way of life and vice versa. The papers by Humphrey and Hugh-Jones provide examples of the personalised nature of the goods involved in barter transactions from both Nepal and northwest Amazonia. Barter thus uses goods to create a relationship of mutual estimation between the self and a partner who is representative of an 'other' set of values. As Woodburn (n.d.) has shown, where there is fear, hostility or status inequality between the parties involved, and where such values involve the stigmatisation of one of the parties, 'silent trade' may result. Here, the avoidance of face-to-face contact may also be a device to maintain the autonomy of weaker, stigmatised groups, such as hunter-gatherers, with respect to their settled neighbours, by reducing the relationship that trade implies to an absolute minimum.

Four: as Sahlins remarked with reference to marital exchange, when unlike, and therefore in some sense unequal, things are exchanged, the lack of a precise balance is of the essence. 'Unequal benefit sustains the alliance as a perfect balance would not' (1972: 222). A 'perfect balance', however, is what is created by immediate barter, because the transactors are quits at the end. If, as we have noted, this tends towards a fragile and unstable bond, it is also essential to note that, in principle at least, the relationship is one of equality. The very act of barter exchange creates equality out of dissimilarity. It does so because the bargain struck is that which satisfies either partner. As Strathern points out in her chapter, one difference between gift exchange and barter is that, by its very nature, the former mode implies some compulsion: ('people must compel others to enter into debt...the recipient's need is forced upon him by the donor'), whereas in barter each side decides their own needs, and the aim is to end the transaction feeling free of immediate debt.

Now it is true that barter can exist within many kinds of wider political relations of inequality: merchants may deliberately employ in-kind payments with indigenous people in order to debar them from the market (Gorer, 1938); or, as the paper by Hugh-Jones (this volume) shows, colonial powers may hijack indigenous barter systems to keep people in thrall by barter credit, often backed by repressive sanctions or an outright reign of terror (see Taussig, 1987); or one community may use force against others to maintain a monopoly of a certain good in a barter system (Jest, 1975). In such situations it is possible for one side to hide information from the other, say about prices in the outside world of the goods they are offering, and thereby exploit them. But this is maintained by forces outside the exchange itself, mainly colonialism and regional balances of power. Barter itself, as a mode of exchange, is a struggle against enforced transactions, though frequently a puny one. The threat never to come back again and the range for bargaining may be small and feeble, more or less illusory in respect of the wider economy, but their existence maintains whatever is possible in the way of equality in the relation between partners.

These four characteristics thus present barter as something which is not stable and self-regulating, but rather dynamic, self-contradictory, and open-ended. Discontinuity, the creation of trust, the interaction with dissimilarity, and the bid for equality are not easy bedfellows. The historical ephemerality of barter may be one reason for the academic neglect of the subject. Yet barter, and the issues it raises, recur sporadically in the literature, and it is to those accounts which have been most influential that we now turn.

The idea that barter is an ancient prototype of capitalist commercial exchange is not yet laid to rest, although it has been the subject of sustained criticism. The theory is as follows: a natural propensity to barter and exchange led people to establish a division of labour whereby separate groups produced different products. Pervasive barter between individuals from these groups soon gave way to fairs, and here one traded item rapidly came to assume the role of a means of exchange. This became money and allowed the development of long-distance trade, and, subsequently, other financial institutions such as bills of exchange and banks. From this emerged the commercial bases of capitalism (see Jevons, 1910; Clower, 1969).

The most forceful critique of the theory was produced by Polanyi, who realised that economic institutions do not just 'arise' in a political vacuum. In his view, the sequence was rather the reverse: ceremonial exchange was primary, political conditions then allowed long-distance trade to arise between geographically different regions, and this was followed by the emergence of money; the existence of money gave people the commercial, profit-oriented attitude, which finally made possible a fringe, low-key haggling and bartering on each occasion (Polanyi, 1957). We do not think it proper to agree with either of these stories, whose foundations lie in so much that is unknown. Indeed, in a daring re-interpretation of the ethnographic data from New Guinea, Gell's paper in this volume actually reverses part of Polanyi's sequence once again – but let us note the key issue of disagreement between them, the alleged propensity of humankind to truck and barter.

Polanyi followed Marx in seeing modes of exchange as determined by the political economy rather than by 'human nature'. Yet on the precise issue of barter itself Marx was ambivalent, as though the ideas of the classical economists were still lingering in him. The idea that barter is 'beyond society' was clearly expressed by Marx in *Capital*, volume I (1954: 91) where he opposed barter to transactions within society and based on communal property rights. He located the origin of barter in exchanges between primitive societies, on the grounds that only in the absence of communal rights to property was it possible for people to alienate their goods. Gregory, elaborating on Marx, has described the relationship between the barter transactors as one of 'reciprocal independence' as opposed to the 'reciprocal dependence' which exists within the 'gift' oriented society (1982: 42). Marx went on immediately to add that as soon as people got the idea of alienated exchange of goods this spread inside society too, because of man's inherent desire for individual acquisition.

This brief account suggests that there are at least two issues: the question of what is individual human psychology as far as acquisition, altruism, etc. is concerned, and the matter of the influence of socio-economic structures. Marx's category of 'use-value' summarises the confusion: is 'use-value' to be located in individual (psychological) evaluations, or in what generally would be the case for a person in a given society? There is a huge literature in many different disciplines which bears on these subjects (Midgley, 1978; Chadwick-Jones, 1986).

We argue against the above theory on the following grounds. Firstly, on the empirical level, it is clear from many ethnographies (Jest, 1975; Orlove, 1986; Fisher, 1986; Gell, this volume) that, whilst barter certainly does alienate goods, it does not entail the reciprocal independence of the transactors, a mutual turning-of-backs when the exchange is over – indeed it may take place within a given society between people who interact on a regular basis (Hugh-Jones and Humphrey, this volume). Quite apart from the likelihood that in a barter system the transaction will be repeated, we have suggested that something much more subtle and interesting is going on, to do with the perception on either side of the 'other', and the location of these perceptions in the economic–political relations between individuals and between social groups.

Secondly, we reject the idea of 'natural' economic propensities as the explanation for any specific economic institution. The point derives not only from the advance made in the political economy approach following Marx and Polanyi, but also from the anthropological view of economies as cultural systems, i.e. economies as taking place within cosmologies and schemes of value (Gudeman, 1986). Nicholas Thomas has pointed out in his paper 'Forms of personification and prestations' (1985) that the culturalist view has implications for the construction of the individual as a person. 'From this alternative point of view', he writes, 'persons do not have some pre-given autonomy and agency but are only constituted as subjects by and through their articulation with language and social relations' (1985: 225). This has particular import for barter, as is implied from Marshall's argument noted above. Not only persons, but also their wants and the types of exchange they create, will always be culturally defined in particular ways. This is not to deny that there are logical constraints on economic activity, nor the existence of economic mechanisms, especially in complex developed economies, which seem to operate independently of minor differences in culture. But it is to say that, in the end, economic actors should not be viewed separately from culturally defined intentions. Different cultural definitions of the persons, processes and intentions involved in barter emerge both in the papers that follow and in our example on p. 6 above where contemporary barter exchange in the United States is specifically designated as being non-commercial.

Another example, from an under-developed society, shows that different kinds of barter may co-exist when social relations themselves are seen differently. A recent study of barter and cash sale of fish on Lake Titicaca shows both to be 'market', i.e. commercial, transactions and they are socially constituted in much the same way (Orlove, 1986: 96). But the difference between this barter among lakeside fishermen and the more socially resonant barter between pastoralists and maize growers in the same region, also described in the Orlove paper, is such that it leads Gudeman, in his comment, to question whether the same thing is going on at all (Gudeman, 1986: 100). It is clear that the socio-cultural context, of which barter is a part, is what matters.

This means that the attempt to establish a universal model of barter, as Anne Chapman has tried to do in her article in *L'Homme* (1980), is not really very useful. She can only do this, because of the difficulties mentioned above, by suggesting that barter as an ideal-type is not embedded in society. 'It stands out by itself as a *purely economic transaction*' (p. 49, our emphasis). The suppositions on which such a model must rest – the non-cultural actors, unspecified values, and, as it were, perfect information – cannot really hold water in a modern anthropological enquiry. Her model might be said to come close to being realised in the rare and exceptional circumstances of one-off barter transactions with strangers but, as she herself says, it 'is not directly applicable to, or representative of, any given case of real ("impure") barter. In the world, barter is a transaction between two living human beings, or groups; it always occurs in a social or psychological situation' (1980: 36).

One reason for the elusiveness of the sort of activities which could be described as 'barter' – also a reason why they are interesting – is their capacity to incorporate different meanings held by the two sides, a condition which is especially marked in the case of barter across ethnic frontiers. Here we should distinguish between differing understandings of the transaction itself, on the one hand, and diverse value systems for the products exchanged, on the other. The first theme is illustrated by the systems of debt-peonage between the native peoples of Amazonia and their White patrons, discussed by Hugh-Jones. These systems, often preceded by the barter of slaves against foreign goods, represent transformations of indigenous barter networks. Today, what one party treats as tantamount to wage labour operating under conditions of labour scarcity and involving a commodity destined for sale in a further monetary transaction, the other may see as a direct exchange of equivalent objects whose values are independent of labour input, and one of which will be used by the transactor.

The second theme, that of diverse value systems for the items exchanged, taken up in the papers by Humphrey and Thomas in this book, has been noted in the literature mainly in relation to non-barter transactions. An example is John Gray's paper 'Lamb auctions on the borders' (1984). The auctions in question are those which take place in Scottish border towns, where lambs are sold for meat to traders from England and the EC countries. For the Scottish farmers sheep breeding is a way of life. Each farm, which normally is in hereditary ownership, has its own combination of pastures, labour is not counted in hours, and flocks, called 'hirsels', are lovingly produced by selection of rams and ewes to make individual types of sheep, instantly recognisable by other shepherds as belonging to particular farms. At the auction, as the lambs are paraded round a ring, the farmer lays his reputation on the line. Before his eyes the value of his lambs is transformed, from 'hirsels' of the lineage he and his ancestors have created, to the external criteria of fat, muscle, bone, length of limbs, etc. in demand among the EC buyers. The traders' criteria sometimes change, but the point is that in any case they are incommensurable with the notion of the 'hirsel'. So bound up is the 'hirsel' with the farmer's notion of self that he will refuse to sell if he feels his reputation is injured by the price offered to him as opposed to other farmers. The auction transforms the lamb from something essentially inalienable in the Scottish context, since all 'hirsels' are recognisably attached to particular farms, to an alienated commodity, a living weight of meat.

From here we are led to consider whole value systems, the maintaining of a separate cultural pattern of consumption, not just for one item, for example sheep, but for the entire range of things and their relationship to one another. Gell in a perceptive recent paper (1986) has shown that for the Muria Gonds, even in the monetised situation of Central India, consumption is channelled in particular cultural forms by 'the paranoia of belonging, which marks all phases of Muria life'. 'Muria consumption is bound up with the expression of collective identity and the need to assert commitment to the village as a political unit and to its institutions. Particular items are singled out from the range of Hindu prestige symbols and incorporated into a collective style, which all Muria try to approximate as best they can' (1986: 122–3). The fact that the Muria economy is almost completely monetised, means that the prestigious and wealthy old men, who enforce the restricted consumption system by a demonstratively simple (i.e. tribal) lifestyle, have to sit on money, and thereby become even richer. Money is a real problem. It can purchase anything from the world economy which reaches the bazaars of Central India. Money is not just wealth, it is also a threat to power legitimated in a particular social organisation.

Gell saw the precariousness of the Muria culture in their being 'newcomers to the world of goods'. It seems clear, rather, that their capacity to negate indiscriminate consumption – their reproduction of the category of the Muria 'person' by particular consumption (the 'forms of categorization, expressions, or arrays of possibilities which exclude others', as Nicholas Thomas, 1985, puts it), indicates that they are, on the contrary, old hands in the world of goods. The paper by Humphrey in this volume discusses the case of 'old hands in the world of goods' as it works out in an economy which is dominated by barter.

Perhaps the closest we can get to genuine newcomers is the paradigm of hitherto isolated tribal societies in their first encounters with colonial powers, a situation discussed by Thomas. Here, according to conventional wisdom, the natives are so impressed by technologically superior tools that they soon lose their heads; exploited by Europeans, their unrestrained hunger for goods soon leads them to lose their culture as well. Without questioning the destructive impact of the colonial encounter, both Hugh-Jones and Thomas throw doubt on the adequacy of a view which locates the dynamics of this transformation in peripheral exchange, and which fails to take into account either the indigenous sense of such transactions or the way in which foreign goods, as novelties, are conceptualised and integrated into autonomous systems of consumption beyond the understanding and control of their alien suppliers.

Still focusing on traditional societies, but this time from an internal perspective, Gell and Strathern, in their different ways, compare barter with 'the gift' in the classic context of Melanesian exchange. Gell argues that the traditional anthropological emphasis on gift exchange has led to a neglect of both the extent and theoretical significance of peripheral trade and barter in Melanesia. Through a critique of the contrast between gift exchange and commodity exchange, he turns the tables on some widely accepted views by suggesting that reproductive gift exchange (exchange associated with marriage and childbirth), far from being the primordial transactional mode in Melanesia, is in fact symbolically derived from a template provided by commodity barter. The real contrast, Gell argues, is not between gift exchange and commodity exchange, but between bride-service and barter. Bride-service implies the subservient status of a son-in-law with an inescapable obligation to provide unreciprocated goods and services to his superior affines, an obligation predicated on the moral idea of sharing and consequent on his relationship with a woman controlled by others. In peripheral barter, partners engage each other freely and as equals, exchanging goods under their exclusive control, goods whose value relates both to their usefulness and to their role in a social transaction which, like 'the gift', is valued for its own sake.

Using the model which barter on the margins of society provides, affinity, with its attendant implications of unreciprocated obligations between unequal partners, can then be reformulated as a balanced and reciprocal exchange of valuables between equal partners on the inside of the group. By mimicking barter, reproductive gift exchange has an ideological function in conveying the impression that social reproduction has been 'detached' from uncontrollable women, and 'attached' to valuable objects controlled by men, and that it is ensured by their exchange activities. Thus, instead of characterising Melanesian social evolution by a series beginning with sister exchange, with bridewealth in the middle, and with the ceremonial exchange of valuables for valuables at the end (see Gregory, 1982 and Rubel and Rossman, 1979) Gell proposes that reproductive gift exchange presupposes the prior existence of the barter exchange from which it extends and on which it is modelled.

Like Gell, Strathern is also concerned to emphasise the continuities and similarities between the gift and barter, but her paper moves in the opposite direction. If Gell uses barter to elucidate the character and genesis of reproductive gifts, Strathern begins with a critique of the 'barter model of the gift', and then provides us with a 'gift model of barter' or, rather, a model which accounts for the specificity of both. But the contradiction is more apparent than real, for Strathern is concerned with a different set of issues, the notion of value and the principles by which comparability is assessed in exchange. The model she criticises is not that of barter itself, but the 'barter model of value', the assumption that, in barter or gift exchanges, the relative worth of things or people is expressed as an exchange ratio arrived at by the simple process of counting things as discrete units which are then calculated against one another.

A word of warning here: when Strathern discusses the 'barter model' this is not what we have in mind. Her 'barter model' is the old stereotype, the transparent, unsocial barter in which people are motivated simply by a desire to get what they want in exchange for what they have to spare. It is this view of barter, in which things with self-evident values are totted up against each other, that Strathern rejects; like the other contributors to this volume, she takes a cultural view of barter, stressing that barter involves relationships and not merely goods. The objects exchanged in barter, like those of the gift, are entities which are compared with their sources or origins – what is exchanged are not things for things, or the relative values of people quantified in things, but mutual estimations and regards. These are unitary entities which are matched and paired together, and in which enumeration serves merely as the metaphor for their substitutability.

This idea of substitutability, as opposed to the calculation of exchange ratios, applies as much to barter as it does to the gift. Substitution is another way of putting the 'accidental equilibrium' of barter arrived at by Marshall. What anthropology can add to the discussion is something which economists do not broach: an understanding of the concepts of relationship implied by barter in various social contexts. Both the gift and barter are modes of non-monetary exchange which derive from, and create, relationships, and in her paper Strathern shows how much they have in common. What differentiates them is the compulsion and 'contrived asymmetry' of the gift, as opposed to the relative freedom and balance of barter.

Let us end with a discussion of this point. Strathern remarks that 'no formal difference hinges on items [exchanged] being similar or dissimilar in themselves'. She is referring here to people's ability to extract objects from one another, necessary in either kind of exchange. In both barter and the gift, objects exchanged against one another are in fact always valued as unlike, because their sources are different, even if they are actually undistinguishable in themselves. As Strathern points out, two identical looking pigs from different families are not socially or qualitatively equivalent. So, it is not because the gift demonstrates asymmetry in a relationship by returning more of the same thing given that Strathern emphasises the compulsion in this mode. The compulsion of the gift, she suggests, lies in forcing others to enter into debt: an object in the regard of one actor must be made to become an object in the regard of another in giving it to them. It is here that the 'contrived asymmetry' lies: one has to accept a gift and hence a debt. But in barter the difference is that items held by others already are objects of desire and this is the only situation in which one will accept an object. Paradoxically, the presence of desire in barter, which might imply an inner compulsion, also suggests its own solution – the exchange – which nullifies demand. In this respect the fact that the objects involved in barter are indeed different is important. This is not to insist on the existence of needs prior to the relationship, but rather that the relationship itself is one which defines the other party as having something one wants. Correspondingly, one must define oneself to the other as a source of what is desirable to them; this is the only 'compulsion' of barter.

So, if the gift defines objects exchanged as being dissimilar because they both come from, and are part of, groups which are distinct from one another, barter adds the idea that in being unlike they are the objects of desire. In this way, the parties stand ready for barter and create the conditions for it. In a sense the very aim of barter is to create and quench desires in oneself and the other. This is what the relationship is about; it is not a mode of negotiating something else (obligation, domination, ostentation, etc.). By definition, the desires created, however unlike one another, are 'symbolically equal'. So, it is because there is no 'contrived asymmetry' in barter that we cannot really talk about compulsion. This being said, any barter transactor should keep their wits about them, as the following story illustrates.

The story concerns Boris Tomashefsky, the great Yiddish actor. He was met backstage one day by an admiring fan, a very pretty girl. Tomashefsky closed the door and the two made love. The next day, the girl returned. She needed help for her sick daughter, she explained, and the actor gave her two tickets for the Saturday matinee. The girls was aghast. 'I need bread, not tickets', she remonstrated. Tomashefsky replied, 'You want bread, screw a baker. Tomashefsky gives tickets' (Matison and Mack, 1984, 237).

REFERENCES

Appadurai, A. (1986) (ed.) *The Social Life of Things*. Cambridge: Cambridge University Press.
Bourdieu, P. (1977) *Outline of a Theory of Practice*. Cambridge: Cambridge University Press.
Chadwick-Jones, J. K. (1986) Social exchange, social psychology and economics. In MacFadyen, A. J. and H. W. (eds.) *Economic Psychology*. Holland: Elsevier Science Publishers.
Chapman, A. (1980) Barter as a universal mode of exchange. *L'Homme*, 20 (3), 33–88.
Clower, R. W. (1969) Introduction. In Clower, R. W. (ed.), *Monetary Theory*. Harmondsworth: Penguin.
Collier, J. F. and Rosaldo, M. Z. (1981) Politics and gender in simple societies. In Ortner, S. B. and Whitehead, H. (eds.) *Sexual Meanings*. New York: Cambridge University Press.
Dalton, G. (1961) Economic theory and primitive society. *American Anthropologist*, 63: 1–25.
Fisher, J. F. (1986) *Trans-Himalayan Traders*. Berkeley University of California Press.
Gray, J. N. (1984) Lamb auctions on the borders. *European Journal of Sociology*, 25(1).
Gorer, G. (1938) *Himalayan Village*. London: Nelson.
Gregory, C. (1980) Gifts to men and gifts to god: gift exchange and capital accumulation in contemporary Melanesia. *Man*, (ns) 15(4), 625–52.
   (1982) *Gifts and Commodities*. London: Academic Press.
Gudeman, S. (1986) *Economics as Culture: Models and Metaphors of Livelihood*. London: Routledge and Kegan Paul.
Hart, K. (1986) Heads or tails. Two sides of the coin. *Man*, (ns) 21(4), 637–56.
   (1987) Commoditization and the standard of living. In Sen, A. (ed.) *The Standard of Living*. Cambridge: Cambridge University Press.
Helms, M. (1988) *Ulysses' Sail: an Ethnographic Odyssey of Power, Knowledge and Geographical Distance*. Princeton: Princeton University Press.
Humphrey, C. (1985) Barter and economic disintegration. *Man*, (ns) 20(1), 48–72.
Jest, C. (1975). *Dolpo: communautes de langue tibetaine du Nepal*. Paris: Editions CNRS.
Jevons, W. S. (1910) *Money and the Mechanism of Exchange*. London: Routledge and Kegan Paul.
Marshall, A. (1920) *Principles of Economics*. London: Macmillan.
Marx, K. (1954) *Capital*. Vol. I (1887 edition). London: Lawrence and Wishart.
Matison, J. and Mack, R. (1984) *The Only Barter Book You'll Ever Need*. New York: Bantam Books.

Midgely, M. (1978) *Beast or Man: the Roots of Human Nature.* Ithaca and New York: Cornell University Press.

Neale, W. (1976) *Monies in Societies.* San Francisco: Chandler and Sharp.

Needham, R. (1975) Polythetic classification: convergence and consequences. *Man*, (3), 349–69.

Orlove, B. S. (1986) Barter and cash sale on Lake Titicaca: a test of competing approaches. *Current Anthropology*, 28(2), 85–106.

Polanyi, K. (1957) *The Great Transformation.* Boston: Beacon Press.

Rubel, P. and Rossman, A. (1979) *Your Own Pigs You May Not Eat.* Chicago: Chicago University Press.

Sahlins, M. (1972) *Stone Age Economics.* Chicago: Aldine Atherton.

Servet, J.-M. (1981–2) Primitive order and archaic trade. *European Journal of Sociology*, 10(4), 1981, and 11(1) 1982.

Simmel, G. (1978) *The Philosophy of Money.* London: Routledge.

Smith, A. (1776) *An Inquiry into the Nature and Causes of the Wealth of Nations.* Harmondsworth: Penguin, 1979 edn.

Tambiah, S. J. (1984) *The Buddhist Saints of the Forest and the Cult of Amulets.* Cambridge: Cambridge University Press.

Taussig, M. (1980) *The Devil and Commodity Fetishism in South America.* Chapel Hill: University of North Carolina Press.

(1987) *Shamanism, Colonialism and the Wild Man.* Chicago: Chicago University Press.

Thomas, N. (1985) Forms of personification and prestations. *Mankind*, 15, 223–30.

Wolf, E. (1982) *Europe and the Peoples without History.* Los Angeles: University of California Press.

Woodburn, J. (n.d.) Hunter-gatherer 'silent trade' with outsiders and the history of anthropology. Ms.

2 The cultural dynamics of peripheral exchange

Nicholas Thomas

Barter has always been associated with social margins. It is paradigmatically the form of exchange which is expected to take place across the frontiers between non-monetised economies, between strangers rather than relatives or friends. From the perspective of a monetised economy, it is also peripheral in the sense that it belongs beyond the domain of currency transactions: it is associated with a marginal, primitive world which we define by the absence of such things as money, writing and the state, rather than by its own positive attributes. That world is no longer purely primitive, and the various forms of colonial penetration and development have clearly had catastrophic consequences for many tribal peoples. In some of these histories, peripheral barter figures as the origin of dependency; the allure of European goods appears as the beginning of asymmetry, the seed of a transformation which some would render positively as progress, and others regret as a corrosion of culture. Does early exchange play this historic role, or does the image turn only on European constructions?

I begin with a string of stories about early exchange on colonial peripheries, that suggest that exchange was not generally dominated by narrow utilitarian interests, and that commonsense interpretations of the functions of articles of trade frequently pass over attributions of value arising from the associations of things rather than their material properties. In the Oceanic cases discussed, these associations arise from prior indigenous attitudes to foreigners and the particular experience of contact with whites.

'In the beginning this island now called Niue was nothing but coral rock.'

So begins a history of the Polynesian island of Niue by John Lupo, a Samoan who settled there as a mission teacher in the 1860s, and, forty years later, wrote down a narrative at the request of a foreigner. He proceeded to describe how the lump of coral was fished up from the ocean by the god Maui, its settlement, the bringing of cultivated plants, various wars and invasions, and the evil work of certain spirits who caused famine.

Then, 'in the later times, there came the mission ships (*vaka lotu*) and the white men (*papalangi*)'.

When the people saw what grand things the *papalangi* had in their ship – the axes, the fish-hooks, the soft cloth – they were crazy to get them. At that time the only axes the *Niue* men had were those made of black stone...and of the big clam-shells...and they desired above everything the sharp hatchets of the white man. They were very anxious to become Christians, because then they would obtain teachers, sharp axes and knives and cloth. And peace ruled over this island where once fighting and man-slaying continually prevailed. (Lupo, 1923: 240)

Here, the indigenous people almost immediately recognise their tech-nological inferiority and form great and insatiable desires for European goods. The difference between their own possessions and those of *papalangi* is simply a matter of objective utility or efficiency: it is self-evident that iron is better than stone, and apparent also that desire should be captured by this difference. The account might in fact be seen to provide a sufficient explanation for the origin of the dependent status of tribal peoples (although that was not its purpose). One can understand that the thirst for objects would lead to the entanglement of indigenous peoples in exchange relations with Europeans, and perhaps also that it would be a motivating force behind the adoption of Christianity, with the broad agenda for change in 'social and domestic habits' (Royle, 1843) which missions brought to Niue and many other places. Islanders, once characterised as those who have no iron, seem ready to be drawn into asymmetrical, and even exploitative, relations. Their naive fascination with Western things can also predictably lead to the 'loss' of their own culture: we can envisage seeing indigenous arts and crafts vanish, while Western clothes and implements are adopted, just as Christianity is substituted for some traditional religion.

The kind of barter described by Lupo this occupies a crucial situation in the liberal representation of the plight of indigenous peoples:

The fur trade forced the Inuit [of Canada] into a symbiotic relationship with the traders: they forsook their traditional hunting ways (in which trapping was unimportant) to trap the furs that would get them trade goods – guns, bullets, knives, flour, tea and tobacco. (Creery, 1983: 4).

There is some uncertainty about native agency here, since the Inuit were at once 'forced' and actively forsaking – but perhaps there is no con-tradiction if one takes the irresistible magnetism of whites' commodities for granted. There is even some congruence between these images and those of some Pacific Islanders, who render their ancestors as victims.

The colonialists...took the best land from us in exchange for items like empty bottles, tobacco, soap, fishing lines and hooks. Then they began to convert proud and dignified Solomon Islanders into a workforce of down-trodden and degraded human beings... (Tuhanuku, 1983: 117).

What is denounced or lamented is partly a gross disparity of value: labour, power, land, or significant natural resources were sacrificed for cheap trinkets or tools.[1] The paradox here is that both Western concern and indigenous hindsight regret that native transactors did not understand the 'real' value of what they gave away, but at the same time fail to raise the correlate of this question: what was the real value of what they received?

A utilitarian viewpoint predisposes us to regard the uses of something like an axe as transparent and intrinsic, but the notable feature of some axes was that they were *not* used –

They possess indeed some tomahawks of European make...These tomahawks however they prize too highly to put them to common use and generally keep as articles of special virtue, hung up in the part of the hut specially devoted to the gods. (J. Renton, 1860s, quoted in Bennett, 1987: 23)

– or rather, their cultural 'uses' are elusive. These considerations threaten to entangle the interpretation of early barter on colonial peripheries in local cultural specificities, but exchange relations demand closer scrutiny if they are in fact the origins of subsequent exploitation and asymmetry; it will be established here that the cultural logic of early exchange often relates more to positive appropriations or constrained management of foreign contact, rather than a mere thirst for superior commodities.

John Elphinstone Erskine was the captain of HMS *Havannah* during its cruise in the western Pacific in 1849. He did not land on Niue, but native men came out to the ship in canoes and barter took place between the ship and the canoes or on deck. Erskine describes a trade which was, at first sight, typically haphazard and typically straightforward: the islanders were particularly interested in knives, fish-hooks, and black bottles, which were probably broken up to make glass cutting implements. Erskine reported that 'their articles of traffic were almost entirely weapons' such as spears; these were evidently of considerable value, some being carefully wrapped in leaves. Others were decorated in a way which linked them distinctly with their owners:

all very nicely made, and ornamented with a few feathers, the arrangement of which, we were told, represented the owner's name, and enabled him to claim the credit for a successful throw in battle. (1935: 27)

Erskine wrote that the 'system of barter was not well regulated', it being 'impossible to fix definite values on the different articles of either side' (*ibid.*) But the islanders evidently had a precise idea of a process of give and take, if not of definite quantitative equivalence. For Erskine, the morality of the act depended not upon the presence or absence of a return, but upon relative values: he admitted that he was 'somewhat ashamed of the trash we had given them' for their weapons, and 'repeatedly' threw out of the stern windows black bottles with a few fish-hooks attached, intending them as a free gift' (1853: 30). This gracious gesture was either rejected or misunderstood by the Niue men: 'invariably one or two spears were thrust upon me, whether I would or no; the canoes which had dropped astern to pick up their bottles paddling with all their might to fulfil their share of the bargain' (*ibid.*).

This insistence on immediate return did not accord with the general pattern of Polynesian–European barter, as documented through mariners' accounts of early contact in larger and more frequently visited archipelagoes, such as the Hawaiian, Society, and Marquesas islands: in the great majority of cases a more diffused, delayed pattern of transactions took place, involving services as well as a broader array of things, including food. Even when the visit of a ship to an island incorporated periods of immediate, organised exchange – often in a delineated space upon a beach – goods changed hands in various ways at other times. It was very common for captains to favour chiefly men and women with particular gifts, which it was hoped would secure their goodwill. Islanders often stole stray objects which a chief, if favourably disposed, might go to some lengths to see returned. The behaviour of the Niue people seems distinguished by a desire to close off the relationship, precluding the emergence of more complicated patterns of indebtedness and association. The islanders evidently wanted knives, as Lupo suggested; in return they gave personalised weapons, which could hardly have been items for exchange within their own system. They were not prepared to give food, which was in day to day exchange, as well as, on larger occasions, the primary expression of social affiliations and obligations throughout Polynesia.

The fact that women played no part in these events is also unusual. A feature of contact in most of the larger island groups in the late eighteenth and early nineteenth centuries was the eagerness of Polynesian women to enter into sexual relations with sailors. The aspect of initial encounters which struck members of Cook's expedition when they visited Hawaii was that no material payment was expected or demanded. This behaviour was attributed to the 'licentious' or promiscuous disposition of Polynesians, and entered the European mythology of Tahiti in particular and the South Seas in general (cf. Smith, 1960: 30). Recently, a more plausible explanation has been put forward: that the women, or their families, wanted children fathered by strangers who were – at least at first – seen as deities. The practice was an extension of 'the offering of virgin daughters to a ranking chief by prominent commoners' (Sahlins, 1981: 40;

cf. Ralston, 1989). A cherished kin connection was established, even though the commoner woman would subsequently take some other husband. Because sailors saw the practice as prostitution, they turned it into an exchange, and, once Hawaiians realised that sexual services could be a commodity, they continued to participate enthusiastically on those new terms. Although foreigners were rapidly stripped of mystical attributes, the link between this exchange and the Hawaiian interest in establishing foreign connections, cannot have been entirely erased for some decades.

Without necessarily assuming that sexual liaisons with men from across the sea had one pan-Polynesian meaning, the absence of such initiatives on the part of Niue women lends support to the notion that the inhabitants were attempting to restrict and foreclose barter. Although they were friendly, and their contact with the *Havannah* was unspoilt by violence, they did nothing toward opening up the relations with Europeans. Given that their internal transactions always involved the larger relations implied by gifts, tribute, and ritual prestations, and also that it would have been hard for them to trade any of their own exchange items in a way divorced from wider social possibilities, it is significant that they seem to have made free, unsocial commodities out of precisely the things they would not have exchanged amongst themselves. This is possible because non-exchange-ability or highly restricted exchangeability is an essential element of the nature of some things which are normally inalienable personal property. Niue weapons were perhaps like Western wedding rings, which are inalienable, but may be disposed of because of financial hardship: under these circumstances the thing immediately loses its principal significance. Although the former owner may experience loss, the object becomes a commodity free of social resonance, and can mediate no connection between former and subsequent owners.

It is fortunate that the missionary William Gill met a Niue man on a ship between Sydney and Samoa in 1838, because what he was told partly explains the particular attitude of the Niue people in wishing to foreclose and restrict barter. Apparently the consequence of one ship's visit had been an outbreak of disease; according to the man they therefore

conceived a dislike to intercourse with [the white man], or to have anything to do with his property. While on board his ship they had also seen him eat '*animal*' food, and had concluded that he was '*a man-eater*' and consequently they resisted every temptation to put themselves within his power. (Gill, 1856: 339)

This attitude had evidently been qualified by the time of Erskine's visit, but most earlier European attempts to make contact seem to have been 'fruitless' (for example Williams, 1838: 296–7).

In some other cases an attitude of resistance arose from earlier violence or disease (for example Beechey, 1831, 1: 43 concerning Easter Island). However more or less severe outbreaks of illness were almost a universal feature of contact, and the distinctive caution of the Niue people with respect to Europeans may rather be explained by the pre-contact character of their representations and experience of strangers. In much of Polynesia (and for that matter in other regions) chiefs were regarded as immigrants or invaders, as sources of extra-local things or powers, to be domesticated and incorporated into an indigenous order (cf. Sahlins, 1985: 73–103). This structure was not always salient, and might be expected to generate rivalries between living local chiefs and the 'chiefly' foreigners who suddenly arrive. But a crucial feature of contact with voyagers – especially in earlier phases – was their transience. Europeans might make unreasonable demands while they were on an island, although these would probably be compensated for with gifts, but for most of the time local chiefs could display their associations with these potent foreigners without having to deal with their presence. Mariners were an absent source of foreign power and special things, rather than a permanent intrusion in the local order. In this sense there could be a congruence between the prior category of extra-local nobility and open and expensive dealings with actual foreign nobles.

On Niue, the conceptual categories were different: there were traditions that their own chiefs had been overthrown, although late in prehistory a new line was reputedly installed, many of whom were, however, assassinated (Thomson, 1902: 34–5). More significantly, there had been a long history of resistance to invaders from Tonga, who were associated with the chiefly line and also regarded, like the white man, as 'man-eaters' (Hood, 1863: 23). Strangers were thus opposed rather than celebrated. The notion that this attitude had a prior political and cultural basis and did not simply derive from the vicissitudes of contact is substantiated by the fact that Captain Cook, the first European to visit Niue, experienced sustained hostility in 1774, and found the place so singular in this respect that he named it 'Savage Island' (Beaglehole, 1961: 434–7).

Lupo's account suggested a shift from hostility based upon elementary ignorance to intercourse based on an equally elementary desire for things. This reappraisal of the encounters which constituted contact reveals the intransigence and hostility rather as an expression of a cultural structure, and its subsequent transformation to be highly constrained: the involvement of these Polynesians in peripheral exchange hardly reflected an unrestrained plunge into the world of commodities.

Just as modern international trade is entangled with foreign policy, the nature of Polynesian–European exchange relations was inextricably associated with representations of others on the part of both Europeans and islanders, and histories of contact and conflict with them. If the restricted nature of the barter carried out by Erskine at Niue in fact reflected an ambivalent compromise around an interest in limited trade, and a desire to disconnect things from their former, potentially dominant owners, then the less restricted, open-ended exchange we find elsewhere in Polynesia might turn out to have less to do with the particular features of the objects, than with the importation of a certain kind of foreignness that was seen as empowering rather than threatening.

In many other parts of Polynesia – and particularly in Hawaii, Tahiti, and the Marquesas – barter was entangled with a process of political transformation. Eighty years after Cook, eastern Polynesian polities were disrupted and elites displaced, but in the earlier decades, before Europeans occupied and restructured island societies, there was space for a dynamic reworking of indigenous systems. This was a space for ambitious chiefs to draw European things, ships and white men, into their own schemes, into projects that entailed the incorporation of some of the symbols and trappings of foreign power towards the creation of centralised indigenous polities on a novel scale.

From indifference to fetishisation: a history of Marquesan barter[2]

In the 1830s and 1840s, foreigners found the inhabitants of the Marquesas Islands to be obsessed with European guns. It might be assumed that this interest was a simple consequence of the technical properties of muskets: they would enable those already engaged in endemic conflict to fight more effectively and intensify their efforts to seize land or expand politically. However, in the early nineteenth century European firearms were often inaccurate; in the sort of hand-to-hand fighting which was usually carried out, they were not significantly more effective than indigenous weapons. The guns which reached the South Pacific were frequently also in poor condition and as likely to injure the user as any prospective victim (cf. Shineberg, 1971). In the early years of their introduction, some battles were clearly won because of the psychological effect of the noise and fire upon those unfamiliar with the weapons, but this must have diminished rapidly, and in any case cannot in itself explain the magnitude of the interest. The argument developed here is that muskets acquired great significance primarily because of their associations with narratives about foreign visitors who appear to have been assimilated to the category of indigenous warrior-chiefs. How this took place is explained in what follows.

The outward appearance of early barter in the Marquesas was much the same as took place elsewhere. Values in the earlier stages were particularly fluid. When Cook first arrived (in April 1744) he initially secured quite a few pigs in exchange for trifles, but the situation changed after the crew had been permitted to barter individually ashore; the next day Cook came back from the beach with only a few small pigs, which he complained had cost more 'than a Doz.^{n} would have done the evening before' (Beaglehole, 1961: 368).

what ruined our Market the most was of them giving for a Pig a very large quantity of Red feathers he had got at Amsterdam, [i.e. the island of Tongatapu] which these people much value and which the other did not know ... Thus was the fine prospect we had of getting a plentiful supply of refreshments of these people frustrated, and which will ever be the case so long as every one is allowed to make exchanges for what he pleaseth and in what manner he please's [sic] (Beaglehole, 1961: 369).

It was indeed a general feature that barter conducted by the crew caused the prices of indigenous commodities to rise; this was here accentuated by the non-correspondence of scales of value. But the difficulty in obtaining pigs endured well beyond these specific misunderstandings.

There was usually a good deal of sexual contact, and voyagers tended to be shocked that girls as young as eight or nine should be involved, and also that husbands should offer their wives, and fathers their daughters. Lisiansky, who with Krusenstern undertook the first Russian circumnavigation, and who visited Nukuhiva in 1804, thought that 'this proceeded from their ardent desire of possessing iron, or other European articles which, in their estimation, are above all price' (1814: 82). It is curious that Lisiansky should say this, since both he and Krusenstern experienced extraordinary difficulty in obtaining any animal food in the Marquesas. It was their own pigs, rather than iron, which the islanders seemed to place beyond price. Pigs were valuable partly because they were individual animals, to be named and nurtured like children, and also because they were killed mainly for grand commemorative feasts for chiefs and shamans, which were probably the most important Marquesan events. Certain animals would have been hard to part with because they were reared for specific ceremonies: to do something else with such a pig would offend the spirit of the person who should have been commemorated, or detract from the significance of the birth of a first-born child. Krusenstern had gathered that 'very few hogs were to be procured', and therefore made it known that only pigs would be accepted in return for axes and hatchets, which he knew the Marquesans wanted. This rule was abandoned when it failed to produce a supply of pork (Krusenstern, 1813, I: 114). An experience at Hakaui valley was typical:

[The chief] was the only one who brought a hog for sale; but he could not prevail on himself to part with his treasure, and after having concluded his bargain four times, and at last on very advantageous terms to himself, he immediately repented of it and returned us our goods, though he was highly pleased with them. (Krusenstern, 1813, I: 132)

This was essentially the experience of every visitor to the Marquesas before 1813. If pigs were obtained at all, they were obtained in very small numbers. It was often thought that this arose from scarcity, but, as a 'clerk' on the Russian voyage discovered, animals were kept well inland, away from the ships, to create such an impression, presumably out of fear that barter would be imposed or pigs stolen (Korobitsyn, 1944: 170; Shemelin, 1815–18, I: 134). In a few cases pigs were obtained for whales' teeth, which were already valuables within the Marquesan system (Appleton, 1799–1801: 10 October 1801). But traders often failed to carry these: Iselin noted that although 'hogs [were] pretty abundant' they could not get 'a very great supply' because they possessed no whales' teeth (n.d.: 39, 43).

A cause of this situation, as well as that on Niue, was that barter with outsiders was in no sense yet a structural element of the indigenous economy. There was no dependence on foreigners for anything which could not be produced on the islands. Since the needs of ships for water and provisions were often pressing, the dependence might rather be the other way around. While Marquesans were clearly excited by iron and trinkets, their own scales of value were not disproportionately subordinated to these new things. Unlike Lupo's Niue men, they were not 'crazy to get' iron tools or axes. What they gave in return were mostly coconuts and breadfruit, which were abundant, and which, in an unprocessed form, encapsulated an insignificant amount of labour.

Moreover, the Marquesans did not care about foreign contact to the extent that they attempted to monopolise it; they displayed no jealousy when visitors moved on to rival bays. In 1791, Marchand was unable to get more than a few pigs at Vaitahu, so he went south along the coast to Hapatoni, where he did obtain a few (Fleurieu, 1798, 1: 67–68). This seems to have been a matter of indifference to the Vaitahu people. Thirty years later things were very different, as I shall explain. But the earlier phase leads one to doubt Lisiansky's view that European things and foreign contact were highly valued. It rarely seems to have occurred to navigators that the things given out as 'trifles' might sometimes have been taken as such.

After 1813 this attitude of indifference was replaced by a preoccupation with contact – not because of a quantitative increase in the frequency of European visits, or any other longer-term trend, but because of the spectacular character of one intrusion, that of Captain David Porter of the US Navy in the latter part of the year. Britain and the United States were at war and Porter, having captured several British whaling vessels, decided to take possession of the Marquesas, and constructed a fortified base at Taiohae, Nukuhiva. Like many other foreign visitors, Porter went through the ritual of exchanging names with the chief Keatonui. In Marquesan terms, this was supposed to create a close identification, the property and interests of one becoming those of the other. Keatonui immediately used this alliance to draw the Americans into his own war: he told Opoti, as Porter was called, that he should help him repulse the Hapaʻa, a group occupying a valley a few miles to the east of Taiohae, with whom the Taiohae people, the Teiʻi, had evidently been fighting: 'he told me they had cursed the bones of his mother, who had died but a short time since, that as we had exchanged names, she was now my mother, and I was bound to espouse her cause' (Porter, 1822, II: 27). Although Porter claimed that he was reluctant to become involved, the Hapaʻa maintained a hostile attitude, and he soon formed the view that 'the sooner they were convinced of their folly, the better' (ibid.). An engagement took place on the hills above Taiohae, and a number of Hapaʻa were killed by musket fire. The Teiʻi then descended upon and ravaged Hapa's settlements.

Since it appears that political groupings and the balance of forces had been relatively stable in this part of Nukuhiva, such a clear-cut military outcome was remarkable. To Keatonui, Opoti's victory 'seemed incredible' (Porter, 1822, II: 36). Shortly afterwards, Porter met the Hapaʻa chief, and agreed to be at peace, provided that the Hapaʻa supplied pork and fruit on a weekly basis, for which they would 'be compensated in iron, and such other articles as would be most useful to them' (ibid.: 38). Everyone treated Opoti as a victorious warrior-chief, so it is not surprising that whereas Marquesans had dictated the terms of barter to previous visitors, new terms were now imposed upon them. Over the following days envoys from other tribal groups similarly paid homage to Opoti and began to bring offerings: the foreigners 'rioted in luxuries which the island afforded' (ibid.: 56). However, offerings from Taipi valley (Melville's Typee), traditionally hostile to Taiohae, were conspicuously absent. Porter complained and gave them the choice of 'peace or war' (ibid.: 67), but the Taipi suggested that the fact that pork and fruit were asked for merely indicated Opoti's inability to come and take them. The head warrior at Taiohae was furious and wanted to make war at once, but Keatonui was saddened and regarded the Taipi's brave words as an expression of their ignorance 'of the dreadful effects of the bouhies', that is, of puhi or muskets. Keatonui's son went to Taipi, in a further effort to induce the people there to submit to Opoti's authority, but returned only to report further defiance: the Taipi asserted that Porter and his men 'were white lizards, mere dirt...the posteriors and privates' of the Teiʻi (ibid.: 69). Keatonui then favoured war, and the head warrior, upon hearing of the report, came into the American settlement, 'boiling with rage, and in a rather peremptory tone insisted on immediate hostilities'. Porter thought that he had to assert himself over the warrior:

I told him...that I did not need his advice, and that I should go to war or make peace when I thought proper, without consulting him; that it was only necessary that he should do as I directed him, and everything must be left to my management. I further told him to leave our village until he could learn to conduct himself more respectfully. He walked off a few paces among the crowd, then turning round, coolly said, he believed I was a great coward.

Porter was again imprisoned by a combination of his own dispositions and Marquesans' expectations of the warrior-chief Opoti, and again he reinforced and extended them: he pursued the warrior, and threatened him with destruction 'upon the repetition of such expression' but immediately acceded to the pressure and prepared for war. This sort of aggression apparently impressed the Marquesans deeply, especially because, after an embarrassingly unsuccessful initial attempt, Porter proceeded to crush the Taipi, destroying their houses and canoes, and desecrating some of their religious sites.

The longer-term effects of this great victory on political relations were limited: Opoti's friends at Taiohae could not sustain any hegemony over the Taipi after the Americans' departure. But it was highly significant in cultural terms: Keatonui, who had exchanged names with Porter, continued to use the name Opoti until 1817, if not until his death. Another kind of association was later emphasised by a chiefly woman of very high rank, Keatonui's grand-daughter Paetini, who in 1836 boasted to Lieutenant Browning 'of having been Com. Porter's girl aged twelve' (Browning, 1833–1836: 11). This assertion conflicts with Porter's own account, in which he said that his attentions were rebuffed 'with sternness' by 'this dignified personage' (1822, II: 107). Whatever the truth of the matter, Paetini's assertion accorded with the construct of Opoti as the warrior-chief invading from foreign shores, whose usurpation was marked by an appropriation of local women. Opoti's aggressive behaviour no doubt fuelled the Marquesan construction of him as an almost mythical hero; he became the focus of a cult which persisted for several decades. During the visit of the US Navy ship *Brandywine* in 1829, the visitors learnt that there would be a celebration:

Tomorrow there will be a great dance and feast in commemoration of Commodore Porter's victory over the Happah's indeed they think that Porter is king of all the world; they venerate his name. (Dornin, 1826–1830: July 1829)

This celebration no doubt took place while the Americans were in the bay precisely because the Tei'i wanted to engineer a repetition of Opoti's partisan involvement. The visitors in fact observed that 'our friends the [Tei'i] are solicitous that we should join sides with them'.

From the time of Porter's visit, a new fear and respect of firearms developed (Shillibeer, 1817: 64–5). Guns had been in use well before Porter's incursion, and the word *puhi* was recorded during the Russians' visit of 1804 (Lisiansky, 1814: 324). It was the distinctive events of 1813 which gave rise to a new set of Marquesan ideas within which muskets had a privileged place. Ambitious chiefs and warriors began to associate their prospects for advancement strongly with personal links with foreigners such as ships' captains, and especially with their own access to muskets. In the southern part of the Marquesas, these notions did not involve specific reference to Opoti, but there was clearly an unprecedented sense that *puhi* were vital. Before Porter, ships experienced considerable difficulty in obtaining pigs; after Porter, almost anything could be exchanged for muskets or gunpowder. As early as 1816, a sandalwood trader noted that

Firearms & ammunition [are] the staple trade of the Islds. and red broad-cloth next in esteem A variety of cutlery and beeds feathers & other articles & ornaments should be provided, and a few whale's teeth (the longer the better) may sometimes produce sandal wood & generally proove [sic] a good article for purchasing hogs & other provisions. (Forbes, 1815: undated entry headed 'Marquesas Islands')

The French trader Rocquefeuil, who visited both the southern and northern parts of the group in 1817, similarly noted that muskets were the basis of trade, adding that they were likely to remain so, 'given the continuous state of hostility in which these people live' (1823, I: 299). The new situation made this utilitarian connection between warfare and a demand for guns eminently plausible, but it would not have made much sense even five years earlier.

Nor did this functional logic subsequently encompass Marquesan uses of firearms. The meanings which arose derived ultimately from efficacy in fighting, but one set of the use-values of an object can often be subordinated or displaced as the thing moves into a new social domain. Postage stamps and money would be meaningless if they could never have been spent or used to send letters, but these functions become elements of meaning without potential social effect when notes and coins or stamps are incorporated into private collections or museums. Their identity is understood in terms of former functions which are actually precluded by subsequent transformation. A chief on Nukuhiva in 1825 made it clear to Captain Paulding of the US Navy that guns and powder were prestige objects for display:

His rank and importance was displayed in the possession of six muskets, and two casks of powder that hung directly fronting the door, and which the chief took occasion to point out to me soon after I entered. To him they were a treasure, and, in fact, the wealth and consequence of every individual seemed to be estimated by this standard alone. The powder was covered over with canvas, and the muskets highly polished. (1831: 59).

But of course these things were not 'status symbols' in the Western sense. The core of that usage supposes that an object stands for a person's aesthetics and ability to purchase such things, but the appropriation of guns as Marquesan things made them bearers of *tapu*. Any activity, including war, which involved the influence of deities, was *tapu*; this state generated restriction around the activity itself, and associated persons and objects (Thomas, 1987). Traditional weapons such as spears and clubs were *tapu*, and acquired the name of a warrior killed with them, or whose blood had stained them, the value of the weapon thereby being 'greatly enhanced' (Porter, 1822, II: 37). The practice of naming was extended to muskets, and it was noted that any animal shot with a *tapu* gun would also become *tapu*, and could only be eaten by men or those of higher rank (Dordillon n.d. quoted in Thomas, 1986a: 116).

At least on Nukuhiva, where Porter had intervened, this was not just a general kind of symbolic value: guns carried a particular historical resonance. In 1825 Paulding had also been told by a warrior or chiefly man at Taiohae

that his father had been a great warrior and a friend of Opotee. Before his door was a swivel and a number of shot, that he said he had obtained from Opotee. He prized them very highly, although they could not be of the least use to him, except as they served to gratify his vanity. (1831: 59–60)

It is perhaps not especially likely that what the chief possessed did derive from Porter's visit, but the fact that the American was represented as the origin of these things is crucial. Possessing them was a way of sustaining a link with an awesome force, a way of repeating a story which might itself be re-enacted. Polynesian genealogy was often a charter for recapitulation (cf. Sahlins, 1985: 47): this chief or his descendant might reproduce the father's victorious alliance with an American warrior. In the 1820s and 1830s, the Marquesans were so deeply preoccupied with Opoti, and with muskets, that it is surprising that Paulding did not recognise that the material remnants of this intervention should not have a use in the expression of a potent association, the value of which was hardly captured by the dismissive notion of 'vanity'.

In the southern Marquesas, Iotete, the chief of Vaitahu bay, gradually acquired, and jealously guarded, a near-monopoly over exchange with European ships. He obtained numerous muskets and, by the late 1830s, controlled the whole of the small island of Tahuata, and was making vigorous efforts to extend his influence to the neighbouring island of Hiva Oa. But his trading activities were motivated neither by simple greed nor narrow political ambition. Rather, he situated himself in a narrative loosely based on the history of contact and chiefly expansion elsewhere in Polynesia. This emerged when he explained his reasons for not adopting Christianity to a missionary:

He has got an idea that the word of God will not grow under his authority, he thinks that his skin is too much marked with tattooing, and that it was at Tahiti when the missionaries first came, old Bomare [Pomare] was taken away before the word of God took effect and grew on Tahiti. It was under Pomare's son that Christianity was embraced. Iotete thinks that it will be under his son that the Gospel will grow at the Marquesas: – this son of his is a lad about 12 years of age called *Timau*, he will not agree at present to have his skin marked as they do in general. (Darling, 1836: 35).

What was envisaged was thus a generationally staged transformation in which Christianity, and the abandonment of certain heathen practices such as tattooing[3] were linked with the formation of a new and extended political order. In this situation 'indigenous' and 'foreign' became, like 'tradition' and 'custom' elsewhere, actively constituted categories: particular practices and objects ceased to be things which were simply used or done and turned into markers of the appropriation of a kind of foreign power and the displacement of a local and now secondary form of power.

In the passage quoted Iotete did not specifically mention muskets, but their significance was evident elsewhere. The same missionary was shown the chief's dead wife.

Iotete took me to the house where his late wife is kept, he prides himself that he has not taken her to the *taha tapu* (sacred place). She has been embalmed and is in a house near to his own, in the same house with her there are 10 or 12 muskets, which were got in her live time, these and many other things are all most sacred, and cannot be touched. (Darling, 1836: 31)

The traditional mortuary place would probably have been in the interior of the island; the fact that this place was by the sea, to which Iotete himself had recently moved, suggests some cultural reorientation associated with the new forms of power and prestige. However, it would be dishonest to claim that the available sources permit a full explication of these distant shifts in Marquesan religion and thought. But there was certainly some ritualisation of the sexual aspect of contact with Europeans: on one occasion the missionaries had to persuade some people at Vaitahu 'to refrain from making something in the shape of a ship…for men and women to go on board in imitation of what they do when a ship comes' (Darling, 1834–35: 10 January, 14 January, 1835).

Muskets were exchange items as well as weapons and stationary things for display. They differed distinctly from most of the objects circulated in earlier indigenous exchange, which unlike many Melanesian trading systems, required no consequential regional specialisation. There were no centres which produced distinct types of valuables to be exchanged against qualitatively different things such as mats, pottery or food. Relationships between localities were therefore not characterised by any sort of dependency, because no place produced important things which were not also produced virtually everywhere else. (There are, of course, other potential foundations for inter-social inequality, but these were not effective in the Marquesas for reasons discussed elsewhere (Thomas, 1986a: 148)). The major presentations between the inhabitants of different valleys took place at competitive feasts at which large quantities of food were offered. The process of competition could produce temporary inequalities of status – which might be reversed at a later 'potlatch' style event – but did not generate any sort of systematic domination.

The circulation of guns could however produce a new kind of systematic asymmetry because firearms were both durable and extra-local. Unlike the cooked food offered at feasts, they did not cease to be exchange items, and could always either be used or passed on to another group. Because, as we noted above, ships called very much more at a few established safe harbours than at any number of other inhabited bays, the point of introduction into the indigenous system was highly localised. The exchange which followed from the fact that demand was widespread also differed from earlier forms of exchange because muskets had a singular status: there was a lack of qualitative equivalence between a gun and anything which might be given in return. In fact, people from other bays mostly made no attempt to give anything in return, but simply came to Vaitahu to 'beg' muskets or powder from Iotete (for example Darling, 1834–35: 1 June 1835). These transactions created indebtedness, and Iotete seems to have successfully turned former equals into dependents of a sort (Thomas, 1986b: 12–16).

There was thus no automatic interest in what Europeans would call 'guns'. The objects that move between groups through transcultural barter may appear valuable or useful in a transparent sense, but it should not be assumed that uses are understood similarly by both sides. The apparent visibility of the worth of a thing masks an analytical trap, because the meanings cannot in fact be specified in the absence of local information about the ways things were actually received. Hence, in this case, the European category of the gun must be displaced by an attempt to grasp the shifting Marquesan conceptions of these objects. *Puhi* became ways of conjuring up a history, things to display in sacred places, and special kinds of exchange items. Their value arose from the indigenous discovery of these prospective uses. It depended upon the intrinsic features of muskets, but did not exist before these attributes were seized upon and recontextualised by Marquesans.

Before returning to the general question of the significance of varieties of peripheral exchange in the history of dependency, I present one further case, in which the argument behind the Marquesan permutations is crystallised. It concerns the politically ambitious and culturally innovative Pomare chiefs of Tahiti, whose deployment of European links exemplifies the symbolically complex aristocratic powerplay which dominated the early history of Polynesian contact with Europeans.[4]

Pomare I was an enthusiastic consumer of alcoholic drinks, which were known as 'ava Peretani or British kava. This might be seen as his own weakness for intoxication, or as part of a general process of 'acculturation', but seems rather to reflect the selective constitution and adoption of 'European-ness' as a Tahitian political symbol, especially since in later years Pomare II actually substituted 'ava Peretani for indigenous kava:

Pohmaree left off drinking Kava, but he afterwards took to European liquors; and it was his delight to sit for long evenings together, along with his chiefs, over a bowl of grog, talking about Buonaparte, Captain Cook, King George, and foreign events. (Henry and Kent, 1828: 351–2)[5]

This was a strategy which had been manifested much earlier, when a British pennant left by Wallis in 1767 was woven into one of the sacred feather girdles which were the most crucial items of Society Islands regalia. Just as Polynesian expansion involved such things as acquiring titles in new districts, chiefs attempted to assimilate the trappings of great foreigners, as represented by naval visitors such as Cook and Vancouver. The social value of alcohol arose because of what it replaced: kava was of political and ceremonial significance throughout Polynesia, and in the Society Islands was more or less confined to those of high rank, the skin condition produced by excessive use being considered a 'badge of honour', as one observer put it (quoted in Oliver, 1974, I: 258). British kava was a special, foreign form of this elite marker. Although it was often given to chiefs rather than directly bartered, the value of the drink cannot be disconnected from this process of substitution which was linked with great foreign names.

At this point it is helpful to raise the question of how novel things are dealt with conceptually. Entities that are entirely strange and new are perceived and need to be named and spoken about. If a thing is initially recognised in a context entailing linguistic interaction with people already familiar with it, their name, or what is taken to be their name for it, may be adopted, but this obviously does not resolve the conceptual question of what kind of thing it is. Therefore, although the Australian marsupial was referred to as a 'kangaroo' in the publications arising from Cook's voyage to Australia, those who first attempted to draw it clearly saw the animal as something like a kind of giant rat (see the George Stubbs painting reproduced as colour plate 1 in Smith, 1960). But the process which is perhaps more common involves an assimilation of the novelty to an existing category. Here, the most useful approach is one which deals with the blurred edges of concepts and semantic indeterminacy.[6] Categories have fuzzy edges and more or less incorporate weaker instances which agree with some, but not all, implicit criteria: neither a boatshed nor a greenhouse is a canonical building, but ultimately the former satisfies key criteria while the latter probably does not.

This is relevant to many forms of barter, as such trade typically involves innovation (cf. Humphrey, 1985: 50), but is quite crucial to the type of peripheral exchange with tribal groups discussed here, because the salient features of many of the items transacted are their exotic origins and their difference from indigenous articles. The 'fuzzy category' approach would suggest that what is unfamiliar is frequently recognised as a form of something known: X is a kind of Y and may be assimilated to Y as a sub-category or marked form. Horses were unknown to Fijians before the nineteenth century and were then called 'large pigs' (*puaka levu*; Maudslay, 1930: 150). A thing may also be taken as a sort of compound of two categories: the Australian platypus was apparently sometimes called a 'duck-mole' (cf. *OED* entry under 'Platypus').

Of course, the fact that a term persists does not necessarily indicate that speakers actually regard one thing as sharing the substance or the crucial attributes of another: it cannot be generally assumed that the meanings are more than shallow and conventional (cf. Keesing, 1985). When English speakers use expressions of the 'duck-mole' type which posit a mating metaphor – the novel thing being a 'cross between' two previously known types – they would not usually believe that anything like genetic trans-mission accounts for the common attributes of the different creatures. But the linguistic process has a cultural parallel, which may exist together with, or in the absence of, terminological inclusion, since in some cases profound identifications are clearly developed between categories. There is no *a priori* element in an entity or a term which permits one to determine whether the process of categorical assimilation is merely conventional or more consequential. The question must be resolved on the basis of usage and practice. It can be established that at a certain phase in Marquesan history guns came to be charged with the set of meanings associated with indigenous Marquesan weapons: this meant that they could not be used effectively unless certain *tapu* restrictions were observed, and that their use had consequences beyond physical killing or injury (cf. above). Certain social meanings, possibilities and constraints are thus carried over from the general type to the introduced thing. In the Tahitian case, alcohol was not simply assimilated to the category of kava in a meaningful way, but was actually substituted for it in practice. The political significance of *'ava Peretani* in the indigenous context of course derived from the fact that it was simultaneously different and the same: it was special not because it was foreign, but because it was a scarce foreign form of something familiar.

What is important in these practical contexts is not the semantic issue of whether an instance is a strong or weak representative of the type, but the potential for a marginal form with particular associations to be privileged in a marked way.

The circumstances of early contact on colonial peripheries are historically singular and might not be thought to indicate much of more general relevance about barter. One principle, however, that emerges in a striking manner in these cases, does have broader pertinence. Use-value is not a stable matter; it derives from, but is by no means intrinsic to, the properties of particular exchange objects. The different parties to various stages of a transaction may have quite different conceptions of the things at issue in exchange. In many instances, these may not be restricted to the material objects that actually move, but may also incorporate aspects of context and prior affiliation. Hence, what for one side is a gift relationship may be barter for the other. This type of perspectival divergence may be more pronounced in novel encounters than in stable and regularised relationships, but could not be said to be restricted to the former.

The interpretations offered here of early contact radically destabilise the image of the naive hunger of newly contacted tribal peoples for iron and trinkets. The moral vision of the injustice of trading in cheap junk itself contains an injustice, in the sense that the indigenous sense of these transactions is forgotten. New things were assimilated to extended categories, appropriated, constituted, and used in ways mostly beyond the vision of the foreign transactors. While native peoples appeared to be being seduced by foreign values, they were actually drawing novelties into persistently autonomous strategies and domains. Of course, the condition of autonomy subsequently came to an end, and action within their territories was transformed and highly constrained by external forces. But this process of dispossession was grounded in another interplay of intrusion and reaction, and did not grow out of the dynamic of peripheral exchange.

NOTES

My appreciation of the issues discussed here benefited a great deal from the other papers presented in the seminar series on barter. Comments from Caroline Humphrey, Stephen Hugh-Jones and Margaret Jolly have been especially helpful.

1 Another substantial point of retrospective indignation has been the alienation of inalienable land on the basis of transactions which islanders saw as involving nothing more than temporary use-rights.

2 The Marquesan material in this paper derives from more extended treatments (Thomas, 1986a, 1990: 131–65) which contain more detail and fuller documentation. A complementary work (1991) links these Polynesian cases to broader issues about material culture and colonialism.

3 Elsewhere the abandonment of certain feasts was mentioned (cf. Thomas, 1986a).
4 For details see Newbury, 1967; Gunson, 1969; Baré, 1987.
5 The male session around a bowl was the usual context of kava drinking in many parts of Oceania, though in eastern Polynesia seems to have been less ritualised than was generally so elsewhere.
6 I refer here to prototype or probabilistic theories of categorisation, but am obviously not concerned in this paper to explore the issues in any rigorous way; see Smith and Medin (1981) for an overview from a psychological perspective and Holland and Quinn (1987) for several papers employing congruent approaches in relation to cultural models.

REFERENCES

Appleton, N. 1799–1801. Journal of a voyage from Salem... Essex Institute Library, Salem, Mass.; Pacific Manuscripts Bureau microfilm 200.
Baré, J.-F. 1987. *Tahiti, les Temps et les Pouvoirs*. Paris: ORSTOM.
Beaglehole, J. C. 1961. *The Journals of Captain James Cook. Volume II. The Voyage of the Resolution and the Adventure*. Cambridge: Hakluyt Society.
Beechey, F. W. 1831. *Narrative of a Voyage to the Pacific... in the years 1825, 26, 27, 28*. London: Henry Colburn and R. Bentley.
Bennett, F. D. 1804. *Narrative of a Whaling Voyage around the Globe... 1833–1836*. London: Bentley.
Bennett, Judith. 1987. *Wealth of the Solomons: a History of a Pacific Archipelago, 1800–1978*. Honolulu: University of Hawaii Press.
Browning, R. L. 1833–1836. Notes on the South Sea Islands. MS, Library of Congress, Washington.
Creery, I. 1983. *The Inuit (Eskimo) of Canada*. London: Minority Rïghts Group (Report No. 60).
Darling, David. 1834–1835. Journal at Vaitahu. In: South Seas Journals, Council for World Mission collection, School of Oriental and African Studies Library, London.
    1836. Report on the Marquesas. In: South Seas Letters, Council for World Mission collection, School of Oriental and African Studies Library, London.
Dornin, T. A. 1826–1830. Journal kept on board US Frigate *Brandywine*. Navy Records, National Archives, Washington.
Erskine, J. E. 1853. *Journal of a Cruise among the Islands of the Western Pacific*. London: Murray.
Fleurieu, C. P. C. de. 1798. *Voyage autour du monde......1790–1792 par Etienne Marchand*. Paris: Imp. de la République.
Forbes, Charles. 1815. Voyage around Cape Horn to the Pacific Ocean...[in the ship *Indus*]. Essex Institute Library, Salem [Pacific Manuscript Bureau microfilm 202].
Gill, W. 1856. *Gems from the Coral Islands*. London: Ward.
Gunson, Niel. 1969. Pomare II of Tahiti and Polynesian imperialism. *Journal of Pacific History* 4: 65–82.
Henry, S. P. and J. R. Kent. 1828. Missions. *South Asian Register* 4: 351–2. Partly reproduced in: *Journal of Pacific History*, 4: 82.

Holland, D. and N. Quinn (eds.) 1987. *Cultural Models in Language and Thought.* Cambridge: Cambridge University Press.

Hood, T. H. 1863. *Notes of a Cruise in HMS 'Fawn' in the Western Pacific.* Edinburgh: Edmonston and Douglas.

Humphrey, Caroline. 1985. Barter and economic disintegration. *Man,* 20: 48–72.

Iselin, I. n.d. *Journal of a Trading Voyage around the World, 1805–1808.* New York: McIlroy and Emmet.

Keesing, Roger M. 1985. Conventional metaphors and anthropological metaphysics: the problematic of cultural translation. *Journal of Anthropological Research,* 41: 201–17.

Korobitsyn, N. I. 1944. [Extracts from his journal] in A. I. Andreev (ed.) *Zapiski. Russiye otkritya v Tikoham okeane i Severnoi Amerike v XVIII–XIX verkakh. Sbornik materialov pod.* [Records. Russian discoveries in the Pacific Ocean and North America from the XVIII to XIX centuries.] Moscow.

Krusenstern, A. J. von. 1813. *Voyage round the World...1803–1806.* London: Murray.

Lisiansky, U. 1814. *A Voyage round the World...1803–1806.* London: John Booth.

Lizot, J. 1985. *Tales of the Yanomami: Daily Life in the Venezuelan Forest.* Cambridge: Cambridge University Press.

Lupo, J. 1923. The story of Niue. *Journal of the Polynesian Society,* 32: 238–43.

Maudslay, A. P. 1930. *Life in the Pacific Fifty Years Ago.* London: Routledge.

Newbury, C. W. 1967. *Te hau pahu rahi:* Pomare II and the concept of inter-island government in eastern Polynesia. *Journal of the Polynesian Society,* 76: 477–514.

Oliver, D. L. 1974. *Ancient Tahitian Society.* Canberra: Australian National University Press.

Paulding, H. 1831. *Journal of the Cruise of the U.S. Schooner Dolphin.* New York: Carvill.

Porter, D. 1822. *Journal of a Cruise made to the Pacific Ocean.* New York: Wiley and Halsted.

Ralston, C. 1988. Changes in the lives of ordinary Hawaiian women. In M. Jolly and M. Macintyre (eds.) *Family and gender in the Pacific: Domestic Contradictions and the Colonial Impact.* Cambridge: Cambridge University Press.

Royle, H. 1843. Results of missionary labour at Aitutaki. *Missionary Magazine and Chronicle,* 7: 116–17.

Sahlins, M. 1981. *Historical Metaphors and Mythical Realities.* Ann Arbor: Michigan UP.

1985. *Islands of History.* Chicago: Chicago University Press.

Shemelin, F. 1815–1818. *Zhurnal pervoyo puteshestviya rossiyan vokrug zemnogo shara.* [Journal of the first voyage of the Russians around the world.] St Petersburg.

Shillibeer, J. 1817. *A Narrative of the Briton's Voyage to Pitcairn's Island.* Taunton: J. W. Marriot.

Shineberg, Dorothy. 1967. *They came for Sandalwood.* Melbourne: University Press.

1971. Guns and men in Melanesia. *Journal of Pacific History,* 6: 61–82.

Smith, Bernard, 1960. *European Vision and the South Pacific.* Oxford: University Press.

Smith, E. E. and D. L. Medin. 1981. *Categories and Concepts.* Cambridge, Mass.: Harvard University Press.

Thomas, N. 1986a. Social and cultural dynamics in early Marquesan history. PhD thesis, Australian National University.

1986b. '*Le roi de Tahuata*': Iotete and the transformation of south Marquesan politics, 1826–1842. *Journal of Pacific History*, 21: 3–20.

1987. Unstable categories: *tapu* and gender in the Marquesas. In C. Ralston and N. Thomas (eds.) *Sanctity and Power: Gender in Pacific History* (special issue, *Journal of Pacific History*, 22 (3–4)).

1990. *Marquesan Societies: Inequality and Political Transformation in Eastern Polynesia.* Oxford: Oxford University Press.

1991. *Entangled Objects: Exchange, Material Culture and Colonialism in the Pacific.* Cambridge, Mass: Harvard University Press.

Thomson, B. 1902. *Savage Island: an Account of a Sojourn in Niue and Tonga.* London: Murray.

Tuhanuku, J. T. 1983. Trade unions and politics. In P. Larmour and S. Tarua (eds.) *Solomon Islands Politics.* Suva: University of the South Pacific.

Williams, J. 1838. *Missionary Enterprises in the South Sea Islands.* London: John Snow.

3   Yesterday's luxuries, tomorrow's necessities: business and barter in northwest Amazonia

Stephen Hugh-Jones

Central to capitalism is a vision of man's limitless needs, needs which lead to his increasing mastery of nature and which propel him onwards and upwards in a spiral of progress. In contemporary Amazonia, and with such progress in mind, missionaries, merchants and government officials vie with each other to bring the material and moral benefits of civilisation to Amerindians. Each mission combines church with store, and even the cocaine-dealers claim a civilising mission as they barter coca leaves for coca-cola.

Long ago, in his Second Discourse on Inequality, and possibly with these same Amerindians in mind, Rousseau questioned this optimistic view of progress and rewrote its history as a tragedy:

This new condition, with its solitary and simple life, very limited in its needs, and very few instruments invented to supply them, left men to enjoy a great deal of leisure, which they used to procure many sorts of commodities unknown to their fathers; and this was the first yoke they imposed upon themselves, without thinking about it, and the first source of the evils they prepared for their descendants. For not only did such commodities continue to soften both body and mind, they almost lost through habitual use their power to please, and as they had at the same time degenerated into actual needs, being deprived of them became much more cruel than the possession of them was sweet; and people were unhappy in losing them without being happy in possessing them. (1984: 113)

Rousseau's pessimistic vision of man's pathological addiction to drug-like commodities is reflected into many a contemporary account of the Indians of Amazonia. Observers frequently mention the harmful impact of Western consumer goods, and often stress the obsessive and insistent manner with which the Indians demand the cornucopia of assorted possessions that travellers bring with them to the forest. Ellen Basso (1973: 7) writes of her experience amongst the Kalapalo of the Brazilian Xingú region 'during the first year of my stay among the Kalapalo, I was inundated with requests for articles of clothing, cooking vessels, food, magazines, and other of my possessions, as well as for presents that I was exhorted to buy in Río de Janeiro' and Napoleon Chagnon (1977: 8) says of the Venezuelan Yanomami:[1] 'The thing that bothered me most was the incessant, passioned, and aggressive demand the Indians made [for goods] ... I was bombarded by such demands day after day, months on end, until I could not bear to see an Indian.'

These demands are so insistent (and I speak here from personal experience) that they form an indelible impression on anthropologists and figure prominently in prefaces, introductory chapters and even whole books which describe the experience of fieldwork in Amazonia. As this 'consumerism' appears to be a characteristic feature of lowland South American Indians, it merits documentation and analysis alongside the more traditional anthropological concerns of subsistence, kinship or myth. Yet when it comes to the main text of the standard monograph, the presence and impact of foreign goods are often strangely absent. As if to bring the image of a 'traditional' society into sharper focus, the ethnographer has tidied away these intrusive objects, like the television cameramen who hide the tin cans from view and plead with Indians to remove their clothes to better present the viewer with untarnished images of the good life.

In this paper, I shall discuss the acquisition, distribution, and consumption of manufactured goods amongst the Barasana and other Tukanoan Indians of the Río Pirá-Paraná in the Vaupés region of Colombia.[2] I shall trace what Kopytoff (1986) has called a 'biography of things' by following the trajectory of manufactured goods as they first pass from White people to Indians in exchange for produce or labour and then get exchanged in a network of barter that distributes them between different Indian communities. Objects may be exchanged either against other foreign merchandise or against goods of local manufacture and may be withdrawn at any point to be put to a variety of different uses.

For ease of exposition, I shall treat this sequence in reverse order. Starting with consumption, I discuss the role and significance of these goods and explore some of the reasons why Indians attach such importance to acquiring and possessing them; I then focus on the use of foreign merchandise in exchanges between Indians and end by relating indigenous barter to external trade between Indians and outsiders.

I have chosen this 'biographical' approach both to emphasise the continuities and interconnections involved between the different parts of the circuit, and in reaction to the fragmentary way that this topic has been treated in the literature on Amazonia. I shall argue that one aspect of the value and significance of manufactured goods lies in the circumstances of their acquisition from White people and also that, by forming trading alliances with White people and by obtaining goods such as guns, Indians can significantly alter the terms on which their own internal trade takes place. This is hinted at when Taussig (1987: 61) talks of the French explorer Jules Crevaux who stayed with a Carijona Indian chief who 'had at least ten rifles and a similar number of cutlasses, together with four boxes of Western goods'. Furthermore, by taking both together, we can see that trade between White people and Indians is continuous with barter amongst the Indians themselves and influenced by it. One consequence of this is that, in trade between White people and Indians, the two sides may not fully share each other's understanding of the objects, values and social relations involved.

Whilst I recognise some very real differences between them, in this context I do not find it useful or advisable to draw a sharp line between Western capitalism and aboriginal economies as ideal types characterised by opposed pairs such as exchange value/use value or market exchange/ indigenous reciprocity (see for example Taussig, 1980; 1987: Part 1). Such contrasts obscure both the relationship and articulation between the peripheries of such economies and the cultural determination of wants and needs which are the focus of my interest here.[3] Instead, I argue that, in practice and at a local level, there is a continuity or 'fit' between capitalist institutions and Indian exchange practices. How this 'fit' works out in practice depends on factors such as the power differential between the individuals and groups involved, and on the nature and intensity of contact between them, and it may vary from predatory slavery, through parasitic exploitation, to something closer to a form of symbiosis. Even under the grossly exploitative conditions of debt-peonage where White traders use manufactured goods advanced on credit to trap Indians in an endless spiral of debt, it is important to look at the situation from both sides. This means bearing in mind that the Indian economy has its own internal logic which reacts and adapts to outside forces, and that the Indians themselves are active agents who often demand the goods they are given, and who sometimes use them to create further debts amongst their own people. Failure to appreciate this point has led to an underestimation of the role and significance of Indian 'chiefs' and other brokers or middlemen in alliance with White traders in some of the recent ethnohistorical writings on NW Amazonia.

Leaving aside personal accounts of the circumstances of fieldwork, in other anthropological writing on Amazonia reference to the Amerindians' involvement with Western goods typically occurs in one or other of three relatively separate areas of discussion devoted either to debt-peonage, or to indigenous trade, or to cultural change and ethnocide.

Accounts of debt-peonage[4] rightly stress the often ruthless exploitation of Indians by White colonists, but frequently fail to deal adequately with the Indians' active role in inter-ethnic trade, with their perception of the objects and exchanges involved, or with the articulation of debt-peonage relations with trading relations between the Indians themselves.[5] By contrast, accounts of indigenous trade tend to stress its more 'traditional' features, often downplay the role and significance of Western goods, and rarely provide a satisfactory account of how such goods are obtained in the first place.[6] Finally, although discussions of cultural change often focus on the issue of manufactured goods and their impact on Indian life and culture, they again tend to omit adequate discussion of how these goods are acquired from White people, and, instead of analysing their significance and value to the Indians, suggest rather that such goods are unnecessary and harmful and that demand for them stems from external pressures. In this latter vein Dumont (1976: 171) writes of the Venezuelan Panaré that 'clothing has recently been adopted because of the constant pressure which has been exerted by the outside world. In fact, not only do the Indians have no need for clothes – clothing is obviously harmful to them and an ethnocentric conception of decency results in gifts which are really poisoned apples'. Others go even further and suggest not only that foreign goods are foisted upon Indians, but also that these Indians are, by nature, uninterested in, or even opposed to, economic and technological change. Of the Tukanoans of Northwest Amazonia, Reichel-Dolmatoff (1971: 310–11) says 'among the Indians there is usually little interest in new knowledge that might be used for exploiting the environment more effectively and there is little concern for maximizing short-term gains or for obtaining more food or raw materials than are actually needed', and, more generally, Lizot (1972: 72) claims that 'primitive societies are characterized by a rejection of technological progress ... their disdain for work and their lack of interest in autonomous technological progress are certain.'

When I began fieldwork in 1968, the different groups living in the Pirá-Paraná basin of the southern Colombian Vaupés – the Bará, Barasana, Makuna, Taiwano, and Tatuyo – had the outward appearance of a traditional Indian society and their contact with outsiders had been quite limited. This appearance was nonetheless deceptive and their enthusiastic reception of the small flock of newly arrived missionaries and ethnographers that descended upon them in the late sixties was not unrelated to the recent demise of a long-declining rubber industry which had hitherto been the Indians' main source of foreign merchandise, a source which had itself been preceded, in previous centuries, by trade with neighbouring Indian groups who obtained manufactured goods from missionaries, traders and slavers.

In 1979, the Barasana and their neighbours began to experience the effects of an economic boom associated with the illicit production of cocaine, a boom which led to a huge rise in the consumption of Western goods amongst all the people of the region, both White and Indian alike. Some measure of the scale of this boom is given by an analysis of the account books of a cocaine dealer trading in the Pirá-Paraná zone. Over a six-month period and in exchange for about 5,500 kilos of coca leaves and just over 2 kilos of cocaine base he gave out merchandise worth some £18,000 to approximately 100 Indians, some of whom had debts of up to £2,000. Although the scale and content of this trade was new, it was no more than a recent transformation of a very old system of debt-peonage which had equally formed the basis for the extraction of slaves, rubber, balata, *farinha* (manioc meal), egret plumes and animal skins in earlier times. Like these previous economic booms, cocaine too was of limited duration: by 1983, a fall in the price of cocaine, rising prices for raw materials, industrialised manufacture elsewhere, increased police control, and the arrival of guerillas of the Colombian Armed Revolutionary Forces (FARC), led to the virtual abandonment of cocaine production in the area. A year later gold was discovered in the south of the region and the cycle began again.

The Barasana speak of manufactured goods as being imbued with *ewa*, an irresistibly attractive and potent force which leads them to act in an uncontrolled manner and to do things against their better judgement. To be under the spell of this *ewa* is to be *bekigi*, a term also applied to people who are mad or drunk. In an apt metaphorical rendering of the fatal attraction of Western goods and of the workings of debt peonage, their myth of *Ibiaka widai* 'the little Sticky Man' tells of a lecherous cannibal living in the sky who fishes up people from the world below using a line baited with shining coins and other gewgaws; his child *Waribi*, conceived by a woman whom he caught in this way, is the ancestor of all White people (see Hugh-Jones, S. 1979: 275).

Amerindians know well that consumer goods bring hardship and suffering. Contemporary Bora and Miraña, southern neighbours of the Barasana, whose forebears were the main victims of the Putumayo atrocities, call the account ledgers of turn-of-the-century rubber traders 'the leaves of painful knowledge' and sing songs of still earlier times when they traded human beings for metal axes (Guyot 1979: 110, 119). According to Hill and Wright (1988: 93), in order to protect their people, the chant owners of the Wakuénai, an Arawakan group living to the north of the Vaupés region, group under 'a single spirit name, *rupápera sru Amáru* ("the paper of Amaru"), the names of exogenous diseases brought to the region by the whiteman. [This category] is used to name all the "hot things" (*tsîmukáni*) introduced by the White man including the powerful but useful steel tools the Wakuénai use in their gardening, fishing, hunting, house-building, and other activities'. Barasana elders often warn against the dangers, to the health of both body and group, of increasing dependency on White people[7] and they too make the same clear association between trade and the spread of disease, an association illustrated by the idea that to dream of a manioc grater, an item obtained exclusively through trade with the Wakuénai, foretells an epidemic.

In the Pirá-Paraná area, the ritual consumption of powdered coca leaves is an obligatory accompaniment to all serious talk between adult men. Each man gives his fellows coca owned by his own group and grown and picked by himself. During the cocaine boom, in an attempt to isolate gift from commodity and to distinguish between the ritual exchange of coca and the commercial sale of coca leaves, I heard a Barasana shaman telling a client suffering from stomach ache 'if you mix together the coca you eat and use for exchange with the coca that you sell to the White people, their illnesses and the chemicals they use to make cocaine will enter your body and make you sick. You must plant the coca you eat and the coca you sell in different places.'

As everywhere the warnings of the elders and shamans went unheeded. A younger Barasana man put it like this: 'to begin with the old people all said "don't work coca, working coca is bad". But those guns and all those other things, they have such *ewa* that everybody – the shamans, the elders, even my old uncle Christo – they're all working coca now. There's no way to avoid it. These White people are really bad but we want their goods so much that we have to act as if we liked them.'

Here then we seem to have a picture of a small-scale society, with simple technology and few possessions, whose members lose their heads and succumb to temptation when set free, like Charlie's companions, in the chocolate factory of capitalism (see Dahl, 1973). It is surely peoples such as these, and not Alfred Gell's (1986) self-denying Muria elders, on the fringes of a great civilisation and already well versed in the perils of the market, who are the real 'newcomers to the world of goods'. But even here a note of caution is appropriate for consumer goods are only relatively new to the Barasana and they are certainly not indiscriminate consumers.

The Indians' demand for goods not only makes life uncomfortable for the anthropologist; more seriously it threatens the integrity of their own society and culture and allows diverse categories of White people to exploit the seductive power of new things to further their own ends. In the Brazilian Amazon, ahead of the road-builders, dam-makers and colonists, government agents charged with Indian protection seduce still isolated and hostile groups from their last retreats by a form of silent trade in which 'presents' are left on forest trails, presents which bear a deceitful and ironic message of peace and friendship. In response to such overtures, some Indians have even produced makeshift 'shopping lists' in the form of scissors, needles, knives and axes modelled with sticks and leaves (see plate 1 facing p. 183 in Cowell, 1975). Missionaries too will often put a material bait on the hook of faith. Metraux (1959: 36) quotes Father Chantre y Herrera, a nineteenth-century priest working in Amazonia as saying 'it is rare that it is divine reasons – which the Indians never understand – which attract them into our missions. They establish themselves there for very

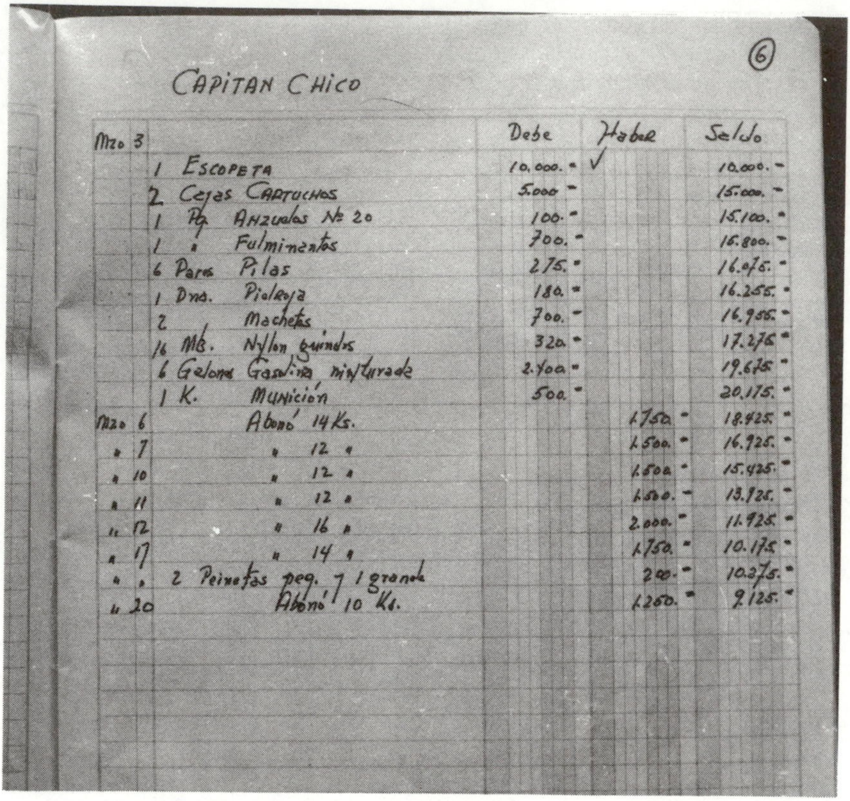

CAPITAN CHICO (6)

		Debe	Haber	Saldo
Mzo 3	1 Escopeta	10.000.-	✓	10.000.-
	2 Cajas Cartuchos	5.000 -		15.000.-
	1 Pq. Anzuelos Nº 20	100.-		15.100.-
	1 " Fulminantes	700.-		15.800.-
	6 Pares Pilas	275.-		16.075.-
	1 Dna. Pielroja	180.-		16.255.-
	2 " Machetes	700.-		16.955.-
	16 Mts. Nylon guindos	320.-		17.275.-
	6 Galones Gasolina mixturada	2.400.-		19.675.-
	1 K. Munición	500.-		20.175.-
Mzo 6	Abonó 14 Ks.		1.750.-	18.425.-
" 7	" 12 "		1.500.-	16.925.-
" 10	" 12 "		1.500.-	15.425.-
" 11	" 12 "		1.500.-	13.925.-
" 12	" 16 "		2.000.-	11.925.-
" 17	" 14 "		1.750.-	10.175.-
" "	2 Peinetas peq. y 1 grande		200.-	10.375.-
" 20	Abonó 10 Ks.		1.250.-	9.125.-

Figure 1. Captain Chico's page in the account book of a cocaine dealer showing his debts for consumer goods (left column), credit for kilos of coca leaves brought in (middle) and balance (right).

Captain Chico

3 March		Debt	Credit	Balance
	1 shotgun	10,000		10,000
	2 boxes cartridges	5,000		15,000
	1 pack no. 20 fishhooks	100		15,100
	1 pack cartridge primers	700		15,800
	6 pairs torch batteries	275		16,075
	1 doz. Pielroja cigarettes	180		16,255
	2 machetes	700		16,955
	16 meters Nylon rope	320		17,275
	6 galons petrol w. oil mix	2,700		19,675
	1 kilo shot	500		20,175
6 Mar.	Delivered 14 kg. coca leaves		1,750	18,425
7 "	" " 12 kg. " "		1,500	16,925
10 "	" " 12 kg. " "		1,500	15,425

down to earth reasons. We could do nothing without the axes which we distribute.' Today too, religious missionaries use their privileged access to goods and medicines as a way of attracting a following.

It is in debt-peonage, however, that material inducements of this kind come most to the fore. Here manufactured goods advanced on credit by White bosses to Indian workers serve to maintain a constant flow of whatever forest product – slaves, drugs, rubber, food, timber, coca leaves, gold... – will fetch a good price on the market of the day. In a parody of the formal procedures of business, complete with separate written accounts for each illiterate worker (see Figure 1), Indians may be kept in a constant state of indebtedness, not knowing if the goods they receive are in payment for last year's work, an advance on the next, or both at once. Of the turn-of-the-century Putumayo region, Taussig (1987: 128) describes such debts as 'a gigantic piece of make belief, ... where the gift economy of the Indian meshed with the capitalist economy of the colonist'; and so it is today.

Of his experience amongst the Yanomami, Chagnon (1974: 29) writes that 'one must always imply that he has many more possessions back home and intends to bring them on his next visit provided the people are friendly. It is like the relationship between the goose and golden eggs. If you want more eggs, be nice to the goose.' This disarming candour underlines the fact that an exchange of goods for hospitality and information also forms part of the anthropological enterprise.[8] But the Indians also know their side of the bargain, as this letter to Dr Patrice Bidou from a Tatuyo Indian of the Río Pirá-Paraná makes clear:

Greetings to all your family and relatives. Through David I'm sending you greetings from the Capitan of Caño Utuya. I want some cigarettes. I want them. Bring them to me. I'm sending you this letter on the 20th of February. The captain of the aeroplane never gave me the cigarettes you tried to send because he didn't want me to have them. My brother David has deposited them in his house. Patrice, bring them to me. I also want a few goods: some beads, two boxes of cartridges, some large fishing hooks, and two reels of nylon line. I want some clothes. I want two pieces of cloth for the women. I will speak again into your tape-recorder. Don't go to B's house. Land at my village, among my people, because that's where I live and that's where I am waiting for you. Come and hear my words. You can stay here, as long as you like, because I am chief of all the people. So you must say to your Capitan [Lévi-Strauss]: 'I'm going.' The Capitan has sent me to tell you I a'm leaving. Tell this to your family too. I also want some boxes of matches. That's all the message I'm sending you. (cited in Gross, 1977: 144; my trans.)

11 "	"	"	12 kg. "	"	1,500	13,925
1 "	"	"	16 kg. "	"	2,000	11,925
17 "	"	"	14 kg. "	"	1,750	10,175
" "	"	"	2 small combs, 1 big comb		200	10,375
20 "	"	"	Delivered 10 kg. leaves		1,250	9,125

Alongside goods or money, the Indians may also receive less tangible benefits in the form of the prestige that accrues to the anthropologist's chief friends and informants; this prestige is also linked with the goods he gives away and may be signified by them.

When Rousseau wrote of the spiral of needs he did not suppose that the members of his original society would be corrupted by outside influences, nor that they would use their leisure time to go off bartering with traders or missionaries. Rather, their boundless needs would come from their own human nature and they would satisfy them with new commodities created by their own wit and invention. In short their world and their demise were both self-contained.

Although they share Rousseau's tragic vision of the effects of consumerism, more recent studies of Amazonian Indians often tell a different story in which apparently stable traditional societies are corrupted and exploited through an externally generated supply and demand.

Citing Sahlins, Lizot (1972: 226) argues that the Venezuelan Yanomami once limited their needs for material possessions so as to guarantee their mobility and to enable them to devote their leisure time to resting and social pursuits. He writes as follows:

During this [early] period, the acquisition of tools fitted into the traditional model of economic and matrimonial exchanges: one traded a piece of metal or an old knife, as before one had traded a bow or a basket. These exchanges occurred without constraint, the Indians did not have to alienate themselves politically or economically, nor to modify their cultural system in response to a pressure put upon them. Henceforth working less, they could devote more time to amusements and relaxation, thus gaining the benefits of a moderate use of manufactured goods, put to the service of a subsistence economy – that is, an economy which is not exclusively oriented towards the production and consumption of material goods. The Indians found a new equilibrium for themselves. And it was a happy one.

This stability came to an end, after the arrival of the first 'whites' when it suddenly became necessary to 'teach the Indians to work'. Non-essential needs were diversified artificially and without discrimination. (ibid: 237)

In claiming that the Yanomami reject technological progress, and in following Sahlins' argument that, with their 'stone age economy', these Indians were predisposed to limit their needs, Lizot is bound to seek some *external* mechanism which disrupted the supposed equilibrium established by the Indians after their initial, moderate, and beneficial acquisition of steel tools. He finds this mechanism in the work ethic that White people impose upon Indians and in the sense of shame they generate by ridiculing and despising Indian customs, habits and behaviour.

There is no doubt that all the Indians are indeed subjected to humiliation and to intense pressures to change their ways and adopt new material possessions. Yet one cannot help feeling that there is something deceptively straightforward about the oft-repeated story of forest Indians, seduced by worthless trinkets, pressured to accept unwanted and unnecessary goods, turned into undiscriminating consumers forced to sell their labour and produce on a ruthless market, who begin by losing their heads, and end up by losing their autonomy and their culture as well. My intention is not so much to deny that something along these lines does sometimes seem to happen, nor to minimise the suffering and exploitation that it entails,[9] but rather to point out that it is a partial and one-sided view which takes both exchange relations and objects exchanged at face value, which sees them through our own eyes, and which risks presenting the Indians as passive victims rather than as active and creative participants in a two-sided process.

The ubiquitous consumer goods that lie around in Amerindian villages are not just blots on the landscape, the sweet-papers of capitalism dropped carelessly in a tropical Garden of Eden; they are also part and parcel of an Indian culture that is constantly being reworked and modified in response to changing circumstances. In following the trajectory of manufactured goods from White supplier to Indian consumer, we must bear in mind both the disjunctions and the continuities involved when the same commodities are exchanged or used in different social contexts.

As ideal types, we may make tidy analytical distinctions between the economy of the Indian and the economy of the colonist, but in reality the boundaries are rarely so clear-cut. In debt-peonage, a chain of indebtedness stretches from urban centres – Manaus, Villavicencio ... to remote frontier areas, and manufactured goods pass down this chain in exchange for labour and produce. The chain binds White patrons to lesser patrons, themselves less white than their bosses, and binds them in turn to the Indians. But this chain does not suddenly stop at an ill-defined ethnic frontier. It stretches on to bind Indian to Indian, so that the morality of the market penetrates that of kinship and the morality of kinship may be extended to dealings with White people. This extension, and the problems it brings, are exemplified in the following letter from a Barasana Indian, once a rubber gatherer and minor patron and later a coca trader, to his classificatory nephew (see Figure 2):

Sunday, 4/11/79,

Dear Ernesto,

In the first place, I want to tell you that the coca we picked weighed only two arrobas [approx. 24 kg].

If you have any doubts about this you can check it by doing the sum for yourself.

Now: the amount still owing to Guillermo [a White cocaine dealer] was a sum of 5.8000 pesos [approx. £580]: I gave you a blanket and a dozen cigarettes so that you would help me pick the coca. I had to pick the coca myself as you are lazy and you said that I owed you the sum of 600 pesos; I did not want to say anything to you because I considered that you were not a thinking being but an animal.

Perhaps it seemed odd to you because you do not know how to do accounts. On the contrary you did not pay me for the blanket and cigarettes which came to a total of 600 pesos.

I must see if I can find some way to solve this problem.

Any patron has the right to charge for food for if we did not give you meals you would be paid 100 pesos a day for food. You get a ten percent discount and if you did not know, you should bear all this in mind.

I'm letting you know all this because, up till now, you have never had to work with a white man worse than me.[10]

Yours sincerely,

José B. and Company.

Note: there is also a letter for Benjamin.

Benjamin,

the merchandise we took out on credit is still to be settled and there are still some 18000 pesos to pay off apart from what you owe. For this reason, I came to pick coca once again to see if I could pay as soon as possible. If the debt does get paid off I will send word to you as soon as possible.

If you had sent coca the account would have been much smaller. As you didn't send any it was a much bigger sum.

José B.

The tendency to overemphasise the disjunction between the economies of Indians and Whites is manifest in a paper by Saffirio and Hames, on the impact of Western goods on Yanomami society, in which they seek to distinguish between Yanomami and Western goods in terms of whether or not they are 'personalised'. Whereas the value of Yanomami goods is held to derive from the person who made or exchanged them, they state that 'since Western goods are impersonal, transactions involving them are impersonal' (1983: 23). But it is not something intrinsically different in the nature of the goods which determines the different qualities of the transactions they enter. Depersonalised Yanomami baskets are on sale as tourist souvenirs in the airport at Boa Vista and can now be bought in New York and London. Their value lies in their being not merely baskets but Yanomami baskets, tokens of a threatened forest and its inhabitants.[11] In a similar way Western goods now play an increasingly dominant role in the personalised exchanges that take place between individual Yanomami (see Lizot, 1984) – they too are not merely 'goods' but also White people's goods (see also Thomas, this volume).

The Barasana often treat manufactured goods as being no less personalised than the manioc graters and vine baskets which they obtain through trade from the distant Wakuénai and Makú. Apart from their

Domingo XI/4-7979

Estimado Benisto:

En primer lugar le quiero decirle que la coca que cogimos salió o pasó 2 arrobas nada más.

Si tiene alguna duda, la cuenta la puede hacerlo usted mismo para que lo compruebe.

Ahora; la cuenta pendiante con Guillermo fué una suma de 68000 pesos; yo le di una cobija y una docena de cigarrillos para que me ayudara a coger la coca. La coca la tuve que coger yo sólo por se perezoso usted ma dijo que yo lo estaba debindo una suma de esa pesos; yo no quise decirle nada porque lo consideré de que usted no era un ser pensante sino un animal.

Tal vez sale extrañado por que ud no sabe hacer cuentas

a lo contrario usted no me pagó la cobija; y la docena de cigarrillos que fueron en total de 600 pesos.

Vea haber si de alguna forma busca solucionar este problema.

Cualquier patrono del trabajo tiene derecho de cobrar la comida por que si no le diéramos la comida se le pagaría 100 pesos diaria por la comida se le descuenta el 10 porciento, por si no sabia Tenga encuenta todo esto.

Lo hice saber todo esto por que ud hasta ahora nunca ha llegado trabajar con un blanco que fuera mas mal que yo.

ATTe José B. y Cía.

nota; también va una carta para Benjamin.

Benjamin la mercancia que sacamos quedarón en tramite como unos 15000 pesos pendientes para cancelar fuera de lo que ud debe, por eso yo vine coger coca nuevamente para ver si puedo pagar las que pronto posible, en caso de la deuda sería cancelada la mercancía información inmediatamente.

si ud hubiera mando coca la cuenta quedaría mas poquito como ud no mando coca entonces fue una suma muy superior.

José B.

Figure 2. Letters from José B., a Barasana Indian coca trader, to two kinsmen concerning outstanding debts.

practical utility, part of the value of all such goods derives from their known association with 'exotic' peoples and, alongside the gourds, baskets, and red paint obtained from immediate neighbours, they acquire a further personal element from the person, White or Indian, from whom they were obtained, whether or not he or she actually produced them. Though the importance attached to this personal element may vary, the source and immediate supplier of all goods, including those obtained directly from White people, is clearly remembered, and the goods are always associated with the people who provided them. The notion of alienation, traditionally used to sort commodity exchange from the gift, is ambiguous in a context such as this for, whilst the goods as such are clearly alienated, they retain a gift-like quality through these memories and associations (see Gell, this volume, p. 145 for the inverse argument with respect to gifts).

It is also important not to assume that the ubiquitous guns and axes, radios and tape recorders, shirts and trousers, sunglasses and watches, which now form part of the paraphernalia of many Amerindian villages, have exactly the same significance or value for the Indians as they do for ourselves. There may be considerable overlap, but when Western goods pass to Indian hands they also pass from 'one regime of value' (Appadurai, 1986: 15) to another, a regime in which they undergo cultural redefinition and may be put to novel uses. However much one might sympathise with statements such as 'their bodies, so elegant, balanced and harmonious, were concealed under filthy rags' (Lizot, 1984: 237) or with phrases like 'tattered garments' or 'European hand-me-downs' (Chagnon, 1977: 140) that are used to describe the Indians' hard-won and much treasured clothes, this language reveals clearly that the clothes in question are being seen through Western eyes. It is hard to square such views with the evident enthusiasm with which the Yanomami wear clothes and trade them with each other.

There are some very real forces which push Indians to accept and demand an ever increasing range of consumer goods. In the Vaupés area, the modern *cocaineros*, heirs of the rubber-gatherers of old, continue to press merchandise onto unsuspecting Indians to create the debts which give the creditor exclusive rights to the coca-leaves and labour of 'his' Indians. Religious missionaries, offended by nudity, concerned with technological backwardness and 'insanitary' conditions and eager to attract a following, ridicule or prohibit old habits and press clothes, new tools and new architecture on their flocks.

But alongside the 'push' to consume provided by the forces of acculturation in the name of 'civilisation' and the market, there is also a significant and important 'pull'. This 'pull' is not simply a blind and mechanical response to alien social manipulation, nor is it simply the reciprocal of the advances which unscrupulous traders force onto unwilling Indians to guarantee their future indebtedness. It is also a demand which has its own internal reasons and which shapes supply.

Using the accounts of early travellers and missionaries, and information from elder Barasana, together with observations made in the field between 1968 and 1984, we can gain some idea of the changes in consumption patterns that have occurred through time, changes which involve both the quantity and range of the goods involved. Initially, steel tools such as guns (with shot and powder), axes, machetes, knives, spear heads, fishing hooks, and chisels for making canoes, provided the bulk of foreign goods acquired by the Barasana. These goods were first obtained through trade with other Indians, but, from around 1920 onward, work for rubber and balata gatherers and a trade in *farinha* became the main sources of supply. Though most of these items were directly related to male subsistence activities and are now central to the economy, the Barasana also acquired less obviously 'useful' goods such as glass beads, mirrors and combs, small amounts of cotton cloth, scissors, needles and thread, matches and salt and, later, torches and batteries.

In 1968, when I began my fieldwork and when the first Catholic and Protestant mission stations were established in the Pirá-Paraná area, the men of each *maloca* community shared a small supply of shot-guns, axes and machetes with each other, the women used digging sticks and broken machete blades for gardening, and clothing was generally limited to a homemade, wrap-around skirt for the women and a cotton g-string for the men. Payments for the Indian labour required to construct mission buildings and airstrips led to a rapid rise in the availability of all the goods mentioned above together with more soap, towels, toothbrushes, medicines and other things. Cotton hammocks began to replace those made locally from palm-fibre string, clay pots gave way to aluminium, women began to make full dresses with puffed sleeves and the men sported shirts and trousers, boots or shoes. Finally, with the arrival of the *cocaineros* in 1979, shoes and underwear, digital watches, radios, tape recorders, outboard motors, large supplies of cigarettes, and black-market shotguns all became freely available and in ever-increasing demand. Also, and for the first time, some Indians began to supplement a diet which, salt apart, was hitherto based exclusively on local produce with small amounts of imported food such as biscuits, rice and tinned fish.

In their analyses of similar data from the Venezuelan and Brazilian Yanomami both Lizot and Saffirio and Hames draw distinctions either between utilitarian objects and those of purely social value (Lizot 1984: 227–8) or between productive and consumer goods (Saffirio and Hames 1983: 15). In each case, the authors appear to espouse a two-stage thesis concerning Indian patterns of consumption: an initial, rational, and internally generated demand for more efficient tools that enhance subsistence production followed by a later, less rational demand for what Lizot (1984: 237) calls 'non-essential needs' stemming from the Indians' response to pressure and ridicule from outsiders. Saffirio and Hames make clear the apparently irrational nature of this demand when they state that:

Consumer goods, with some exceptions such as medicine and some items of food and clothing, have very little utilitarian value for the Yanomami in that they do not enhance subsistence effort, diet, or provide protection against the environment. For example, Yanomami carrying baskets, houses, tobacco, and hammocks are just as good as their Brazilian equivalents. In addition, the labor to produce some traditional artefacts is less than the labor one must perform for Brazilians to gain money to buy Brazilian goods. (1983: 18–19)

Although such arguments make some sense, they nonetheless ignore other factors and, rather than reflecting an Indian perspective, they seem to be more influenced by the authors' own views of what a sensible Indian ought to want, thus missing the point. I use a Yanomami carrying-basket as a waste-paper basket. In one respect it is less good than its Western equivalents – it has a round bottom and constantly falls over, spilling its contents on the floor – but that's not the point either.

Beside their association with subsistence activities, most of the initial items of Western manufacture acquired by the Barasana were also associated specifically with men (and the same appears to be true of the Yanomami also). Over time, there was an increase in goods associated with the women's activities of cooking and food preparation, and an increase in items of female dress. Part of the reason for this early dominance of men's goods lies in the fact that it was largely the men who travelled abroad to trade and make contact with White people and it was they who were recruited to work in the forest-based activities of rubber-tapping and hunting animals. Even though such activities depended on supplies of *farinha*, produced by the women and used to feed the Indian labourers, it was still the men who traded *farinha* with White people and in their own name.

With the establishment of mission stations and, latterly, cocaine laboratories, close to the Indian communities, women now have more access to manufactured goods and have begun to take a more active part in acquiring them through the new employment opportunities of cooking, cleaning, and teaching in mission schools. But access is not the whole story for, at the same time, the women's use of such things as underwear reflects changes in their own view of themselves.

Although coca leaves were traditionally an exclusively male crop, when the *cocaineros* arrived this did not stop Barasana men from ordering their women to pick coca to pay off their debts, nor did it prevent some women from planting and picking coca for sale on their own account. These changes in the accessibility of goods are also associated with political changes in the relations between men and women brought about by contact with outsiders and actively encouraged by the missionaries. This is most strikingly illustrated in the changes in women's dress: whereas women once went naked and men had exclusive rights to wear the finery of ritual, today women too have access to their own kind of finery. Many of the younger girls use mission-education and work for White people as a way of escaping from the clutches of their menfolk, and as a way of improving their status. The new clothes they flaunt aggressively speak of this freedom.

Consumer goods also express and reflect changes in the balance of power between young and old. Traditionally, valuables in the form of feather headdresses and imported guns were controlled by the older men who dominated trade and the ritual avenues to prestige. Today, prestige within the community accrues more and more to the younger, mission-educated men whose knowledge of Spanish and experience of White society enables them to deal with outsiders and to mediate with them on their community's behalf. Travel to local towns and work amongst White people is now part of the typical career of young bachelors, and is partly motivated by a spirit of curiosity and adventure and by the status and glamour it confers. It also provides opportunities to acquire consumer goods and to meet young women, activities which are linked by the fact that such goods are used as courtship gifts and as a substitute for brideservice. The clothes they bring back, and the radios which they play ostentatiously before dawn and during sacred rituals, proclaim the increased power and importance of these younger men and bear witness to the periods they spent away from home amongst powerful foreigners.

A further complication in the picture of a progressive shift from productive to consumer goods is suggested by the fact that items for dress and display – beads, combs and mirrors and the like – figure amongst the very first goods obtained from White people. In fact the distinction between these two kinds of goods is impossible to maintain, for not only do items such as shoes and clothing serve the utilitarian function of protection, but so also may objects used in subsistence enter simultaneously into the arena of prestige and display to take on symbolic functions. On social occasions Barasana men are rarely parted from their guns, but not because they fear attack. Rather these prized possessions are like dress-swords in the West, complex signs of power, valour and the capacity to hunt, which often serve as an index of the fact that their owner has spent a period of time working for White people and has the ability to do business with them on equal terms. They have not only displaced bows and blowpipes as hunting weapons, but have also displaced hardwood sword-clubs of exclusively ceremonial use.[12]

In Barasana myths of the origins of White people and their possessions it was the fact that their ancestor chose the gun over the Indians' bow which led to the present differences between them. Guns are the source and symbol of the power of the White people, or 'Fire People', and their clothes, those cotton skins that can be shed at will in the manner of snakes, give them their longevity (see Hugh-Jones, S. 1979: 181 ff.). Guns, clothes and all manufactured goods were created through the shamanic powers and knowledge of ~Waribi, an ancestral hero and the 'father' of White people, and they come from spirits in the world of the dead, a world represented in myth as identical to the White people's towns (see Hugh-Jones, S. 1988; Guyot, 1976). It is for this reason that they are imbued with the *ewa* which makes them so powerful and attractive. To possess such goods is to share in the world from which they derive, and to appropriate some of the transformational power that is used to make them.

Factors to do with increased efficiency and durability certainly underlie the demand for steel tools and aluminium cooking pots and, in acquiring items like clothing and watches, the Barasana do indeed respond to pressures to imitate White people and to appear more 'civilised' (though their interpretations of 'civilisation' are not always the same as the 'civilisers'). But between the apparently self-evident rationality of a demand for subsistence goods, and the puzzling irrationality of an alien consumerism, there are other factors at work. If guns are better than bows as hunting weapons, so too do clothes offer novel and more varied forms of self-decoration than bark-cloth g-strings and body paint and feathers, especially as all can be used together or put on at different times. Both sexes have used imported cloth and clothing to evolve their own styles of dress which display neither indiscriminate, nor wholly derivative, choices. The Barasana know well that it is only Indians who wear white glass beads round their necks, towels on their shoulders and clean white handkerchiefs perched on their heads, but that has not so far diminished their enthusiasm for these imported goods. If occasionally the Indians dress up for White people, most of the time they do it for each other.

Finally it should be added that curiosity and inventiveness also play their part, and that foreign items are often treated in the creative and adventurous spirit of Lévi-Strauss' *bricoleur* – acquired and kept because they might one day come in useful. When the proper apparatus is unavailable, old socks and empty oil cans may be used for sieving coca powder, and a further collection of bizarre and so-far useless items, gleaned on visits to White settlements and now talismans which evoke their strange origins, lurk in odd corners of Indian houses waiting each day for some as yet undiscovered use.

In sum, there are clearly a host of reasons why Amazonian Indians should want manufactured goods and why their demands for them should change through time; to explore all of these reasons is beyond the scope of this paper. What is clear, however, is that demand is neither Rousseau's limitless product of individual human nature and needs, nor is it merely a response to external pressure. Furthermore, demand is neither indiscriminate nor simply a reflex of increased availability. Coming from within, it is motivated by the logic of a particular culture and, if it comes from without, it is still mediated through that culture. The response of Amazonian Indians to the large and novel range of commodities made increasingly available to them by White people suggests that their image as tribal societies with some inbuilt propensity to limit their needs requires revision. In particular, it should be borne in mind that, prior to the advent of Europeans, most of these groups were surrounded by peoples whose technologies and material repertoires were not markedly different from their own. Western goods provided new and increased opportunities for both technological and symbolic innovation.

In addition to a demand for goods for immediate consumption, the Barasana also seek goods for use in exchange. Indeed it is their supreme exchangeability, above and beyond any practical use they may have, that makes Western goods so eagerly sought after. These exchanges serve variously to obtain other goods, to keep up social relationships, to make payments for the services of ritual specialists, and to fulfil social obligations such as gifts to future wives and to parents-in-law.[13] They also form the focus of an exchange network: in writing about the Tukanoan Cubeo, Goldman (1963: 68–9) states that

the entire Northwest Amazon region is a vastly complex trading network. Objects of every description, household implements, ornaments, musical instruments, ceremonial objects, plants, pets, and magical substances are in constant circulation from tribe to tribe, from sib to sib. Indians who are in contact with the trading centers of Colombians and Brazilians are often middlemen, pumping manufactured goods into the stream of trade – cloth, salt, fish-hooks, guns, machetes, as well as cheap ornaments.

The Barasana are part of this network and trade extensively among themselves and with members of the other groups with whom they have contact. I know of no examples of Vaupés Indians acting as specialist traders in chains of formalised trading partnerships, and being involved in long-distance trade of the kind reported for the Guianas (see Colson, 1973, Thomas, 1972, and Mansutti Rodriguez, 1986) but people do use the opportunities of travel to obtain goods of localised distribution, such as yellow ochre, stones for burnishing clay pots, and panpipe reeds for trading onwards. Thus the Makuna, southern neighbours of the Barasana, obtain curare from groups of Makú further South. When the Barasana visit the Makuna, they acquire curare for barter with groups further to the North. Similarly, in working for White people, Indians will obtain goods both for immediate use and for future exchanges. The local towns are also important distribution centres, not only for manufactured goods, but also for indigenous artefacts; White traders buy such artefacts both for sale to the cities and for sale to other Indians, and they have inserted themselves into the chain which brings manioc graters from the Arawakan Wakuénai to the north.

In the literature on the Vaupés region there are frequent references to the specialised production of certain artefacts by different 'tribes' or exogamous groups (see Chernela, 1983: 127 ff.; Jackson, 1983: 99; Ribeiro, 1980: 423 ff.). The Tukano are known for their wooden shamans' stools, the Desana as makers of flat *balaio* baskets, the Uanano as makers of strainers for manioc mash, the Tuyuka as the makers of canoes, the Wakuénai as makers of manioc graters, and the Makú as the source of blowpipes, curare, and vine carrying baskets. Whether this specialisation was once part of a formalised system of inter-tribal trade similar to that which occurs in the Xingú region of Brazil (Basso, 1973), or whether it is simply part of a wider 'totemic' system that also allocated such things as language or varieties of cultivated plants between different groups, is now hard to tell. Today, at least, although such goods (alongside smoked fish and meat or ants, caterpillars, frogs or raw forest fruits) sometimes figure as emblematic markers in ceremonial exchanges or *dabukuris* between exogamous groups and although there is still extensive individual barter of Wakuénai graters and Makú baskets, the rest of the 'system' is more a matter of an ideal, ancestrally ordained association between group and object, and not one of exclusive right to manufacture or trade.

Members of the same community living in the same longhouse are expected to share food and to lend or give their possessions freely, and no barter occurs between them – barter is thus isolated from obligations of helping and sharing amongst co-residents. It also has connotations of equality, so that husbands and wives would give to, rather than barter with, their spouses' parents. Otherwise there are no restrictions, and in practice, no preferences as to who should barter with whom – it takes place between friends and between strangers, within the group and beyond it. A relationship of formal friendship between men and women is established at the close of male initiation rites when young men give women baskets in exchange for garters and red paint (see Hugh-Jones, S. 1979: 96). Although formal friends are expected to exchange more frequently and more generously, and though the garters that the women give to their male partners are not usually bartered with others, in other respects their exchanges do not differ markedly from those with other people.

Barter is initiated by one party asking for objects owned by the other; the asker may offer goods in return or wait for a request. There is no expectation that either requests or exchanges need be simultaneous, the transaction rests on trust, and there is often considerable delay before the two sides of the transaction are completed. A person may also commission another to make a specific object at a later date in exchange for one offered on the spot. There are no set rates of exchange,[14] bargaining happens discreetly or not at all, and it is often difficult to know that a transaction has occurred. Each transaction is self-contained and between individuals, features that mark them off from the ceremonial exchanges of food and ceremonial goods which occur between longhouse communities acting as units.

Those who are stingy are unpopular and come in for heavy criticism, so that it is hard to refuse a request or an offer. For this reason, people are cautious about what they display to whom and keep some possessions, especially stocks of Western goods, hidden away in dark corners of the house. But stinginess also carries with it the connotation of being unsociable in a more general sense – above and beyond any utilitarian motivation, bartering is often an end in itself, a mark and device of sociability which people engage in for its own sake and as something appropriate to dances, feasts and other social occasions. As Gell points out for New Guinea 'commodity exchange or barter in itself confers value on goods which they would otherwise not possess' (this volume, 148). On the basis of personal experience, I suspect that much of the 'pestering' experienced by foreigners amongst Amerindians is motivated as much or more by this desire to make social contact, as it is by a desire for exotic goods themselves.

People are nonetheless cautious for, if they ask for things, they are both exposed to reciprocal requests and must bear in mind considerations of status and respect. Younger men, who would think twice about asking for things from their elders, may be rapidly relieved of their hard-won possessions as they return from work amongst White people. Besides request for barter from older men, they must accede to the demands of the shamans who officiated at their birth and initiation, and fulfil obligations to their parents-in-law if married. By contrast, feared and respected shamans rarely get asked for their possessions and can often accumulate large quantities of goods given them in payment for curing and other services, or offered as gifts to ensure their goodwill.

Status and closeness of social relations may also affect what is exchanged and on what terms. The Tukanoans treat the semi-nomadic Makú as their inferiors and will exchange *farinha*, manioc bread and manufactured goods with them in return for meat, baskets and agricultural or house-building labour. Amongst the Tukanoans themselves, food is only normally exchanged ceremonially and on a group-to-group basis, food items other than salt, smoked chili peppers and *farinha* do not normally enter into barter transactions, and labour can only be repaid with labour.

As condiments, neither salt nor chili peppers have the status of proper foods, and it is probable that the limited bartering of *farinha* is linked with its commoditisation by White traders. True food is either shared within (and occasionally between) households, or exchanged in the context of ritual. Significantly, on the one occasion on which I saw a Barasana exchange beads for cassava bread, the bread was requested by a hungry member of the Wabea clan who the Barasana consider to be like the Makú (Hugh-Jones, C., 1979).

Ceremonial valuables (*he ˈgaheudi*) such as sacred flutes and trumpets, feather headdresses, tooth belts, bark-cloth aprons, ankle rattles, and maracas are collectively owned by the clan and embody its spiritual essence and power. These inalienable items are never bartered between individuals, but may be ceremonially exchanged as gifts which establish ties of ritual affinity (*he ˈteyia*) between the parties involved.

Apart from food and collectively owned valuables, all other possessions can be bartered. In practice, some items – basketry (carrying baskets, sieves, strainers, manioc squeezers or *tipitís*, and flat decorated *balaios*), bark-cloth bags of smoked chili peppers or red paint, gourds, and balls of string for hammock-making – are more frequently bartered than other goods, and are often made specifically for exchange. Although people may barter different locally produced objects or different manufactured goods for each other, the vast majority of such deals involve the exchange of manufactured goods against local artefacts. In the same vein, although local products are acceptable as payments to shamans or as gifts to in-laws, manufactured goods are more commonly used and often preferred. Such goods may also be exchanged for non-material possessions in the form of songs, chants, and spells, and are the preferred form of payment when shamanic knowledge is transmitted between unrelated individuals.

Money (Colombian pesos) very rarely changes hands. When it does, notes may be bartered alongside other items; coins themselves are valued as decorations worn on necklaces either in their 'raw' state or beaten into silver triangles called 'butterflies'. As they are both highly valued and easily divided, strings of imported glass beads (preferably small white rocaille), worn round the neck and wrists, are a frequent item of exchange. People may occasionally state that an object will fetch so many strings of beads but, in practice, the rates and contents of particular exchanges depend on the relation between the parties and on what they have to offer. As the most highly valued objects, guns are typically paid for canoes and for major shamanic services, and are usually demanded when Indians agree to sell their 'inalienable' feather headdresses to White people.

From what has been said above it should be clear that manufactured goods play a key role in indigenous exchange in the Vaupés region.

Because of the absence of money, fixed rates of exchange, and formal partnerships, I have chosen to call this exchange 'barter' rather than 'trade' but, in this context, it would be mistaken to assume that the term implies exchanges which take place on the margins of the society, between people with minimal social obligations, and in a spirit of self-aggrandisement or profit. Most barter takes place between people who live close to one another, who interact frequently, who belong to a dispersed community formed by the *malocas* (longhouses) located around a particular stretch of river, and who are linked by a network of kinship relations – it is both the result and the mark of their sociability.

How things are requested, who gives what to whom, and on what terms, are all bound up with the nature of the goods involved, the amount each person possesses, their relative status, and the particular relationship between them. Usually goods are bartered between people of approximately equal status who seek to substitute one kind which they possess for another they want. Alternatively, one party may feel an obligation to part with valued Western goods for indigenous goods they want less, and those with large amounts of Western goods may willingly exchange them for less wanted indigenous products as they are more interested in the social benefits that accrue from the exchange. Finally, things offered for little or no return may be variously interpreted as a sign of weakness, respect, generosity, or strength.

Given this range of behaviour and underlying motives, it is often difficult to know where barter ends and more socially embedded forms of exchange begin, and in many of these barter transactions, the objects concerned are simultaneously both 'gift' and 'commodity'. In her paper on barter, Chapman considers that barter is either very marginal or absent amongst the Yanomami. She bases this view on Chagnon's account of 'artificial' village specialisation in the production of certain goods which allow trade to function as a starting mechanism in the formation of alliances (Chapman, 1980: 45). It is clear that manufactured goods now play an important role in these exchanges, and that those with ready access to such goods use them to create and cement alliances with their less fortunate neighbours (see Chagnon, 1974 and Lizot, 1984). But one suspects that alongside the motives of politics and prestige, here too there operates the more mundane desire to swap one useful object for another and that, as in the case of the Barasana, the dividing line between gift and barter would often be hard to draw.

Since the ending of rubber production in the late sixties and a ban on the trade in animal skins soon after, the Indians of the Pirá-Paraná region have obtained most of their manufactured goods from Protestant and Catholic missionaries, from cocaine dealers, or from working gold. Goods are obtained in exchange for coca leaves, for small quantities of cocaine paste, or gold; for labour (housebuilding, airstrip construction, making gardens for manioc and coca, processing cocaine and mining gold); for services (as guides, porters, boatmen, cooks, cleaners, etc.); for food (smoked fish and meat, fruit, manioc bread and *farinha*); and for artefacts (mostly basketry, blowpipes, dart cases, pottery, stools, canoes, and paddles), animal skins and the odd live pet. It is notable that in offering coca-leaves, food, and labour to White people in exchange for consumer goods, the Indians are making exchanges which they would not normally make with each other.[15]

The Protestant missionaries, and to a lesser extent the Catholics also, have a policy of introducing and teaching the use of money, and both they and the cocaine dealers and gold miners calculate the value of goods and services they buy and sell in monetary terms, but for a variety of reasons money itself rarely changes hands.

The area is remote, on the periphery of the monetary system, and the scale of commercial operations is small. There is little money in circulation and what there is is held mainly in the hands of the White people. As neither side usually has enough cash, the result is that consumer goods are typically given out on credit or bartered directly for Indian labour or products, with the White people and some of the Indians, using pesos as a numeraire. Though Indians will accept money and a few have small savings, most prefer payment in kind and spend what money they get as soon as possible. Besides a windfall mentality and an ignorance and suspicion as to the value of paper notes, money is of little use to them, for the modest stores of the missionaries are widely separated and the nearest town with shops is a week's journey away. In addition, supplies are unpredictable and notoriously unreliable, for they are subject to government controls (in the case of guns), to the vagaries of the weather, the whims of the pilots who fly them in, not to mention inflation.

To break the tradition of debt-peonage, and in order to teach the Indians good financial habits, the Protestant and Catholic missions try to make it their policy not to extend credit to Indians. As they are used to credit both in their dealings with each other and with White traders, the Indians often resent this and accuse the missionaries of meanness. The traders have fewer scruples, so that credit is the life-blood of cocaine and gold production as it was of rubber beforehand.[16]

Besides factors to do with the absence of money and markets, there are a number of other reasons why credit is favoured by Amazonian traders. By advancing goods on credit to largely illiterate and innumerate Indians, the traders can manipulate profits on both the goods they sell and the labour and produce they buy. Under extreme conditions, the value of goods given out is so minimal compared to the value of the produce received, and the sanctions against refusal to produce so severe, that the system is tantamount to forced labour or outright slavery. This was the case with rubber in the Putumayo district in the 1900s (see Taussig, 1987) and again in parts of the Vaupés as recently as 1971 (see Gossain, 1971). A constant state of indebtedness, backed by a general state of fear and the threat of specific physical sanctions, also serves to guarantee that Indians who are self-sufficient in food, unused to the concept or regular habits of wage-labour, and who normally choose to work for White people only in order to obtain specific items, will, nonetheless, deliver a constant supply of labour or produce.

The system also serves to regulate relations between the traders themselves. By giving out goods on credit, each cocaine dealer could claim exclusive rights over the labour and produce of 'his' Indians; if they then sold their coca leaves to another dealer, he would both punish them and fight with his rival. This use of credit as a device for establishing rights in labour and produce against other competitors was a conscious strategy on the part of the cocaineros. It was particularly important in the illicit production of cocaine where, by definition, the traders had no legal rights, but it was also employed in the legitimate rubber business and deserves more attention in the literature on debt-peonage as a whole.

In a discussion of the debt-peonage connected with rubber production in the Putumayo earlier in the century, Taussig observes that the notion of debt and of a trade in goods for rubber hides what is really going on: 'Everything in this "system" depends on the appearance of trade in which the debtor is neither slave nor wage labourer but a trader with an ironclad obligation to pay back the advance' (1987: 54). He argues therefore that 'in the debt peonage system, as befits a system built around the fiction of traders and not commodities, it is the debt and not the commodity that is fetishized' (*ibid*: 70). But if such trade is a fiction in the economy of the trader, it is certainly real in that of the Indian and this is part of its seductive efficacy. What in effect happens is that the White patron or trader appropriates and subverts the Indians' barter network which is extended to him.

We can represent the economic activities of the cocaine dealers who exchange consumer goods for coca leaves as follows:

$$M - Cg - (m) - Cc - Cc' - M'$$

(where M = money, Cg = goods, (m) = money as a unit of account, Cc = coca leaves, Cc' = value-added cocaine and M' = profit).

This circuit bears a formal resemblance to that of barter transactions in which money is used simply as a numeraire or measure of equivalence, but *not* as a medium of exchange and which can be represented as:

$$(c - (m) - C)$$

(where C = commodity and (m) = money as numeraire).

As alienable products intended for exchange, and as objects representing congealed labour, both manufactured goods and coca leaves are here commodities, and the aim of the transaction, at least as far as the cocaine dealer is concerned, is quite clearly profit. Most importantly, despite their formal parallels with barter, the cocaine dealers treat these exchanges as merely a specialised form of monetary or commodity transaction.

However, when seen from the perspective of many Indians, who are interested in neither money nor profit and who are often unable to read or follow the calculations involved, the same exchange can be represented simply as:

$$Cc - Cg$$

(where Cc = coca leaves and Cg = goods).

Apart from the presence of raw coca leaves which are never exchanged or bartered between Indians, this transaction is otherwise identical to their own barter transactions. The coca is commoditised in that it is produced specifically for exchange, but only those with mission education or long exposure to wage labour will relate the prices of the goods they receive to the hours it takes to pick the equivalent quantity of leaves. Many Barasana have only the vaguest of notions concerning the monetary aspects of the exchange and are not concerned with monetary value or profit: the object is simply to swap *anything* that White people will accept for the goods they want. As one of them put it 'first they wanted rubber, then it was jaguar skins, then it was coca. What else will they want? The only thing left is our shit!'

The Barasana are, however, well aware of the fact that their coca leaves are being alienated and this causes them some misgivings. Like feather headdresses, coca plants form part of the spiritual heritage, identity and substance of each clan and are bound up with its mythical origins. In this sense, coca is inalienable, which is partly why it plays such a key role in ritual exchanges between individual men. Awareness of the problem is revealed in the shamans' injunctions to keep coca for ritual exchange separate from that for sale (see p. 47 above) and in the arguments they produced that although selling coca leaves to White people was acceptable, the sale of coca plants was not. This argument can be interpreted both at a symbolic level – the sale of plants being literally the sale of the clan's body and soul – or at a strategic, economic level – without access to coca plants, White people would be unable to establish their own plantations and thus unable to convert the Indians into mere labourers who could no longer barter coca leaves for goods.

The similarity between barter and this external trade is even clearer when locally produced artefacts, rather than coca leaves or labour, are offered to White people in exchange for manufactured goods for, as was shown above, this is also the pattern of most exchanges between Indians. It is also borne out by the fact that Indians often extend the personal bonds that characterise relations with other Indians to those White people with whom they interact frequently and from whom they get most of their manufactured goods. Sometimes this personal aspect seems paramount, so that when I was pestered for things like books in English for which the Barasana had no conceivable use, I felt at times that their requests came as much from the desire to establish a social bond as from a desire for the object in question.

Individual Barasana often refer to rubber-gatherers, cocaine-dealers, missionaries, anthropologists or others with whom they have frequent dealings as *yi gawi/o*, 'my White man/woman' and they treat them with a kind of bantering familiarity. They may ask such people to give names to their children, and talk about them amongst themselves in a way which serves to boast of their familiarity with the outside world. This personal aspect is reinforced when White traders take Indian women as concubines and have children by them. The most successful cocaine dealer in the Pirá-Paraná region owed much to the mediatory role played by his popular son, who was both the child of an Indian mother and had a Barasana girlfriend himself. It is in this kind of way that the morality of kinship mingles with that of the market.

As from each other, the Barasana expect trust from outsiders and consider the missionaries' refusal to give credit as a sign of their stinginess and lack of sociability. For the same reason, they express anger and resentment when White people refuse to part with their goods or turn down things offered to them – so much so that the missionaries sometimes feel themselves under pressure to create employment simply in order to satisfy demand for the goods in their stores.

Visiting, working, and trading with White people is simultaneously a means of acquiring consumer goods, a popular pastime and entertainment, a way of making social contacts with foreigners, and an end in itself. Many Barasana actively seek association with White people, travelling long distances to see them and then simply hanging around their establishments. For adolescent men this forms part of an informal rite of passage.[17] Association with foreigners brings with it the opportunity to learn Spanish and Portuguese, to acquire knowledge and experience of the outside world, and to gain status and prestige in the eyes of both Indians and White people. It is for this reason that I argue that part of the value of manufactured goods lies in the act of acquiring them, the context in which they are acquired, and in the people from whom they derive.

Despite these similarities, I do not wish to suggest either that there are no differences between indigenous barter and trade with White people or that the Barasana see no differences between them – they do. A key difference lies in the fact that whereas barter takes place between approximate equals, each of whom has a roughly equivalent say in the deal, and ends with each side feeling that they have made a fair swap, trade with White people is fundamentally asymmetrical and it is usually they who set the terms of exchange.

Barter between individuals has its counterpart in the reciprocal and roughly balanced exchanges of food and goods between whole groups (see p. 60 above). The asymmetrical exchange between Indians and Whites also has its counterpart, for when ceremonial exchange takes places not between affinally related exogamous groups of equal status, but between the ranked clans within one such group, the exchange ceases to be balanced and the lower-ranking clan gives more to their seniors (see also Chernela, 1983: 130). In Vaupés society, the extreme case of such asymmetrical exchanges is the 'tribute' in food (meat) and labour that the riverine Tukanoans extract from the semi-nomadic Makú living in the interfluvial zones. Significantly the Barasana employ the verb *hoso* – 'to be made into Makú', to describe their own situation *vis-à-vis* White people.

Although the Indians have little direct bargaining power, a combination of market and moral forces has, at times, given them some measure of indirect power. In the past, the presence of missionaries provided a certain measure of restraint on the worst excesses of the rubber gatherers. Their successors, the cocaine dealers, were in competition with each other, and the price they paid for coca leaves was subject to market forces operating in the region as a whole. There was also competition from the missionaries as supplier of consumer goods, so the cocaine dealers' prices were roughly on a par with those at the mission stores. Furthermore, although the missionaries were powerless to stop the illegal cocaine trade entirely, their presence in the immediate area, and the uneasy truce that operated throughout the region, meant that the cocaine dealers were restrained from applying the violence and physical sanctions necessary to enforce a harshly exploitative regime. Paradoxically, it was the very legality of the previous rubber industry and the active role of the police in forcing Indians to deliver on their 'debts', that led to some of the worst abuses of the early 70s. Although they were well aware of the cocaine dealers' greater profits, the Barasana often commented on the fact that they themselves had to work much harder and under worse conditions when tapping rubber.

Caroline Humphrey has pointed out that debt relationships are typically associated with barter across ethnic frontiers in which one side has a monopoly over certain goods (1985: 60–1). Although control of the means of exchange allows profit, she argues that the system is self-limiting because 'the trust required for barter to include credit effectively circumscribes economic operations' (*ibid*: 67). It is precisely when violence and terror masquerade as the trust they subvert and replace, that the limits break down and the system becomes one of gross exploitation (see also Anderlini and Sabourian, this volume, on the subject of enforcement).

A comparison between rubber production in the Pirá-Paraná area, and the cocaine industry that replaced it, suggests that there is a continuum between barter and debt-peonage depending on the asymmetries of power and differences in economic system between the parties involved. At one extreme there is egalitarian barter, simultaneous or delayed, within the Indian community, and at the other there are the worst excesses of hierarchical and exploitative debt-bondage.[18] In between lie the relations between Indian entrepreneurs and their kinsmen, direct exchanges between Indians and missionaries, and the credit arrangements between Indians and White traders.

Whilst the advance of goods on credit is an integral part of debt-peonage, allowing manipulation of prices and serving to perpetuate ties between debtor and creditor which guarantee a regular return of labour and product, the case of cocaine production in the Pirá-Paraná area shows also that similar credit arrangements may operate in a system which is not markedly more exploitative than the commonplace, but equally profitable, sale of goods for cash elsewhere in the world. Credit may be forced upon unwilling recipients and clearly lends itself to gross exploitation, but it exists also for other reasons which themselves make it open to abuse.

In addition to the near absence of money and markets for goods and labour in frontier zones, we must also take into consideration the fact that the Indians actively seek credit both because it gives them instant access to desirable goods of uncertain supply, and because it fits in with the patterns and habits of their own barter. Furthermore, the transitive nature of debt-peonage, and the power imbalances caused when Indians acquire guns or become allied with White people, means that debts can be passed on so that the clients of White men become the patrons of Indians in their turn.[19] This chain may be institutionalised by Indian rubber gatherers and cocaine dealers like José B. (see the letter on p. 51 above), or it may be disguised under ties of kinship and affinity that allow individuals to demand the 'help' of their household and neighbours in picking the coca leaves needed to pay off their guns and outboard motors. Behind the name of each individual in the cocaine dealer's ledger there hides a small community of such helpers, so that the Indians themselves find it hard to disentangle help, reciprocity, and debt.

In saying this, I do not intend to be an apologist for debt-peonage, nor to imply that White people and Indians, by matching their complementary demands, simply barter away happily in a system of enlightened self-interest. The many, and often horrifying, accounts of Amazonian debt-peonage have already shown that this is far from the truth. I do want to suggest, however, that, unless we try to disentangle our own views as to whether or not Indians *should* want consumer goods, from an understanding of why they *do* want them, and unless we begin to examine debt-peonage and other inter-ethnic economic exchanges from both sides, Indian as well as White, they will continue to have the deceptively transparent but nonetheless mystified appearance that Taussig (1987: 63) detects but does not fully explain. In particular, it will remain very hard to understand why Indians often continue to be involved in a system, which is often patently exploitative, even when they are not under duress.

Although they stem from an admiration of Amerindian cultures and societies, an understandable and proper reaction to past and present abuses committed against them, and a laudable desire to further their interests, all of which I share, I nonetheless feel that the tendency to blame Indian 'consumerism' on outside pressures, do dwell upon the more 'traditional' aspects of Amerindian exchange, to draw sharp and sometimes morally loaded lines between two economies signalled by 'gift' and 'commodity', and to underplay the Indians' active involvement in trade with White people, including their roles as chiefs, patrons and middlemen, all stem from a misguided liberalism. These views do not accurately reflect the past history and present circumstances of the Indians of Amazonia, nor will they help them in their future struggles, and they run the risk of presenting them as passive victims rather than as active agents in their own destinies.

It is folly to pretend that guns and machetes reproduce Indian culture, whilst clothes and digital watches do not: all four serve useful functions, all may be worn on the body as symbols of power, and all represent creative experiments. Such objects, traded between Indians and White people alike, are both the symptoms and the causes of profound changes in the Indians' economy and society and it is for these reasons that I have chosen to discuss the acquisition, distribution and consumption of consumer goods together. Barter plays a key role in this circuit, providing both the hinge between two economies and the door whereby they penetrate one another.

NOTES

1 For convenience, I shall use 'Yanomami' to cover all the different sub-groups and different orthographies concerned and have altered quotations accordingly.

2 The Barasana are one of a number of exogamous groups, each speaking an eastern Tukanoan language and belonging to the same general culture, who live in the basin of the Río Vaupés/Uaupés, along the equator and straddling the frontier between Colombia and Brazil. Traditionally these groups lived in dispersed communal houses (*malocas*) with an economy based on the

cultivation of bitter manioc and supplemented by fishing and hunting. This paper is focused on those groups – Tatuyo, Taiwano, Barasana, Bará, Makuna – living in the basin of the Río Pirá-Paraná in the southern Colombian Vaupés. For further ethnographic details see Århem, 1981 – Makuna; Bidou, 1976 – Tatuyo; Chernela, 1983 – Uanano; Goldman, 1963 – Cubeo; Hugh-Jones, C. 1979 – Barasana; Hugh-Jones, S. 1979 – Barasana; Jackson, 1983 – Bará; and Reichel-Dolmatoff, 1971 – Desana.

Research by C. and S. Hugh-Jones was variously supported by the Social Science Research Council (now ESRC); King's College, Cambridge and the British Museum. This support is gratefully acknowledged.

In writing this paper I have received helpful comments from Mauro Barbosa, Patrice Bidou, Dominique Buchillet, Philippe Descola, Chris Hann, Keith Hart, Christine Hugh-Jones, Caroline Humphrey, Margaret Jolly and Peter Rivière. This too is gratefully acknowledged.

3 See Sahlins, 1976: 148 ff. on the ethnocentrism latent in the notion of 'use value'.

4 Also known as debt-slavery, debt-bondage, *enganche, endeude, habilitación* and *aviamento*.

5 Chevalier (1982: 197 ff.) does briefly discuss the misappropriation of the Campa *ayompari* relationship between trading partners. Taussig (1987) also gives some consideration to these issues, but his claim that 'what is so painfully absent from the Putumayo accounts, namely the narrative mode of the Indians themselves' (1987: 134–5) is belied by Guyot's work (1972, 1976, 1979) on the Bora and Miraña. This material, surprisingly ignored by Taussig, provides important data on their own perceptions of their dealings with the Casa Arana, a useful complement to Taussig's account.

6 Perhaps the most striking example of this is Colson's (1973) account of trade in the Guiana highlands, but the same is also true of Thomas (1972) on Pemon trading and the brief discussion of intervillage trade in Basso (1973: 147 ff.). By contrast, Bodley (1973) on the Campa, Harner (1972) on the Jivaro, and Mansutti Rodriguez (1986) on the Uwotjuja, and Taylor (1981) on the Achuar all make clear the importance and significance of manufactured goods in indigenous trade, with the last two authors also providing information on how such goods are obtained from White people.

7 See also Albert, 1988 and the references to other similar cases contained in his footnote 7.

8 Payments made by tourists, anthropologists and film-makers may, at times, make up a significant part of the total income of manufactured goods in isolated tribal societies. Chagnon says he was 'identified by the Yanomami as an inexhaustible fount of goods' (1974: 165, fn. 2).

9 See Taussig's (1987) powerful account of the depths to which such exploitation may sink.

10 This last phrase is unclear: I take it to mean 'you have never had to work with a White man and they are worse than me'.

11 It is by no means always the case that Western goods are impersonal. An obvious example would be Christmas and birthday presents; more germane to the present discussion would be the examples of South African fruit and Nicaraguan coffee. Alongside the purchaser's intended effects on the economies

concerned, for some at least, such commodities became tokens imbued with the positive or negative associations of their origins.

12 See also Harner, 1972 for photographs of Jivaro Indians 'wearing' guns, and the brilliant watercolour sketches by Goodall (1977: 63, 70) showing the same habit amongst Guyana Indians.

13 Lizot reports that the Yanomami also seek manufactured goods for use in future exchanges and comments that it is for this reason that those villages with greater access to the sources of such goods possess greater quantities of locally produced artefacts as well (1984: 229). Much the same is also true of the Tukanoans.

14 Chernela does mention set rates for exchange amongst the Uanano – one grater for one canoe, one strainer for one *balaio*, one strainer for one Makú basket, one manioc grater for six Makú baskets or six strainers – but I have my doubts that such rates are really 'set'.

15 Some Indian patrones do in fact attempt to buy food and labour from their fellows in return for goods advanced on credit. Because this conflicts with other expectations between the parties concerned, they find it hard to make such deals stick and they often lead to quarrels. The letter cited on p. 51 was part of such a quarrel.

16 Jean Jackson (pers. comm.) reports that Indians in the main Vaupés area demanded cash and would no longer accept advances on credit for work in the cocaine business.

17 The Piro of the Bajo Urubamba have a similar view, namely that working in lumbering for White or mestizo *patrones* is a vital part of adolescence. So important is lumbering to manhood that the expression 'ya es madrero', 'he is now a lumberer' is equivalent to saying 'he is now a man' (Gow, 1987: 133).

18 A Bora myth from the Putumayo explains the origins of commerce with White people and the cruelties perpetuated by the Casa Arana. The myth describes how manufactured goods, created by a culture hero, were exchanged first for *cumare* string ('raffia') and other local products, then for human beings and finally for rubber in a repressive regime invented by the same culture heros (Guyot, 1976). Barter, slavery and debt-slavery are thus put into a historical sequence which would accord with our own histories of NW Amazonia.

19 The same Bora myth that accounts for the atrocities of the Casa Arana also underlines the active role of Indians as intermediaries and middlemen in the trade in manufactured goods. This point is also made when Guyot writes that 'flight was the solution of those who had nothing to lose, but the most influential, chiefs of the most important *malocas* thought they could find a compromise and an advantage in their commerce with the White people' (1976: 381).

This passage also hints at an allied point – that of the need for compromise. Many Indian chiefs and middlemen have little alternative and are effectively forced into their role. But the same can also be said for many White people in similar situations.

REFERENCES

Albert, B. (1988) La fumée du metal. *L'Homme*, 106–7: 87–119.

Appadurai, A. (1986) Commodities and the politics of value. In Appadurai, A. (ed.) *The Social Life of Things*. Cambridge: Cambridge University Press.

Århem, K. (1981) *Makuna Social Organization*. Stockholm: Almqvist and Wiksell International.

Basso, E. (1973) *The Kalapalo Indians of Central Brazil*. New York: Holt, Rinehart and Winston.

Bidou, P. (1976) Les Fils de l'Anaconda Céleste (Les Tatuyo). Thèse du 3ieme cycle, University of Paris.

Bodley, J. (1973) Deferred exchange among the Campa Indians. *Anthropos* 68: 589–96.

Chagnon, N. (1974) *Studying the Yanomami*. New York: Holt, Rinehart and Winston.

(1977) *Yanomami* (2nd edn). New York: Holt, Rinehart and Winston.

Chapman, A. (1980) Barter as a universal mode of exchange. *L'Homme*, 20 (3): 33–83.

Chernela, J. (1983). *Hierarchy and Economy Among the Kotiria (Uanano) Speaking Peoples of the Northwest Amazon*. Ph.D. dissertation, University of Michigan.

Chevalier, J. M. (1982) *Civilization and the Stolen Gift*. Toronto: University of Toronto Press.

Colson, A. (1973) Inter-tribal trade in the Guiana Highlands. *Antropológica*, 34: 5–70.

Cowell, A. (1973) *The Tribe That Hides from Man*. London: Bodley Head.

Dahl, R. (1973) *Charlie and the Chocolate Factory*. London: Allen Lane.

Dumont, J. P. (1976) *Under the Rainbow*. Texas: University of Texas Press.

Gell, A. (1986) Newcomers to the world of goods. In Appadurai, A. (ed.) *The Social Life of Things*. Cambridge: Cambridge University Press.

Goldman, I. (1963) *The Cubeo*. Urbana: University of Illinois Press.

Goodall, E. (1977). *Sketches of Amerindian Tribes 1841–1843*. London: British Museum Publications.

Gossain, J. (1971) 'Compran a los indios por $10' and 'De Planas al Vaupés: desalojo y esclavitud'. *El Espectador*, Thursday 18 February, Friday 19 February. Bogotá.

Gow, P. (1987) *The Social Organization of the Native Communities of the Bajo Urubamba River, Eastern Peru*. Ph.D. Thesis. London School of Economics.

Gross, C. (1976) Introduction de nouveaux outils et changements sociaux: le cas des indiens Tatuyo du Vaupés (Colombie). *Cahiers des Amériques Latines*, 13–14: 189–236. Inst. des Hautes Études de l'Amérique Latine.

(1977) La fin d'une autonomie indienne: le cas des indiens Tatuyo du Pirá-Paraná (Amazonie Colombienne). *Cahiers des Amériques Latines*, 15: 113–46. Paris.

Guyot, M. (1972) Le recit d O'ioi. In Jaulin, R. (ed.) *De L'Ethnocide*. Paris: Union Generale d'Editions.

(1976) Le travail du cautchouc chéz les Indiens Bora et Miraña. In *Hommage à Roger Bastide: L'Autre et L'Ailleurs*. The Hague: Mouton.

(1979) La historia del mar de Danta, el Caquetá. *Journal de la Société des Américanistes*, 66: 99–124.

Harner, M. (1972) *The Jivaro*. London: Robert Hale.

Hill, J. and Wright, R. (1988) Time, narrative and ritual; historical interpretations from an Amazonian society. In Hill, J. D. (ed.) *Rethinking History and Myth: Indigenous South American Perspectives on the Past*. Urbana and Chicago: University of Illinois Press.

Humphrey, C. (1985) Barter and economic disintegration. *Man*, NS. 20 (1): 48–72.

Hugh-Jones, C. (1979) *From the Milk River*. Cambridge: Cambridge University Press.

Hugh-Jones, S. (1979) *The Palm and the Pleiades*. Cambridge: Cambridge University Press.

   (1988) The gun and the bow; myths of White men and Indians. *L'Homme*, 106–7: 138–56.

Jackson, J. (1983) *The Fish People*. Cambridge: Cambridge University Press.

Kopytoff, I. (1986) The cultural biography of things. In Appadurai, A. (ed.) *The Social Life of Things*. Cambridge: Cambridge University Press.

Lizot, J. (1972) Economie ou societé? *Journal de la Société des Américanistes*, 60: 137–74.

   (1984) *Les Yanomami Centraux*. Paris: École des Hautes Études en Sciences Sociales.

Mansutti Rodriguez, A. (1986) Hierro, barro cocido, curare y cerbetanas: el comercio intra e interétnico entre los Uwotjuja. *Antropológica*, 65: 3–75.

Métraux, A. (1959) La révolution de l'hache. *Diogène*, 25: 32–45.

Reichel-Dolmatoff, G. (1971) *Amazonian Cosmos*. Chicago: University of Chicago Press.

Ribeiro, B. (1980) *A civilização de Palha: a Arte do Trançado dos Indios do Brasil*. Ph.D. Dissertation, University of São Paulo.

Rousseau, J.-J. (1984) *A Discourse on Inequality*. London: Allen Lane.

Saffirio, J. and Hames, R. (1983) The forest and the highway. *Cultural Survival Report* no. 11/*Working Papers on South American Indians*, 6: 152.

Sahlins, M. (1972) *Stone Age Economics*. Chicago: Chicago University Press.

   (1976) *Culture and Practical Reason*. Chicago: Chicago University Press.

Taussig, M. (1987) *Shamanism, Colonialism and the Wild Man*. Chicago: Chicago University Press.

   (1980) *The Devil and Commodity Fetishism in Latin America*. Chapel Hill: University of North Carolina Press.

Taylor, A.-C. (1981) God-wealth: the Achuar and the missions. In Whitten, N. (ed.) *Cultural Transformations and Ethnicity in Modern Ecuador*. Urbana, University of Illinois Press.

Thomas, D. (1972) The indigenous trade system of southeast Estado Bolivar, Venezuela, *Antropológica*, 33: 3–37.

4 Some notes on the economics of barter, money and credit

Luca Anderlini and Hamid Sabourian

1 Introduction

Barter, and more generally the question of the organisation of exchange, have attracted the attention of economists for a long time. These notes are an attempt to show how some of the problems concerning the organisation of exchange can be addressed from the perspective of modern economic theory and to summarise our own views on the topic. We have endeavoured to avoid technicalities at all costs, and hence omissions have been inevitable.

In a sense these notes contain nothing new. We have pieced together various insights (old and new) which economic theory offers about barter and the organisation of exchange. The result is, we hope, a totally non-technical view of how some of the problems of the organisation of exchange can be addressed from the perspective of economic theory. Some reflections which are, if not novel, not entirely stale, have emerged along the way. The reader accustomed to the style of modern economic theory will be disappointed, however. We do not 'work out' these ideas rigorously, but just suggest how they may be used to further our understanding of the issues at hand.

After apologising to economic theorists for the lack of rigour, let us apologise to anthropologists for the lack of references to the 'real world'. The approach which we have taken in these notes is rather abstract. This is in the tradition of both orthodox and unorthodox economic theory. A highly abstract framework has its costs as well as its benefits. The approach taken here allows us to address questions which would be difficult to analyse in a less stylised framework. However, this does not mean that we think of cultural and historical factors as being unimportant in, say, determining whether or not money will emerge as a medium of exchange. On the contrary, some of the results which we report below, we believe, reinforce the important role of cultural and historical factors (we are referring in particular to the multiplicity of equilibria which emerge in dynamic models, cf. sections 3 and 4).

We devote the next section to setting out the categories of barter, money and credit. Using a simple example we argue that these can be viewed as trading arrangements satisfying a more or less stringent set of constraints. One word of warning is appropriate here. Throughout these notes we use the term credit to denote trade arrangements which involve any form of deferred payment. In other words we mean any departure from an instantaneous satisfaction of a 'quid pro quo' constraint.

In section 3, we analyse a rudimentary 'evolutionary' model of money. It should be emphasised here that we are *not* sympathetic to the view that, since monetary exchange is 'better' than barter, the former will necessarily evolve out of the latter.[1] The issue is a lot more complex than this simple view would suggest, and the model which we analyse supports this stance. In section 4 we analyse the problem of 'enforcement' associated with any credit system. This is simply the problem of finding arrangements which ensure that (implicit or explicit) debts are paid up in due time. Scrutiny of this point leads us to say that which arrangements are, or are not, viable, crucially depends on the size of the community involved and on the degree of anonymity of the system.

Finally, in section 5 we discuss the interaction between the way the exchange of commodities is carried out and the ratios at which such commodities are exchanged.

In section 6 we offer some concluding remarks.

2 Barter, money and credit

We begin this section by setting out in as precise a manner as possible the categories of 'money' and 'barter' which we will subsequently use. This is best done in a simple set-up. Throughout these notes, we will be concerned almost exclusively with the problem of exchange and its relationship with money. Thus, we will largely ignore the additional problems introduced by explicit consideration of production. This is a substantial omission, but it is a necessary one for reasons of both clarity and space. First, we will look at the problems of exchange, taking the ratios at which goods are exchanged as given, uniform throughout the system, and consistent with the exchange wishes of the traders.[2] Taking exchange ratios as given and independent of how actual exchanges are carried out, is perhaps a worse sin than ignoring production, and we shall return to the problem of exchange ratio in some detail in section 5 below.

What we have in mind at this stage is a set of traders who know at which ratios commodities are exchanged, and who meet each other in pairs in order to carry out exchange.[3]

The first point to make is that barter is not simply non-monetary exchange. Barter is one form of non-monetary exchange. One example of non-monetary exchange which in no way could be called barter is that which could arise in a world in which all traders are perfectly trustworthy. All transactions could then be run on a 'credit' basis, and no role for a medium of exchange would ever arise.[4] Barter is a form of non-monetary exchange in which all trades are required to balance in some appropriate sense. In other words each bilateral trade has to be such that, at the given exchange ratios, the value of what each trader sells equals the value of what he buys.[5]

Moreover, in our view, any strict definition of barter for the framework which we have just described must include the stipulation that no trader acquires any commodity for the purpose of selling it again to some other trader.[6] Resorting to economic jargon we shall call bilateral trades which do not involve a medium of exchange, in the above sense, excess demand diminishing trades. We shall make clear what we mean presently. Suppose a trader starts off a sequence of bilateral trades wanting to acquire 1 apple and willing to supply 1 orange in exchange, while not wanting to buy or sell any pears. We shall call excess demand diminishing trades, exchanges after which the trader's demand or willingness to supply has not increased for any commodity. For instance exchanging the apple for, say, a pear would not be an excess demand diminishing trade for the trader in this example, since his initial demand for pears is nil.[7]

It is not difficult to see that the two (types of) constraints on bilateral trades, that they should be both balanced *and* excess demand diminishing, can make the organisation of exchange very difficult indeed. We shall illustrate this by means of a simple example (Ostroy, 1973, Ostroy and Starr, 1974). Consider an 'economy' made up of three traders and in which three commodities are the object of exchange. Let the traders be named A, B and C, and the commodities as p, q and r. Imagine also that the appropriate exchange ratios have been 'announced' to all. By changing the units in which we measure the commodities there is no loss of generality in stipulating that the exchange ratios are all 1.[8]

Suppose now that the demands of each trader are as follows:

$$Z_A = \begin{bmatrix} +1p \\ 0q \\ -1r \end{bmatrix} \quad Z_B = \begin{bmatrix} -1p \\ +1q \\ 0r \end{bmatrix} \quad Z_C = \begin{bmatrix} 0p \\ -1q \\ +1r \end{bmatrix}$$

These numbers should be interpreted as follows. The demands of trader A are denoted by Z_A. In this example, trader A wants to buy 1 unit of commodity p, zero units of commodity q, and wants to sell 1 unit of commodity r. A positive (negative) demand is thus interpreted as willingness to buy (supply). The demands of traders B and C should be interpreted in an analogous way.

Before proceeding further it should be pointed out that these demands are consistent in two precise ways. Firstly, each trader's demands are balanced. At the given exchange ratios, the value of what, say, B wants to buy is equal to the value of what he wants to sell. (Recall that 1 unit of commodity p exchanges for 1 unit of commodity q). Secondly, for each commodity the total amount which the three traders want to sell equals the amount which they want to buy. (The numbers in each row of Z_A, Z_B, Z_C add up to zero.)

Consider now a sequence of pairwise meetings A and B, A and C and B and C.[9] Let us now impose the condition that each bilateral trade satisfies both constraints of being balanced and excess demand diminishing. In other words, let us examine what are the exchange possibilities of the three traders under our strict definition of barter.

Take for instance the meeting between A and B. Trader B wants to sell 1 unit of commodity p, and trader A wants to buy one unit of commodity p. On the other hand there are no commodities which trader A wants to sell and trader B wants to buy. The only possible excess demand diminishing trade between A and B is the exchange of commodity p, but there is no other commodity which can be used to 'balance' such trade. One can then conclude that there is no trade between A and B, which is at the same time balanced and excess demand diminishing.

It is quite easy to see that analogous considerations apply to the meetings of A and C and B and C. Thus, in the above example, we have reached the extreme conclusion that under a strict barter regime of exchange, no exchange will actually take place. The conclusion is rather extreme and the example has no aspirations of realism, however we believe that this illustrates well what one could call the 'difficulties of barter'.

The rest of this section is dedicated to an examination of the two routes which are available to resolve the difficulties of barter in our example (and more generally): credit, and money.

Let us consider the case of credit first. One way to think about the system of exchange which we are about to describe is the following. Each individual has an 'account' denominated in some abstract numeraire.[10] For the sake of simplicity, let us imagine that commodity one is the abstract numeraire. Each individual is allowed to have a positive balance or to overdraw by as much as he wants during the course of the exchange process. However, each individual is required to have a zero or credit balance by the time the sequence of pairwise meetings has been completed. How such a requirement may be enforced is the subject of our focus in section 4 below, for the time being we simply assume that it is enforced in some effective way.

It should by now be clear that we are introducing credit as a way of relaxing the constraint that all bilateral trades be balanced. With credit we no longer require that trade be balanced at each paired meeting, but merely that each individual's trades be balanced over the *whole sequence* of pairwise meetings that they undergo. Relaxing in this way the constraint that each bilateral trade be balanced, is enough to make exchange possible through any given sequence of pairwise meetings, while satisfying the constraint that trades be excess demand diminishing. This would be true in fairly general models and in particular it is true in our example.

Consider the meeting between A and B. The only possible excess demand diminishing trade between the two is a transfer of 1 unit of commodity p from B to A. This is now feasible on its own, simply adding that B's account will have a credit balance of 1 and A's account a negative balance of 1. As a result, after the meeting with B the demands of A are

$$Z_A = \begin{bmatrix} 0p \\ 0q \\ -1r \end{bmatrix}$$

and his account has a balance of -1.

Consider now the meeting between A and C. The only possible excess demand diminishing trade is the transfer of one unit of commodity r from A to C. Again, this is now feasible on its own because of the credit possibility we have introduced. The result of this transaction is that A's account will now have a zero balance, and that C's account will have a balance of -1. Also A's demands now are

$$Z_A = \begin{bmatrix} 0p \\ 0q \\ 0r \end{bmatrix}$$

Hence A's demands are satisfied after the given sequence of two pairwise meetings with B and C, and his account has a balance of zero. Thus, as far as A is concerned, the objective of carrying out trades within the given constraints has been achieved. It is very easy to check that after B and C have met they will also be in a similar position as a result of the transfer of one unit of commodity q from C to B. Hence the introduction of credit makes it possible to carry out the given trades without violating the constraint that trades be excess demand diminishing in one 'round' of pairwise meetings. Abstracting from the fundamental problem of enforcement mentioned earlier, we seem to have resolved the 'difficulties of barter' simply by introducing credit. We want to stress at this stage that this is quite distinct from the introduction of a medium of exchange.

Let us now look at the effects of relaxing the requirement that bilateral trades be excess demand diminishing. We are now allowing traders to acquire commodities for the sole purpose of exchanging them again against other commodities. Hence we are allowing traders to use one or more medium of exchange. The case in which all trades are executed using a *single* medium of exchange we call 'monetary exchange'.[11] We now want to look at the exchange possibilities in our example when all bilateral trades are required to be balanced, but the constraint that they should be excess demand diminishing is relaxed.

Consider again the meeting between traders A and B. The exchange of one unit of commodity p from B to A, together with one unit of commodity r from A to B, is a balanced transaction. It is now allowed since we are not requiring that bilateral trades be excess demand diminishing. Notice in particular that trader B has taken on one unit of commodity r, while ultimately he has no demand for it. Thus, if we are to end up with all traders having zero demand for all commodities, trader B must be taking on one unit of commodity r for the sole purpose of exchanging it again at a later stage of the trading process. Commodity r is now acting as the medium of exchange.

Let us follow through to the end the execution of trades in our example. After their meeting, A's and B's demands are

$$Z_A = \begin{bmatrix} 0p \\ 0q \\ 0r \end{bmatrix} \quad Z_B = \begin{bmatrix} 0p \\ +1q \\ -1r \end{bmatrix}$$

Since A's demands are now all nil, it is natural to imagine that during the meeting between A and C no trades are executed. Consider now the meeting between B and C. Upon meeting their demands are

$$Z_B = \begin{bmatrix} 0p \\ +1q \\ -1r \end{bmatrix} \quad Z_C = \begin{bmatrix} 0p \\ -1q \\ 1r \end{bmatrix}$$

and hence a balanced transaction of 1 unit of commodity q from C to B, and 1 unit of commodity r from B to C, will ensure that all traders' demands are fully satisfied. Allowing non-excess demand diminishing trades, while still requiring that all bilateral trades be balanced, is thus enough to resolve the difficulties of barter as we defined them earlier. This conclusion is true in our simple example, but could be shown to be valid in a much more general framework.

We want to point out that our example suggests that it is always possible to execute trades using a single medium of exchange, and at the same time meet the constraint that all bilateral exchanges be balanced. This can be done in a more suggestive way by introducing a 4th commodity (call it s) which we stipulate should also be measured in units such that its exchange rate with commodities p, q and r be 1.

We want to imagine our 4th commodity,[12] s, as one for which no trader has an actual excess demand.[13]

At the start of the trading process our 3 traders now have the following demands:

$$Z_A = \begin{bmatrix} +1p \\ 0q \\ -1r \\ 0s \end{bmatrix} \quad Z_B = \begin{bmatrix} -1p \\ +1q \\ 0r \\ 0s \end{bmatrix} \quad Z_C = \begin{bmatrix} 0p \\ -1q \\ +1r \\ 0s \end{bmatrix}$$

Our concern now is to show that it is enough to relax the constraints that trades be excess demand diminishing as far as the 4th commodity is concerned, in order to fulfil traders' demands via a sequence of bilaterally balanced trades.

Consider the meeting between traders A and B. As far as the first 3 commodities are concerned there is only one possible excess demand diminishing trade: one unit of commodity p from B to A. Let us now balance this with the transfer of one unit of the 4th commodity from A to B. The reader will already have noticed the analogy between the present case and our previous illustration of exchange patterns when credit is allowed. The trades described here are the same as in the credit case, with the addition that the 4th commodity is now used as a 'record-keeping' device for the traders' credit accounts. By this we mean that the same trades as in the credit case can now be executed. Traders in credit of 1 unit will have 1 unit of commodity s for supply. Traders with a credit balance of -1 will have a demand for 1 unit of commodity s. We leave it to the reader to check that this is indeed the case.

It is quite easy to see that what we have just said applies to much more general situations than our simple example. One can always imagine trades as being carried out via a sequence of bilaterally balanced exchanges which use a single medium of exchange. It is natural to call such medium of exchange money, and such sequence of bilateral trades monetary exchange. There is, in general, no cogent reason why bilaterally balanced execution of trades which allows for non-excess demand diminishing transactions should involve a single medium of exchange. The reasons why one might (or might not) expect the emergence of a *single* medium of exchange are beyond the scope of our simple example. Many more considerations need to be brought into the picture. We return to this problem in some detail in section 3 below. The task for our example is of preliminary clarification of the issue.

There is one important point which needs to be raised about the patterns of exchange which we have just described. We have implicitly assumed that, while all traders have no excess demand for commodity s, they all possess at least one unit of it at the beginning of the exchange sequence. If, say, trader A started the exchange sequence with $1/2$ units of commodity s, it would have been impossible to balance the whole of his one unit of commodity p trade with B. Difficulties for the whole sequence of trades would have ensued. One condition which will ensure that monetary exchange in the above sense is always possible is that all traders should start the exchange sequence with at least as much of the 4th commodity as the total value of the positive components of their demands.[14] More generally, the conclusion that monetary exchange always ensures that given trades can be carried out must be qualified by requiring that all traders should have 'enough' money at the beginning of the trading sequence. We have then reached the conclusion that, in order for a medium of exchange to serve its function efficiently, not only should it be supplied in sufficient quantity, but it should also be appropriately (not 'too unequally') distributed among the traders. This problem is all too often ignored in the economic literature. Some of the extreme 'monetarist' conclusions, for instance, rest upon a complete disregard of these issues.

To conclude this section, let us sum up what we believe to be the main insights of our discussion so far. In some sense there is a decreasing degree of 'difficulty' between barter, monetary exchange and credit. These alternative regimes of organising the exchange of commodities, can be seen as satisfying different *constraints*. Barter is a way of organising exchanges so as to make sure that both the quid pro quo and the excess demand diminishing constraints are satisfied. Monetary exchange is a way to organise transactions so as to satisfy the quid pro quo constraint, but in which violation of the excess demand diminishing constraint is allowed.[15] Finally, credit is a way to organise exchange in which the quid pro quo constraint may be violated. All that is required in this case is that agents' trades be balanced overall – agents are only required to satisfy their lifetime *budget constraint*.

To what extent do money and credit resolve what we have called the difficulties of barter? The ordering which we have given above is reflected in the answer to this question. What we mean is that a full credit system can be said to resolve the difficulties of barter, and no major qualification needs to be added to this statement. In the case of money, it is true that the difficulties of barter are in part (and may be fully) resolved, but two important qualifications need to be added. The first one we have discussed already and has to do with the quantity and distribution of the medium of exchange across the agents. The second qualification we have not properly addressed before. It is related to problems arising from the explicit consideration of a time dimension in analysing the process of trade. There is a distinct asymmetry between money and credit in this case. Consider a system in which some agents want to trade commodities available in the future against commodities currently available. Among others, it seems appropriate to single out one reason why the consideration of such intertemporal exchanges should be relevant; what we have in mind is a production process which *takes time*. The difficulty with money is that, while it will allow agents to purchase commodities in the future by selling commodities now, it will not suffice for the reverse. By holding money, traders can transfer wealth through time, but they will find it difficult to transfer to the present wealth which will be available to them in the future.[16] Such asymmetry would clearly not arise in the case of credit.

3 Dynamics

Barter makes exchange difficult. Using a generalised medium of exchange resolves (at least in part) the difficulties of barter. It is then tempting to conclude that there will be a natural tendency for money to evolve out of barter situations.

In the social sciences one should always be at least sceptical of any argument based on the view that because some state of *society* is 'better' than another, then the better state will be an equilibrium in some appropriate sense.[17] The argument that because a better state of economy exists (even if it is an equilibrium), a natural dynamic path leading to it can be identified, would be even less convincing. We believe that this scepticism is well placed in the case of the evolution of money out of barter.

Our first aim in this section is to address the question of which dynamic forces are at work on the exchange arrangements starting from barter. After having identified such forces we will try to draw some general conclusions as to where they may lead.

An initial word of caution is absolutely necessary. There are at least two important reasons why what follows may seem incomplete. The first is that rigorous analysis of any 'dynamic' problem, like the one at hand, quickly leads to the use of fairly high-powered mathematical tools which we have striven to avoid. The second, and perhaps more important, is that on this issue the body of literature from formal theoretical economics on which one can draw is quite small (Jones, 1976; Nagatani, 1978; Iwai, 1988). A lot of what we say in the sequel is based on Jones (1976), but of course we alone are responsible for the present treatment of the problem.

Consider a situation of barter in which it is actually feasible for agents to carry out their desired trades. (We are thus considering a situation in which the difficulties of barter are less acute than in our example of section 2.) To make sense of the statement that barter makes exchange difficult, one needs to make explicit the notion of costs (in a very general sense, as will be clear below) associated with the execution of transactions. The claim that monetary exchange is superior to barter could then be rephrased as the claim that the costs of carrying out given trades using monetary trade arrangements are smaller than the trading costs associated with barter.[18]

The first important point which we wish to stress is the following. It is not the case that considering any kind of trading costs will lead to the conclusion that monetary trade arrangements are superior to barter ones.

Consider an individual who wants to exchange one unit of commodity p for one unit of commodity q.[19] Suppose that the individual has two alternative plans between which he has to choose. One plan is to first exchange one unit of commodity p for one unit of a third commodity, which acts as a medium of exchange, and then exchange the third commodity he has acquired for one unit of commodity q. The alternative plan is to simply exchange directly one unit of commodity p for one unit of commodity q.

Suppose now that trading costs are simply such that each and every transaction costs a fixed amount. Then clearly the individual will opt for the direct exchange. Hence, if it is to be the case that monetary exchange is better than barter, a transaction involving the purchase or the sale of the medium of exchange must be 'cheaper' than transactions between two non-medium of exchange commodities.

The obvious candidate for a type of trading cost which will favour monetary exchange over barter is the cost of *finding* someone wishing to make the complementary exchange to one's wanted transaction. It should already be clear that some specification of the cost of searching for trading partners is what we have in mind.[20] There are many possible ways to make this notion precise. Obviously, they all need some specification of the way in which traders meet each other. We will illustrate one such way while trying to keep matters simple. We do not claim that the example is realistic, but we believe it captures some of the essential features of the difficulty of finding a 'double coincidence of wants'.

Imagine a set of M[21] traders who want to carry out exchanges concerning 3 commodities of the following kind. A fraction f_{pq} of the traders only wants to exchange one unit of commodity p for one unit of commodity q. A fraction f_{pr} of the M traders wants to exchange one unit of commodity p for one unit of commodity r. Analogously let f_{qp}, f_{qr}, f_{rp} and f_{rq} be the fractions of the M traders who wish to exchange one unit of commodity q for one unit of commodity p, and so on. Let us also imagine that the wishes of these traders are consistent[22] so that there are just as many traders who want to exchange one unit of commodity p for one unit of commodity q, as there are who wish to exchange one unit of commodity q for one unit of commodity p, and so on for all commodities. In other words we will assume that $f_{pq} = f_{qp}$, $f_{pr} = f_{rp}$ and $f_{qr} = f_{rq}$.

Suppose now that each of the M traders is faced with the following problem. Before the trade process he has to decide whether to look for a complementary trader or to opt for indirect exchange. Throughout the illustration of this example we shall assume that the decision is *irrevocable* for the trader. So for instance a trader who wants to exchange one unit of commodity p for one unit of commodity q, has to choose either to wait until he meets a trader who wants to exchange one unit of commodity q for one unit of commodity p, or to first wait for a trader who wishes to exchange one unit of commodity r for one unit of commodity p, and then to wait for a trader wishing to exchange one unit of commodity q for one of commodity r.

Let us suppose that any given trader knows, at the beginning of the trading process, that he will meet other traders in a totally random order. Moreover, we want to imagine a trader's transaction costs as being proportional to the total amount of time he spends carrying out his exchanges. For simplicity suppose that traders meet randomly at regular time intervals. Then one can imagine agents choosing among the possible ways (direct or indirect) of carrying out exchange so as to minimise the number of traders they have to meet in the process of exchange. Notice that the number of meetings that a trader will in fact need is not known to him in advance. Hence one has to qualify the above by saying that traders will try to minimise the *expected* numbers of traders they have to meet in order to carry out their desired exchange sequence.

Let us now go back to our trader who wants to exchange one unit of commodity p for one unit of commodity q. If he decides to wait until he meets a trader wishing to exchange one unit of commodity q for one unit of commodity p, the expected number of traders he has to meet is[23] $1/f_{qp}$. If he decides to wait first for a trader wishing to exchange one unit of commodity r for one unit of commodity p and then (that is after he is in possession of 1 unit of commodity r) wait for a trader wishing to exchange one unit of commodity q for one unit of commodity r, his expected number of meetings is $1/f_{rp}+1/f_{qr}$. It follows that our trader will plan to use commodity r as a medium of exchange

$$\frac{1}{f_{qp}} \text{ is greater than } \frac{1}{f_{rp}}+\frac{1}{f_{qr}}$$

and this is clearly possible as long as f_{qp} is 'low' and f_{rp} and f_{qr} are 'high'.

Some comments are in order about the manipulations which we have been carrying out. The intuition behind the proposition that sometimes indirect exchanges will be easier (faster) than direct exchanges is the following. If there are few traders wanting to exchange commodity r for commodity p and commodity q for commodity r then, on average, it will be easier (faster) to carry out trades using commodity r as a medium of exchange. This basic observation is the key to understanding the dynamic process which we are about to describe.

Consider a situation completely analogous to the example which we have just illustrated, but where there are many commodities.[24] In Jones' (1976) framework two propositions can be demonstrated. Firstly, if a trader is planning to use indirect trade he will always plan to exchange via the most frequently traded commodity rather than any other medium of exchange. Secondly, it is never the case that the trader will plan to execute his trades using more than one medium of exchange, one after the other. This will never require a smaller number of expected meetings than using the most frequently traded commodity as a medium of exchange.

We have now arrived at a point where it is possible to loosely describe the dynamic process governing the evolution of the patterns of exchange. Suppose, for simplicity, that all traders initially know which fraction of other traders wishes to execute a given trade. In terms of our earlier example, we are stipulating that initially traders know the values of f_{pq}, f_{pr} and so on. It is *possible*, as we have shown in our example, that these values of f_{pq}, f_{pr} etc. will make it convenient for some traders to execute their transactions via the medium of exchange.[25] For convenience only, let us identify the latter with a commodity named m. It follows from the above that the fraction of traders actually transacting commodity m *may* be higher than that which the traders initially expect. Thus the demand for commodity m can now be divided into two components. The first is the demand of those traders who wish to ultimately hold (i.e. consume) commodity m, and the second is the demand generated by those traders who wish to use commodity m as a medium of exchange.[26]

Let us now imagine that as traders execute each 'round' of trade, they have a chance of updating their beliefs[27] about the number of traders who transact commodity m. In other words, in executing their exchanges, the traders realise that the fraction of people transacting commodity m has increased because some traders are using it as a medium of exchange. We are now through to the next 'round'. The traders' updated beliefs *may* cause even more people to start using commodity m as a medium of exchange. Executing their exchanges, traders will again have a chance of updating their beliefs, and so a third round of the dynamic process can be defined.

There is an obvious way to define what is a resting point for the dynamic process which we have outlined. This is simply a point at which traders' beliefs about the fraction of people transacting commodity m are the same as the fraction of people *actually* executing transactions using commodity m. We shall call any such point an equilibrium pattern of exchange.

Of course the interesting question now is whether there are general conclusions which one can draw about the nature of equilibrium patterns of exchange. Let us call complete barter a situation in which no medium of exchange is used at all and completely monetary exchange a situation in which commodity m appears, as either bought or sold, in all transactions.

The first general conclusion which can be drawn is that it could well be the case that complete barter *is* an equilibrium pattern of trade. In our earlier example take, for instance, $f_{pq} = f_{pr} = f_{qr}$. Then no commodity is transacted sufficiently often as to ever induce any traders to use it as a medium of exchange. The pattern of exchange is in some sense 'trapped' into a barter situation.

The second general conclusion is that completely monetary exchange is always one possible equilibrium pattern of trade. In other words, if traders know that all other traders want to exchange via commodity m, it will be the case that all traders will use commodity m in their exchanges.[28]

The third general conclusion is that there may be one or more equilibrium pattern of exchange. Moreover, in most cases, equilibrium patterns of exchange will be characterised by a coexistence of monetary exchange and barter. By this we mean that some exchanges will be carried out using a medium of exchange and some exchanges will be direct. This is a comforting feature of the model which we are describing, as it seems to reflect some general patterns of many societies, both 'primitive' and 'advanced'.

The final conclusion which can be drawn from the nature of equilibrium patterns of exchange is that, in equilibrium, a commodity plays (fully or partially) the role of a medium of exchange because individuals *believe* that the commodity plays the role of a medium of exchange. In other words, an agent may accept more of a commodity than he desires for consumption because he believes that other agents will also accept more of that commodity than they desire for consumption. It is this 'bootstraps' mechanism in beliefs which lies at the centre of the determination of the equilibrium patterns of exchange. If all agents believe that a certain commodity is the medium of exchange, then it is 'rational' for each individual to accept such a commodity whenever it is offered to him as a means of payment. Once one begins to think of money as a commodity, the value of which is sustained by this type of 'bootstraps', it becomes clear that any (storable) good which is not too abundant, divisible, easily transportable and so on, can become money. This not only explains the multiplicity of equilibria which are obtained in this model, but it also explains how it has been possible historically that different commodities have been used (in some cases simultaneously) as money or near-money (Polany, 1957). Furthermore, there is nothing in the 'bootstraps' ex-

planation of the possibility of monetary exchange which indicated that the
commodity used as a medium of exchange should have any use-value to
any of the individuals concerned. Paper money ('fiat money') will be
accepted as a means of payment by agents who believe that other agents
will accept it as a means of settlement of exchanges.

Before turning to the dynamics of the model, let us mention one point
which has puzzled economic theorists for some time. If the economy is
modeled as being of finite duration, then at the last date no agent will wish
to hold any commodity as money.[29] (No agent will accept a commodity in
order to use it to buy another commodity in the future.) Let us now turn
to the moment just preceding the final date. If agents can foresee that, in
the final period, no one accepts money, then it would not be 'rational' for
them to accept money in the penultimate period: since money is held to buy
something in the future, they would be foregoing current consumption for
no future benefit. Hence, no one will wish to hold any commodity as money
in the penultimate period, and the 'monetary value' of any commodity
must be zero. Proceeding in this way, and assuming that agents can
forecast correctly the future value of money, we can easily deduce that no
commodity will be used as money in any period.[30] Economic theorists have
suggested many different solutions to the above problem (see Hahn, 1982).
The important point to note here is that, if we are to explain the value of
money in terms of some 'bootstraps' mechanism in expectations, then it is
clear that at any stage of the trading process we need a future date in order
to give a role to money.

Let us now turn to the dynamic properties of the equilibria which we
have claimed exist. These are unfortunately rather difficult to explain
intuitively. All the equilibria which we have mentioned may in fact be the
outcome of the dynamic evolutionary process which we have described,
starting from a barter situation. This is of course saying much more than
simply asserting that these are equilibrium patterns of exchange. We have,
for instance, pointed out that full monetary exchange can always be an
equilibrium pattern of exchange. However, it may well be the case that the
dynamic evolutionary process which we have described will never reach a
full monetary exchange. Such a process could find another resting point
first, which is some mixture of barter and monetary exchange, or even
never take off from complete barter. It could indeed even be the case that,
because of changes in the basic features of the economy (for example
changes in technology, transaction costs interpreted in a broad sense,
needs and tastes of consumers, etc.), the 'parameters' of the model (the f_{ij}'s)
could change in such a way as to take the economy away from monetary
exchange after this had been established. The net result of these changes
may well be towards a different equilibrium, entailing more barter than

before. However, the simple dynamic system which we have described will have the following feature. Starting from a barter situation, the resting point which the system will actually reach is the equilibrium pattern of exchange with the lowest (amongst the equilibria) use of the medium of exchange.

Of course, it follows from the definition of equilibrium that if one starts from any equilibrium trading arrangements, the system will perpetuate itself. The next natural question to ask is then whether the equilibria which we have identified are 'locally stable'. In other words, starting from any equilibrium point, and given a 'small' change in the parameters of the model, will such equilibrium trading arrangements survive? One pre-liminary answer to this question can be provided returning to our example. Suppose, for instance that

$$\frac{1}{f_{qp}} \text{ is smaller than } \frac{1}{f_{rp}} + \frac{1}{f_{qr}}.$$

Recall that this implies that the owner of commodity p, who desires commodity q will try to achieve a direct barter rather than try to use commodity r as a medium of exchange. If similar inequalities hold for other commodities, barter trading is in equilibrium. If the inequalities are strict, as we have supposed above, then a small change in the parameters will leave the inequalities intact. Thus barter trading will survive such a small change in the underlying conditions of the economy. In such a case, only a large shock (a large change in the parameters) can move the system away from the existing equilibrium and start a dynamic process taking the economy away from barter. One possible example of what we have been trying to explain could be a 'backward' economic community with no established central authority (state) in which trading takes place using a mixture of barter and monetary exchange (see, for example, Humphrey, this volume). A minor shock to such economy may not affect the trading arrangements. However, a major shock, such as the establishment of a central authority which 'protects' and taxes agents in the economy, may have a dramatic effect on the established trading arrangements. If such an authority demands the payment of taxes in a certain commodity (this could, for instance, be gold, wheat or paper money printed by the state itself) then the underlying demand for such a commodity will rise by a large amount. This will affect inequalities such as the one above. As a result the 'optimal' way of trading for some (or all) individuals may change. In particular it may be that now it pays (in terms of expected trading costs) some (or all) individuals to accept and use the commodity in question to buy all that they desire. This will increase the demand for such a commodity, which in turn will justify further use of it as a medium of exchange. How large the fraction of individuals using such medium of exchange will be at the end of this dynamic process will of course depend on the demand for other commodities, on how individuals learn about the widespread use of media of exchange, etc.

To conclude this section, let us remark that what we have just outlined is one possible and very stylised way to look at the dynamic forces which operate upon exchange arrangements. However, we believe that the main feature of the argument, which emphasises the role of expected trading costs and of beliefs, is a very general one. Also, as we remarked at the beginning, the conclusion that it is not necessarily the case that social exchange arrangements evolve towards more efficient states is not surprising and in line with many of the findings of modern economic theory.

4 Enforcement

In section 2, we claimed that the difficulties of barter can be fully resolved by introducing a credit system encompassing all agents. We already mentioned that the difficulty in running such a scheme would lie in enforcing the stipulation that debts are paid up in due time. This, in our sample example, took the form of the assumption that each agent's credit balance be zero at the end of the exchange process.

The viability of the credit system obviously hinged on the fact that such a constraint be satisfied. Clearly, if agents do not trust that other agents' credit balances will be zero by the end of the trading process, some of them at least will be reluctant to participate in the credit scheme in the first place.

If all agents were perfectly trustworthy, the running of a credit system would clearly not generate a problem of enforcement, and the credit system itself would always be viable. The problem arises when some or all agents may not honour their debts if appropriate sanctions are not imposed. In the rest of this section we shall be concerned with the latter case.[31] We shall discuss some possible enforcement mechanisms and analyse conditions which would make them viable.

The first, and preliminary, observation which seems relevant concerns our approach (which we discussed in sections 3 and 2) of taking the ratios at which commodities are exchanged as given. It is clear that when one is analysing the problem of enforcement (and hence of possible *default*) the two-way relationship between the equilibrium exchange ratios and the process of exchange may become important. The first relationship arises from the following obvious observation. If some (or all) agents are allowed to default on some (or all) of their debts, it is not necessarily the case that the exchange ratios which guarantee that the quantities demanded and supplied by the traders are consistent in the aggregate (cf. section 2) will be the same as in the case in which all debts are honoured. In other words different credit arrangements and associated default possibilities may quite obviously change the 'equilibrium' exchange ratios.

The second possible connection between credit arrangements and exchange ratios is in some sense a consequence of the first one. If it is the case that some (or all) agents are not insignificant in size relative to the whole set of traders, then they may be aware of the fact that *their own* decision of whether to honour their debts will affect the ratios at which commodities are exchanged. As a consequence, the decision of whether to honour debts may become strategic in the sense that agents may take into account the effect of their decision to default on exchange ratios of commodities and on other traders' behaviour.

Having issued the above warnings about the possible problems of taking exchange ratio as given, we shall proceed to do just that. The reason for this is two-fold. In the first place there is a straightforward need to simplify our discussion of the enforcement of credit arrangements, which would become quite untransparent if the above considerations were brought directly into the picture. Secondly, we dedicate the next section entirely to the formation of commodities' exchange ratios and their interrelation with trade and credit arrangements.

Let us now go back to the problems of the enforcement of credit arrangements. We shall start with a pair of totally self-evident observations and subsequently build on these. The first observation is simply that, in order to force traders to comply with arrangements which may be against their immediate interests (such as paying up debts), one needs some form of punishment, however defined.[32] The second observation, which follows from the first one, is that, in order to punish traders who do not comply with their obligations, it may have to be the case that the interactions of the traders are not totally anonymous. Clearly, in the case of complete anonymity, only sanctions which apply to all traders are possible, and there are two obvious difficulties with these. The first is that to always have to punish everyone in the set of agents considered is a very costly and wasteful way of dealing with 'deviant' behaviour. The second is that the intensity of punishment which can be obtained may be severely limited if one is not able to aim it at one agent in particular, rather than the whole set of traders.

Let us expand on the first of these two observations. Throughout what follows we shall imagine that the traders' interactions are in fact not anonymous, so that the 'punishment' of single individuals is possible in principle. We shall only return to the question of anonymity briefly at the end of this section.

Consider two[33] self-interested agents who meet to trade in two commodities, and who know that they will never meet again and that their actions in this bilateral meeting are not going to affect them in any way in the future. Then it is certainly the case that these two self-interested traders will take actions which give them the maximal *instantaneous* benefit. At the risk of becoming pedantic, let us explain more. For concreteness imagine the above situation to be one in which trader A wants to exchange two apples for one orange with trader B, and trader B agrees with such an exchange in principle. Suppose now that the exchange is sequential in the sense that first trader A gives one orange to trader B, and then trader B gives the two apples in exchange. Notice then that in some sense, between the two transactions, B is in debt to A to the extent of two apples. In the extreme situation which we have depicted, B has strong incentives to, and indeed if he is purely self-interested will, default on his debt towards A, since he has nothing to lose but something to gain from it. What is needed to convince B to pay up is the threat of losing something in the *future*, as a consequence of his default. This loss is what we have so far been calling punishment. Therefore, by punishment we mean 'stick' and/or withholding 'carrot'. The point which we are trying to stress here is simply that, in order for it to be possible that self-interested agents forego opportunities for immediate gain, which is essential to the viability of any credit arrangements, a time dimension in the relationship between traders is needed. Traders' actions have to have future consequences as well as current ones. One situation in which it is easy to imagine this to be the case, is, for instance, one in which the same group of traders meets repeatedly through time in order to carry out exchanges. In such cases, individuals may not default on their debts for fear of punishment by some or all the other agents in the future. There are several questions one may ask at this stage. What are the punishments? Who are the enforcing agents (those who carry out punishments)? Why should some or all agents punish someone who has defaulted? Or, putting the last question differently, are the threats of punishment credible?[34] Punishment can take many forms: legal penalties, refusal to enter any further credit or even trading arrangements with the defaulter, social ostracism, physical harassment, etc. The punishers can be the injured party, a group of agents, or all individuals in the community. The identity of the enforcers could be decided tacitly, or the community could formally delegate the punishment of deviators to a (presumably small) subset of agents in the economy (for example the state).[35]

The recent literature on repeated games (see Sabourian (1989) for a survey) provides a natural framework for the analysis of the repeated interaction among participants in a credit system and the rest of society, and in particular for the analysis of the credibility of punishments. In this literature two reasons are usually offered to explain why individuals may follow norms which are not in their immediate interests. The first tries to explain the adherence to such norms in terms of a straightforward threat of future punishment by some or all other agents. Such a threat is credible because, if any member of the community who is supposed to punish a deviator does not so do, he in turn will be punished by some or all agents. This explanation justifies the adherence to norms by appealing to the possible existence of 'a potential sequence of successively higher order punishments, where the punishment at each level is carried out for fear that the punishment at the next level will be invoked' (Fudenberg and Maskin, 1986).

The second explanation of adherence to norms which are not in one's short-term interest is in terms of acquiring and sustaining a reputation for being 'trustworthy'. In models in which individuals are not certain of each other's motives (games of incomplete information), it may pay individuals to acquire a reputation for being a type of individual which he, in fact, is not. In such contexts, agents want to know what sort of person is the individual that they are dealing with. They form an opinion on the basis of what they know of him. This opinion, as Dasgupta (1986) puts it, 'is based, amongst other things, on the theory we hold of the effect of culture, class membership, family life and the like, on a person's motivation (his disposition) and thus his behaviour. This opinion, which is publicly held and formed, is this person's reputation.' Clearly, how other agents treat a person depends on their opinion of that person; as a result, the person might follow certain norms in order to influence the others' opinion of himself. In other words, one can explain adherence to norms which are not in one's immediate interest by looking at reputation as a capital asset. As with other capital assets, one can build it by following certain behaviour, and one can destroy it by following other behavioural patterns.

Clearly the above observations provide a good framework for thinking about the problem of enforcement in the context of credit arrangements. The enforcers may punish a defaulter because of the fear that they may be punished for not punishing (for example if the state does not apply the appropriate legal penalties to those who have clearly violated legal agreements, the state itself may be in a vulnerable position in the future).

Turning to the reputation explanation, suppose that a trustworthy man is one who always settles his debts, while untrustworthy people never do so. Clearly, if an agent is thought to be untrustworthy, no one will wish to provide credit for that person (they, of course, may also impose other punishments on him). In such a case, an agent who has acquired a reputation for being trustworthy (by 'luck', or by behaving in the right way for some length of time), will always settle his debts for fear of losing his reputation for being trustworthy. The latter would not be in his interest since it would entail being treated as untrustworthy in the future.

There are several further points to notice about the above explanation of the possibility of credit enforcement:

(1) If a self-interested individual is allowed to run up a debt and he has the knowledge that there will be no future consequences whatsoever for his behaviour towards his creditor, then he will default. As a result, the potential creditors will not enter a credit arrangement with such fly-by-night operators in the first place.

(2) The larger the cost of observing a deviation for the enforcers, the less severe the potential punishment which can be credibly imposed on a deviator may have to be. As a result, the larger this cost, the less likely the possibility of credit arrangements. (Observational costs will clearly grow with the size of the economy and with its degree of anonymity, and we will return to this point later.)

(3) In repeated interaction between agents (repeated games) there are generally many possible equilibria, each with different enforcement mechanisms.[36] In some equilibria the deviator is punished by the injured party only, in some others a group of individuals punish the deviator and in some others, all agents punish the deviator. Clearly the severity of potential punishments will increase with the number of individuals who threaten to punish.

The last point takes us back to the question of delegation which we mentioned before. A useful distinction to make in this respect is the obvious one between systems which delegate the punishment of deviators to a (presumably small) subset of agents in the economy, and those systems in which no particular group of agents is delegated to carry out punishments. A prime example of a system of the first type is the one in which the punishment of deviators is carried out using a body of *legal penalties*. A good example of a system of the second kind is a group of sovereign nations, which, almost by definition, cannot apply legal penalties to each other, and hence punish or threaten to punish deviators by, say, excluding them from future trades with the group of countries in question.

Let us try and examine more closely what might generate such diverse punishment systems, in the sense of delegated ones versus non-delegated ones. Two categories which will be useful for such a task are those of the *observation* costs and *verification* costs of a deviation. The cost of observing such a deviation does not need any further explanation, except perhaps for the remark that if the deviation is a debtor's default, then the creditor will automatically (that is at no cost) observe such deviation, and one only conceive of observation costs of default as far as a 'third party' is concerned.

Of course it is possible that something is easy to observe, but that it is rather difficult (or even impossible) to produce 'hard evidence' of it. This observation underlies our distinction between observation and verification costs. By the cost of verifying a deviation, we mean the cost of producing evidence of such deviant behaviour which would be accepted in a court of law. This can of course be a lot higher[37] than the cost of simply observing such behaviour.

Consider now the example of a large economy, let us say that of an advanced capitalist country. To make an undelegated system of punishments viable large numbers of agents would have to observe (and remember) the identities of the deviators. In the aggregate, the resource cost of running such a scheme would be very high. Hence, despite the fact that the cost of verifying deviations may be considerably higher than the individual cost of observing them, it is highly likely that a delegated system of punishment will be the most efficient in the aggregate. On the basis of what we have just said, it would be tempting to conclude that if the aggregate cost of observation of deviators is higher than the cost of verifying deviant behaviour, then a delegated enforcement system will emerge. However, we believe that this conclusion would be far too bold for at least two reasons. Firstly we believe that it would be obviously wrong to claim that the only reasons governing the emergence of legal systems are economic ones. Secondly, as we pointed out in section 3, we believe that it is wrong (but an unfortunately common mistake) to say that simply because a more efficient social state exists, then the system will evolve towards it. The analysis of section 3 is a good example of how wrong such an assumption can be. Perhaps minimalistically, we would like to conclude only that the relative sizes of the aggregate observation costs and of the verification costs of deviant behaviour are important in determining whether a system of delegated punishment will have a *tendency* to emerge, leaving the *actual* emergence to be influenced by a host of historical and social factors largely outside the realm of economic analysis.

Summing up, it seems that the viability of a trading system based on credit hinges on two prerequisites. Firstly, agents must not meet in a totally anonymous way. Secondly, there must be a temporal dimension to the relationship between agents. The trading process is *repeated* over time. Moreover, the ways in which the punishment of deviators is carried out will be affected by the relative size of the aggregate cost of observation and of verification of deviant behaviour. In particular, then the size of the system considered will have an effect on the tendency for a delegated punishment system to emerge.

To conclude this section we want to point out instances in which the above observations may afford some insights into the workings of exchange systems. Our remarks, for instance, seem to explain well the fact that, within families and small communities, exchange is most often carried out on what could appear to be a 'gift' basis, but which we would prefer to call a long-term credit and debit basis. It is interesting to notice that the punishment of deviators in these contexts is largely undelegated, and often takes the form of non-pecuniary sanctions as well as pecuniary ones (such as being barred from future exchanges). Social ostracism can be a very effective form of punishment.

A second example in which the repeated nature of the relationship and the small number of non-anonymous participants, together with other restrictions, favour the emergence of trade on a credit basis is that of a group of sovereign nations. Bilateral, or multilateral, transactions in which *first* one good is delivered from one Government to the other, and *then* some other good is given back in exchange is of course a credit-based form of exchange.

Credit transactions have been expanding very rapidly indeed in advanced capitalist economies in recent years. It is easy to ascribe this phenomenon to the rapid recent advances in the technology for the transmission, retrieval and storage of information. In particular, both the costs of verification and of observation of deviant behaviour have been greatly reduced in recent years.[38] The importance of the decrease in the verification costs is obvious since such large systems are run using delegated legal penalties. The role of the decrease in what we have been calling observation costs is more intriguing, however. What has become easier and cheaper is the cost of observing and producing credible *signals* of credit worthiness (what are credit cards after all?).

We believe that a possible ceiling to the expansion of a generalised credit system in a large advanced economy can be provided by our remarks on anonymity and credit. As long as some agents have interest to keep some (or all) of their transactions anonymous, it is unlikely that paper money will disappear. It is a most convenient and anonymous way to satisfy the quid pro quo constraint of section 2.

5 Price formation

Our analysis in this paper has so far suffered from a weakness which we have pointed out at various stages. In our discussion of different ways in which exchange can be carried out we have maintained the stipulation that the exchange ratios, for commodities which guaranteed that the wishes of the traders were consistent in the aggregate, were *given* throughout, and *independent* of, exchange arrangements. In the jargon of economists we have been taking equilibrium relative prices as given, and independent of how transactions are carried out (and hence of the cost of such transactions). This problem turns out to be a hard and under-researched one. We cannot claim that this section offers an answer to it, or even a unified framework in which it would fit. We shall do no more than discuss some examples of how one could try to start attacking the issue.

Before we discuss any actual mechanism of interdependence between the organisation of exchange and relative prices, a few general points are in order. Consider for instance our arguments of section 2, and in general the 'difficulties of barter'. The crucial point there was that a trader would take on a commodity which he does not ultimately want if he knew that he could exchange such commodity for something which he did ultimately want. Clearly it is rather unrealistic to say (as we implicitly did in section 2 for analytical convenience) that the trader in question will think of the relative prices as *given*, and then consider whether or not at the given prices he can rid himself of what he does not want for something which he does want. The correct way to think of the question that the trader will ask himself is, what exchange ratio with commodities which he does want will the commodity which he holds eventually fetch? Thus the problem of not finding a buyer for something you want to sell can actually be seen simply as the problem of finding buyers only at very disadvantageous prices.[39]

More generally, the interconnection between the ratios at which commodities are exchanged and trading arrangements can, roughly speaking, be summarised as follows. The way in which exchanges are carried out (for example barter, money or credit, and the costs incurred) clearly depends on what (and in which quantities) agents want to trade, and on the exchange ratios. The way in which exchanges are executed, and the costs of such execution, obviously affect the ratios at which commodities are exchanged. Lastly, the ratios at which commodities are exchanged affect what (and in what quantities) agents want to trade.[40] The purpose of this section is to report some of the insights offered by economic theory on the second of the above connections, namely how trading arrangements will affect the formation of the exchange ratios which prevail in the economy. The first connection we have explored in sections 2, 3 and 4. The last connection is what economists would call 'demand theory' and 'supply theory'.

The obvious starting point for a review of the theories of price formation is what one could call the demand and supply approach. This approach, until relatively recent times, has not just had a dominant place among theories of price formation, but had come dangerously close to a monopoly position, and, as everyone knows, one should beware of that. The story goes, roughly speaking, as follows. Each individual trader takes commodities exchange ratios as *given* and formulates his desired demands and supplies on the basis of such ratios. Such relative prices give rise to desired demands and supplies for each trader, and hence will entail an aggregate demand and supply for each commodity. If desired demand is equal to desired supply for all commodities, then the story ends. If, however, for some commodities, say, demand exceeds supply, 'the market' will make sure that the relative price of these commodities rises (falls if supply exceeds demand) until the process converges[42] to a set of prices which guarantee that demand equals supply for each and all commodities.

What we have just described seems to provide an explanation of how relative prices are established without any reference to the actual trading process. This is of course wrong, and a number of such assumptions are implicit in the standard supply and demand story. Let us try and disentangle the matter. The first thing to notice is that the assumption that individual agents take the ratios at which commodities are exchanged as given needs justification. That a trader takes relative prices as given, means in particular that he does not perceive himself and his trades as able to affect such relative prices in any way. This is an appropriate assumption for a quite restricted class of situations. The obvious counter-example is that of the sole seller of a commodity who, of course, should, and will, take into account the effect of how much he sells on the relative price of the commodity he sells.

It is intuitively appealing to say that the assumption that individual traders take relative prices as given is appropriate in situations where there are 'many small buyers' and 'many small sellers'. Albeit with some qualifications this intuition turns out to withstand rigorous analysis.[43] The second step, which deserves closer attention in the supply and demand approach which we have outlined, is the one which claims that the ratios at which commodities are exchanged respond to *aggregate* demand and supply. Whatever story one tells about how the relative prices are actually adjusted,[44] this obviously conflicts with the possibility of envisaging completely decentralised trade where agents meet, say, pairwise and carry out exchanges.

The standard supply and demand story is thus seen to embody at least two crucial assumptions about the organisation and nature of exchange. Firstly it requires a large number of 'small' buyers and sellers. Secondly it requires some mechanism for aggregating individual demands and supplies so that relative prices can respond to them. The easiest way to imagine for such process to take place is that of a central warehouse where all exchanges take place. It should then be quite clear by now that the standard supply and demand story in some sense assumes away the problems connected with how exchanges are actually carried out, which are our main concern here.[45]

It should be pointed out that the standard demand and supply story can, and has, been integrated with the consideration of transaction costs (Hahn, 1971; Hahn and Starrett, 1973). The analysis of such systems yields a number of interesting propositions. However, it necessarily relies on 'exogenously' given transaction costs. In other words, the way in which such costs depend on transaction arrangements is not addressed in these works. This seems to be in some sense a natural consequence of the supply and demand approach.

We now turn to the considerations of situations in which individual agents do not take the ratios at which commodities are exchanged as given. As we pointed out earlier, any situation in which individual agents are not small and 'insignificant' relative to the market, should not be analysed by assuming that individual agents take relative prices as given. Hence, we are now turning to what ought to be considered the more general case.[46]

Consider a 'small' group of agents who meet *repeatedly* to exchange commodities. Since we know that the traditional supply and demand story does not make much sense here, what can be said in general terms about the relative prices which will prevail? The answer that can currently be given to this question suffers from at least two major drawbacks. Firstly, as we shall see, it has very little *predictive* power. Secondly, what is predicted to happen, is, except for one special case (to which we shall return shortly), not particularly related to actual real world exchange arrangements. This is simply a largely under-researched area.

The main prediction of a game-theoretic analysis of the situation depicted above is that virtually any set of relative prices could emerge.[47] Moreover, there is no reason why different agents should not be able to exchange the same commodities, fetching different exchange ratios with other commodities. In other words, there is no need for the emergence of prices in the traditional sense, a unique set of exchange ratios between commodities, prevailing throughout the system.

Closer scrutiny makes the above statements more interesting than they may appear at first sight. Indeed the result which we have cited (cf. Sabourian, 1989) can be interpreted as saying that in many situations virtually any set of 'exchange norms' could be maintained in 'equilibrium'. The mechanism which enables such norms to be sustained is one of punishments for deviating from the group norm, which is almost completely analogous to the one which we have mentioned in section 4 above.

Let us now turn to the special case which we mentioned before. The special case is that of two agents bargaining over, say, the exchange ratio of two commodities. For concreteness, imagine one agent starting off with one unit of one commodity, and the other agent starting off with one unit of the other commodity. Also, we want to imagine both agents as being interested in both commodities, so that mutually advantageous trade is possible in principle.

In the special case which we have outlined, if the bargaining process is a sequence of offers and counter-offers, and if both agents are interested in agreeing on a price early, rather than late, a game-theoretic analysis of the situation will yield a precise and unique prediction of the price on which the agents will agree (Rubinstein, 1982; Sutton, 1986).[48] It is important to point out that the feature of unique prediction of a price hinges on the fact that *two* bargainers are involved and not more. The problem of so-called multi-person bargaining is still an open one. This, of course, should somewhat dampen one's enthusiasm about the ability to predict precisely the outcome of bargaining price-forming situations.

Despite the above caveats it is of course possible to proceed to use the result which we have just cited in a wider context. The context is similar to the one which we envisaged in sections 2 and 3: a group of traders who meet pairwise to carry out exchanges. The bargaining result which we have cited can then be used to predict the outcome of each pairwise meeting, and hence ultimately to predict the aggregate patterns of exchange. These may or may not match the predictions of the traditional supply and demand story.[49] Embedding bargaining situations in a more general set-up at this stage seems a promising way to analyse how actual trade arrangements affect the relative prices which will prevail in the economy.

6 Conclusions

The fact that barter makes the exchange of commodities difficult is best viewed as a result of the fact that barter is a way to organise exchange so as to satisfy 'many' constraints. Monetary exchange allows some of these constraints to be relaxed, and credit only requires one constraint to be satisfied. In these notes we have elaborated considerably on this main theme. However, with the exception of some parts of section 3, we have not expanded on the origins of such constraints. We would like to conclude these notes with some remarks about this matter.

The different degrees to which trading arrangements are constrained can be viewed as originating in different degrees of *trust* present in the system.[50] Barter is the extreme case in which no trust is present in the system, and hence traders will not be allowed to run up debts, and will not want to take on commodities which they ultimately do not want. In the case of monetary exchange, traders trust the medium of exchange. We have emphasised elsewhere the crucial role of beliefs in this matter. Monetary exchange is possible when agents trust that other agents will accept money in exchange for goods at some future date. Finally, in the case of credit, traders trust each other. If the necessary conditions for the enforcement of credit arrangements (cf. section 4 of these notes) are satisfied, agents trust that other agents will pay up their debts in due time. The only constraint that traders have to satisfy in this case is what economists would call a 'lifetime' budget constraint.

NOTES

1 The view that monetary exchange does not need to evolve out of barter seems to be well established in the anthropological literature (see Humphrey, 1985).
2 We shall, in other words, take equilibrium relative prices as given and uniformly established throughout the system. The classic reference for a formal treatment of conditions which guarantee the logical consistency of this assumption when 'competitive' conditions prevail is Debreu (1959). Addressing the question when markets are 'small' and not competitive is a much harder problem, see Hart (1985).
3 One does not need to imagine that traders strictly only meet in pairs. All the remarks that follow essentially apply if one imagines traders meeting in 'small' groups. (Small here is intended as small relative to the whole set of traders.) Centralised exchange obviously never presents particular difficulties. If all traders can be imagined to meet at a central 'warehouse' all the problems of exchange automatically disappear. Hence, throughout the paper we shall be thinking of exchange which is in some way decentralised.
4 We believe the question of 'trust' to be central to the problems addressed in this paper. We shall return to it many times, particularly in sections 4 and 6 below.
5 Some authors (for example Ostroy and Starr, 1974) have called this a quid pro quo constraint.
6 Of course if, say, prices are not fixed and an explicit time dimension is added to the analysis our definition would also rule out any kind of speculative hoarding. Hence in a more general framework a more detailed definition of barter would be needed. However, given the set-up with which we are concerned in these notes, the above seems to be adequate.
7 A brief digression is in order. Early writers in the economics tradition (see for instance Jevons, 1883) took the restriction that trades should be excess demand diminishing as given and proceeded to use it to illustrate the difficulties of barter. (This is in fact not very different from our treatment of the problem in this section.) However, modern economic theory has at various points sought an *explanation* of the restriction that bilateral trades be excess demand diminishing. The obvious (with hindsight) route to follow, is that of making relevant to their exchange decisions in bilateral encounters the information that traders have about possible future trades (Ostroy and Starr, 1974; Starr, 1976; Starr, 1986). Roughly speaking, restrictions on what 'unwanted' commodities traders are willing to take on during the exchange sequence can be related to the fact that traders may not know that they will in fact have an opportunity of exchanging the unwanted commodity for something which they ultimately want. The more recent literature which we have cited is quite technical in parts.
8 Suppose for instance that 1 orange exchanges for 2 apples. Then by measuring apples in pairs and oranges in single-fruit units, one can obviously say that one unit of oranges exchange for one unit of apples.

9 The reader can check that what we claim in the sequel does *not* depend on the *particular sequence* of meetings which we have chosen to illustrate the point.

10 This is only an accounting device for amalgamating entries originating from the exchange of different goods and should not be intended as money in any sense.

11 Unfortunately our example is too simple to show appropriately the difference between exchange organised using multiple media of exchange and monetary exchange proper. In particular, this is due to the small number of commodities and traders involved in the example.

12 Some comments are in order about the intrinsic nature of our commodities. The first two cases which we have illustrated need no special attributes for any commodities. In the third case we have obviously implicitly assumed that commodity r is not instantly perishable, since it is used as a medium of exchange. Our 4th commodity, however, we imagine as having a number of special attributes. This commodity is best thought of as non-perishable, easily transportable and recognisable throughout the system. Moreover, let us stress again that we are abstracting from problems of production. This means in particular that we imagine the total quantity of each commodity in the system as given. In any generalisation of our example it is important to stipulate that any medium of exchange, and hence our 4th commodity, is 'difficult' to produce. Using economic jargon this would be expressed by saying that our 4th commodity should have an 'inelastic supply'.

13 Zero excess demand does not entail that our traders do not derive consumption value from the 4th commodity, merely that the amount of the 4th commodity in their possession at the start of the trading process is precisely the amount which they desire. It is, however, important to notice that a commodity which no trader has desire to ultimately consume (fiat money) can also be used as a medium of exchange. This case will be discussed in the next section.

14 Notice that we have stipulated at the beginning of this section that the value of the positive components of traders' demands be equal to the value of the negative components of their demands.

15 As we have pointed out earlier, strictly speaking, monetary exchange should be defined as one particular way of organising transactions, so as to ensure that the quid pro quo constraint is satisfied and so as to use a *unique* medium of exchange.

16 Unless, of course, they are allowed to hold a *negative* amount of money. But this would entail a 'capital market' for borrowing and hence would fall in our credit category rather than in the money one.

17 We shall use the word equilibrium, in this section especially, as having a precise meaning. An equilibrium state of an economy is a state which, once reached, will have a tendency to persist through time. Expanding on this naturally leads one to define an equilibrium state of an economy as a resting point of some dynamic process which governs changes in the economy itself. A simple *example* of such process is to imagine agents which pursue *given* objectives. What agents are able to do depends on the state of the economy, and what they do affects the state of the economy itself. One could then imagine that the state of the economy ceases to change as soon as agents' actions are consistent in the sense of, say, aggregate feasibility conditions (that is, for instance, that aggregate consumption of a commodity does not exceed the total quantity of

that commodity which is available). An equilibrium is then a state of the economy in which all agents are doing the best that they can given their objectives, their beliefs, and the state of the economy itself, and such that agents' actions are feasible in the aggregate. Below, in this section, we apply a concept of equilibrium based on a dynamic process to traders' beliefs about the pattern of exchange. It must be pointed out that we are here only scratching the surface of a very complex and important issue which has received distinguished attention in the economic literature; a classic reference is Hahn (1981).

18 Of course one has to be careful in specifying *whose* costs would be smaller. One example of unambiguous gain would be the one obtained if exchange costs were lower for each individual trader when monetary exchange is used. Failing such 'lucky' outcomes one would have to define some sensible measure of overall social gain obtained from the knowledge, amongst other things, of the changes in all traders' exchange costs.

19 We adopt the same convention here as we did in section 2, that commodities are measured in such a way that all exchange ratios between them are 1.

20 Several comments are in order. The specific cost which we will consider below is the cost of time spent searching for trading partners. (In such cases as that of the Lhomi (this volume) where regular networks of barter exist these costs may be minimal.) There are of course other possible sources for these costs. These can range from the cost of information gathering before and during the search process, to the actual cost of, say, transport incurred during the search. The costs which we have in mind are best imagined as being, among other things, increasing with the size of the economy (and hence low for small communities), and increasing with the degree of anonymity of the system.

21 Throughout the rest of this section we implicitly consider a set of traders which is 'large'.

22 cf. note 2 in section 1 on this point.

23 The mathematics behind these claims is very simple indeed. However, we do not think it appropriate to reproduce them here since we endeavoured to avoid formalities as much as possible. Our claim is consistent with the so-called 'sampling with replacement' procedure.

24 Unfortunately, from this point onwards a precise description of what we have in mind which makes no use of mathematical notation would be virtually impossible. In the rest of this section we will try to appeal to the reader's intuitions which we hope have been enhanced by our initial example.

25 Notice that the medium of exchange is now unambiguously identified as the most frequently traded commodity. This is very convenient, but of course depends on our simplifying assumptions like, for instance, the one that all traders initially have the same beliefs about f_{pq}, f_{pr}, etc. However, the basic argument above will apply more generally than the one which we are discussing in our example.

26 Towards the end of this section we discuss the possibility of a medium of exchange which no trader wants to ultimately consume.

27 The original paper by Jones (1976) on which we are freely drawing uses an 'adaptive' expectations rule. Many alternatives would be possible.

28 Clearly, it is possible to imagine that the economy be sufficiently 'simple' so that what we have just asserted is not in fact true. Take, for instance, the

example of an economy with two commodities only. Our assertion above implicitly assumes that there are 'enough' commodities, 'enough' traders and that the economy is such that the initial holdings of commodities 'vary sufficiently' between agents.

29 In the case of paper money, no one will wish to hold any of it, and paper money will be worthless in the last period.

30 In the case of paper money, it will be worthless in every period.

31 We shall call traders with this type of preferences 'self-interested' agents.

32 Punishments, of course, need not be actually carried out. In this sense we shall be using punishment and punishment threat quite interchangeably.

33 The fact that we refer to two agents rather than any finite number of them is completely inessential.

34 Credibility of the threats is of the utmost importance, because otherwise the threats are obviously devoid of any value.

35 We shall return to the question of delegation at some length very shortly.

36 Which equilibrium actually occurs, as in the previous section, will depend on what each individual expects others to do.

37 We do not think that this is the right place to explore the reasons why this may be so. It is obvious, however, that if legal procedures were too 'easy' the possibilities and/or incentives for the misuse of legal penalties, on the part of those delegated to administer them, could cause great difficulties for the proper functioning of the system.

38 Of course, the cost of book keeping has also been greatly reduced, and this has obviously worked in favour of a credit system as well.

39 Care should be taken with this point if, for instance, the 'quality' of what you want to sell is uncertain for the buyer. Under certain circumstances, being willing to sell at a very low price may become a signal of low quality, thus deterring potential buyers. If this 'vicious circle' is sufficiently strong, it is possible that a seller may simply not find any buyers at any price. This problem has been extensively studied in the economics literature in very different contexts. See, for instance, Akerlof (1970), Stiglitz and Weiss (1981) or the pioneering Arrow (1963).

40 Of course there is nothing 'circular' in what we have just described. Many 'variables' are involved in the determination of demands, supplies and exchange arrangements, and they all affect each other. The solution to the problem will have to take into account many requirements, as well as the values of many variables, all *simultaneously*. Provided that a solution to such a problem exists, it is clear that there is nothing circular about it!

41 Demand and supply theory is a quite settled and 'standardised' piece of economic theory. References range from the highly elegant and formalised work of Debreu (1959) to undergraduate (Gravelle and Rees, 1981) and graduate (Varian, 1978) textbooks.

42 Even with the most generous assumptions, it is by no means straightforward that the process will in fact converge (see Hahn, 1981 for a survey of the necessarily very technical literature on this question), but this is of relatively little interest to us here.

43 The *Journal of Economic Theory* dedicated a whole issue in 1980 to a symposium on this matter. We refer the reader to the discussions of the problem contained in there.

44 The reader may have already noticed that there is a missing piece from the supply and demand story which we have told. In a world where everyone takes relative prices as given, who changes the prices? This is what our previous reference to 'the market' was hiding. In the economics literature there is a long tradition of resorting to a fictitious 'auctioneer' figure, who is not involved in the trading, and merely 'adjusts' prices. The advantage of such an obviously surreal story is, we believe, that precisely its lack of realism reveals that this is a *real* problem of the supply and demand story. The discussion of this problem is beyond the scope of this paper, however. A survey reference is Hahn (1981).

45 The requirement of a large number of small buyers and sellers also obviously makes the supply and demand story less interesting to anthropologists since it rules out the study of 'small communities'.

46 The tool, by now commonly used in economics, to analyse situations in which agents are aware that their actions influence the fate of other agents and vice-versa, goes under the name of Game Theory. The literature is vast, but we recommend Luce and Raiffa (1958) and Binmore and Dasgupta (1986).

47 We are implicitly assuming that the agents in this economy are, at any point in time, sufficiently 'concerned about the future'.

48 The actual outcome will depend on a number of factors, such as who makes the first offer and the relative degrees of 'impatience' of the two bargainers, as well as on the precise 'rules' of the bargaining game. What is of interest here is that, as a function of various 'parameters' of the model, a *unique* prediction will be obtained.

49 Under which conditions this is precisely true is a question which has aroused noticeable interest and debate among economists in recent years. A discussion of this point is clearly beyond the scope of this paper. A couple of, inevitably technical, references are Rubinstein and Wolinsky (1985), and Gale (1986).

50 The analysis of the question of trust is not new in economies. Many references could be given, but we shall limit ourselves to Dasgupta (1986), and Gale (1982).

REFERENCES

Akerlof, G. A. 1970. 'The market for "lemons": quality uncertainty and the market mechanism', *Quarterly Journal of Economics*, 84, 488–500.

Arrow, K. J. 1963. 'Uncertainty and the welfare economics of medical care', *American Economic Review*, 53, 941–73.

Binmore, K. and Dasgupta, P. 1986. 'Game theory: a survey', in *Economic Organizations as games*, eds. K. Binmore and P. Dasgupta. Oxford: Blackwell.

Dasgupta, P. 1986. 'Trust as a commodity', *Economic Theory Discussion Paper*, no. 101, University of Cambridge.

Debreu, G. 1959. *Theory of Value*. Yale: Yale University Press.

Fudenberg, D. and Maskin, E. 1986. 'The folk theorem in repeated games with discounting and with incomplete information', *Econometrica*, 54, 533–56.

Gale, D. 1982. *Money: In Equilibrium*. Cambridge: Cambridge University Press.
1986. 'Bargaining and competition (part I and part II)', *Econometrica*, 54, 785–819.

Goodhart, C. A. E. 1977. 'The role, functions and definition of money', in *The

Microeconomic Foundations of Macroeconomics, ed. G. C. Harcourt. London: Macmillan.

Gravelle, H. and Rees, R. 1981. *Microeconomics*. London: Longman.

Hahn, F. H. 1971. 'Equilibrium with transaction costs', *Econometrica*, 39, 417–39.
   1973. 'On transaction costs, inessential sequence economies and money', *Review of Economic Studies*, 40, 449–61.
   1977. 'Keynesian economics and general equilibrium theory: reflections on some current debates', in *The Microeconomic Foundations of Macroeconomics*, ed. G. C. Harcourt. London: Macmillan.
   1981. 'Stability', in *Handbook of Mathematical Economics*, vol. II, eds. K. J. Arrow and M. D. Intrilligator. Amsterdam: North-Holland.
   1982. *Money and Inflation*. Oxford: Blackwell.

Hart, O. D. 1985. 'Imperfect competition in general equilibrium: an overview of some recent work', in *Frontiers of Economics*, eds. K. J. Arrow and S. Honkapohja.

Humphrey, C. 1985. 'Barter an economic disintegration', *Man* (N.S.), 20, 48–72.

Iwai, K. 1988. 'The evolution of money: a search theoretic foundation of monetary economics', *CARESS Working Paper*, 88–103, University of Pennsylvania.

Jevons, S. 1883. *Money and the Mechanism of Exchange*. London: Macmillan.

Jones, R. A. 1976. 'The origin and development of media of exchange', *Journal of Political Economy*, 84, 757–76.

Luce, R. and Raiffa, S. 1958. *Games and Decisions*. New York: J. Wiley and Sons.

Nagatani, S. 1978. *Monetary Theory*. Amsterdam: North-Holland.

Ostroy, J. M. 1973. 'The informational efficiency of monetary exchange', *American Economic Review*, 63, 597–610.

Ostroy, J. M. and Starr, R. M. 1974. 'Money and the decentralization of exchange', *Econometrica*, 42, 1093–1114.

Polany, K. 1957. *The Great Transformation*. Boston: Beacon Press.

Rubinstein, A. 1982. 'Perfect equilibrium in a bargaining game', *Econometrica*, 50, 97–109.

Rubinstein, A. and Wolinsky, A. 1985. 'Equilibrium in a market with sequential bargaining', *Econometrica*, 53, 1133–1150.

Sabourian, H. 1989. 'Repeated games: a survey', in *The Economics of Information, Missing Markets and Games*, ed. F. H. Hahn. Oxford: Oxford University Press.

R. M. Starr. 1976. 'Decentralized nonmonetary trade', *Econometrica*, 44, 1087–1089.
   1986. 'Decentralized trade in a credit economy', in *Equilibrium Analysis: Essays in Honour of K. J. Arrow,* eds. W. P. Heller, R. M. Starr and D. A. Starrett. Cambridge: Cambridge University Press.

Starrett, D. A. 1973. 'Inefficiency and the demand for money in a sequence economy', *Review of Economic Studies*, 40, 437–48.

Stiglitz, J. E. and Weiss, A. 1981. 'Credit rationing in markets with imperfect information', *American Economic Review*, 71, 393–410.

Sutton, J. 1986. 'Noncooperative bargaining theory: an introduction', *Review of Economic Studies*, 53, 709–724.

Varian, H. L. 1978. *Microeconomic Analysis*. New York: W. W. Norton and Co.

5 Fair dealing, just rewards: the ethics of barter in North-East Nepal

Caroline Humphrey

This paper discusses some implications of barter for morality and ethnicity. In the Arun Valley of North-East Nepal barter is not a haphazard expedient, but is the major type of economic transaction both between and within ethnic groups. This paper shows what kind of social relations are created by barter when it is a constant feature of the regional economy. In barter, unlike many gift-exchange systems, people transact different items (they acquire what they have not got and vice versa) and thus barter tends to link micro-economies which, at least in this respect, are dissimilar from one another. Towards the end of the paper it is suggested that the shifting ethnic identities for which highland Nepal is so well known can be seen as consequent on the dependencies and enmities created by barter. Here, the more marked ethnic distinctions need not imply hostility. People define themselves as different from those with whom they exchange products in long-term relations, but they are also dependent on, and need to maintain trust with such groups. On the other hand, they are in frequently hostile competition with the groups which have a similar economic niche and economic values to themselves. To demonstrate these points the paper will focus on the Lhomi, a group of farmers and traders, in their situation in the vertical Himalayan economy.

In relating such a system to morality, one could make the point that ethics in any culture must extend *even* to what has been seen in Western tradition as typically amoral, i.e. barter, simply because it is a regular part of social life; or, that any deal once accomplished is 'fair', since the two parties have accepted it. But this paper makes the stronger point that it is because barter is essentially a voluntary, ungoverned agreement between individuals, a choice to agree, in a situation which has variable consequences for both parties, that it becomes a crucial arena for ethical action. In societies which live mainly by barter it can be seen, both systematically and from the point of view of the actors, as having, even engendering, a morality[1] of its own.

Barter in non-market economies is not the mutual handing-over of objects of externally defined equal value. In true barter systems (those with

107

no numeraire, monetary or otherwise) there is no criterion by which a general value may be established. Objects always have different statuses in the micro-systems of each of the transactors, but in a barter economy there is no mechanism to measure individual bargains whereby they can be compared with one another, either across the range of goods or through time (see Introduction and Strathern, this volume). Therefore in barter the two sides must *agree*, and agree each time anew, that their transaction is fair. It is because barter in farming economies tends to be repetitive and to operate with known partners (Humphrey, 1985), because a transaction may really advantage or disadvantage people, and because of the absence of any sanctions outside the fact of the agreement, that we can speak of morality in this context. The moral obligation, in the case of the Lhomi, is to create or preserve a mutual sense of 'fairness' and trust, in which each side takes responsibility as recipient both for his/her satisfaction and that of the other.

Something like this may apply in barter systems in general, but in the Buddhist cultures of North-East Nepal it rests on a particular social organisation built of nested, yet discrete and 'closed' units: the adult person, household, village, clan, and ethnic group (von Furer-Haimendorf, 1965 and 1975). The household is the most important of these transacting units, since it is the major locus of property rights (Ortner, 1978) and barter almost never takes place between its members. In general we can see groups at each level from the household and above as nested 'moral' as well as economic communities. The individual acts both for himself or herself and a representative of any or all of these communities. Any given transaction can be seen by particular transactors as simultaneously self-oriented *and* fair, precisely because their interests, as members of different communities, are dissimilar.

In this paper the term 'barter' will be used in an inclusive sense following the practice of the people concerned. They do not separate the direct swapping of goods from delayed exchange (the return is made after some time), nor from the transfer of goods against labour or services, repaid simultaneously or later. The element of delay, made inevitable by the timing of harvests in the vertical economy, requires trust (Anderlini and Sabourian, this volume). This means that 'barter' includes what Sahlins (1972) calls 'primitive trade', i.e. where exchange rates are subordinated to the social relations between the actors.

The direct involvement in barter of one's work or its products engages any individual in his or her identity as a specific person. Both this, and the frequent need to involve trust, raise the ethical stakes, as it were. We might also say that barter involves ethics in a general and systemic sense, because the exchange of unlike objects and services in a historically established pattern creates the identities of communities, and engenders regional dependencies between them (as well as those between households). These have the character of organic solidarity, that is reciprocal dependence, which engenders regard for the other as a necessity for long-term preservation of a given economic specialisation. This reciprocal dependence, which Gregory (1982) claims is characteristic of 'the gift' as opposed to 'the commodity', I would see as equally present, in a different form, in barter.

As Parry (1986) has pointed out, there are important differences in the ideology of 'the gift' between its classic tribal home (Melanesia, Polynesia) and the regions of Asia dominated by world religions. In India the gift (*dana*) does not constrain a return, but is rather a religious transfer without return, embodying the sins of the donor, a surrogate for sacrifice. The gift is separated from other transactions of the complex economy precisely by its religious connotations. The Lhomi have a tribal society, but they are also Buddhists, i.e. adherents of a religion which pervasively ethicises actions. I suggest that there it is not just goods in the form of gifts which embody the moral person (1986: 460), as in urban India, but the entire range of tribal products involved in barter as well as presentations. Furthermore, religious ideology does not stop short at a conceptualisation of 'the gift', but encompasses all transactions. As Parry rightly points out it is only in the Christian, not the Asian, world that the theory of pure utility has developed, making the things of this world antithetical to the person's true self (1986: 468). In the tribal world of North-East Nepal, essentially without markets or complex urban economic organisations, and also without the Melanesian-type institution of 'the gift', all transactions, including barter, cannot but involve the person, and hence intentions and obligations, subject to religious values.

In the Buddhist worldview, I suggest, an analogy can be made between the ethics of barter and aspects of the local understanding of the doctrine of *karma*. Fürer-Haimendorf (1984), Ortner (1978) and others have noted the dominance of this idea in the Tibetan-type societies of North-East Nepal.

The entire moral system is dominated by the belief in merit and sin...Every individual has a kind of spiritual account and every act of virtue adds, every sinful act diminishes, this valuable store. The addition and subtraction of merit are more or less mechanical. Throughout a person's life appropriate points result from good or bad deeds. After death the balance of good or bad marks influence the fate of men and women, expressed in good or undesired reincarnations. (Schrader, 1988: 237–8)

Morality in Buddhist culture gives far greater priority to the perfection of the self, as opposed to disinterested action in favour of the other, than in most Western traditions. Yet few things are more 'moral' in the sense of spiritual benefit to the self than compassion for the other. In other words the obligation in Buddhist culture is to have regard for the other, which in the end is reducible to preserving the capacity of the other to act in the way appropriate for that other (for example, a hare must be allowed to act as a hare should). Fulfilling this obligation, which is nevertheless a matter of choice, is of inevitable religious advantage to the self. The moral obligation here is not so much a matter of charity, so emphasised in Christianity, as of justice.

This is different from the fundamentally altruistic character of morality as it is popularly understood in the modern West. But, as Williams points out discussing Plato and Aristotle, egoistic considerations need not contradict ethics. The Grecian tradition, for example, rejects the idea of justice as founded purely on external convention, something one would not want to follow if one did not have to. So ethics can be based, as in Buddhism, on an idea of internally generated spiritual self-improvement. This has an important implication. It cannot be presumed that there is some universal self, some set of individual satisfactions which is well-defined before ethical considerations appear. 'Their [Plato's and Aristotle's] aim is not, given an account of the self and its satisfactions, to show how the ethical self luckily fits them. It is to give an account of the self into which that life fits.' (Williams, 1985: 32)

What is suggested here is not of course that the prevailing socio-economic conditions explain the morality of *karma*, which is a much wider phenomenon, but that barter exchange does engender its own obligations, and that these can readily be understood by people in terms of *karma*. Thus the task of this paper is not only to describe the ethics of barter, but also to explain the Lhomi 'self into which that life fits'. It is important to note at the outset a point I shall return to at the end, that the self appears not just as a single 'individual', but also as the representative of social groups, and that *karma* can apply to communities as well as to individuals.

Barter in society

First of all, what is the social context in which barter exists in North-East Nepal? As Strathern (1986) following Collier and Rosaldo has pointed out, it is useful to distinguish societies with brideservice from those with bridewealth and/or dowry – that is, to distinguish those systems where obligations are fulfilled in labour, while goods, hardly subject to a concept of property, stand only for themselves, from those where goods not only are owned, but also substitutable for people. The societies I shall be discussing are clearly of the latter type. The presence of clan exogamy, brideprice, and 'women's goods' (principally jewellery) are the conditions for marriage as a transfer of women between groups. Barter in this kind of society involves the transaction of 'characteristic goods', the products of specific labour processes and environments, identified with their community of origin, in much the same way that a bride is identified with her clan or village.

The analogy between barter and marriage can be taken further. Marriage in this region is not really an 'exchange' in the sense that brideprice is considered equal in value to the bride. The brideprice, as in most Tibetan societies, is a fixed sum in money, often a relatively trivial amount.[2] It is an obligation, the payment of the right kind of thing in the right amount to the bride's side, just as she is in effect a payment to the groom's side. Barter has this character of *mutual payment*, as opposed to *equal exchange*, too. One hands over what one is obliged to hand over in the specific relationship with a partner. Where barter and marriage have been thought by anthropologists to differ, lies in the fact of the unequalness of the transaction in marriage and its long-term and systemic consequences (for example alliance), as Levi-Strauss and Sahlins have pointed out, whereas in barter the transfer is agreed to be one of balance – quits, in effect. But this distinction, though it may hold at an abstract level (see Introduction) does not apply to the societies of North-East Nepal: here, on the one hand, barter has long-term 'organic' results, and on the other, marriages are often short-term and considered as finite relations between households.

The Lhomi in this respect are similar to the Sherpas as described by Ortner (1978). She argues that the 'private-property-owning family household' is the significant unit of exchange, that both individuals and households tend toward social closure and resistance to exchange, and that there is a dominant exchange strategy, *yangdzi*, which both reflects and reproduces these tendencies. *Yangdzi* entails softening up the hardness of others to gain their cooperation and it is also a finite contract.

Yangdzi operates at the level of individuals, overcoming their presumed closure to one's appeals for goods or assistance, and it also operates at the level of families: the marriage process may be described as a sort of giant extended *yangdzi*... And just as *yangdzi* leaves individuals independent after the fulfilment of the contract, so it does with families, where once the new couple has finally been established, there are no residual bonds between their respective groups. (1978: 160–1)

My argument is that the finite contractual mode in both marriage and barter in fact masks underlying, deep-moving, relations between groups created by such contracts.

What makes barter among the Lhomi more complex than simple mutual payment is the fact that the barter of objects for use is not differentiated by the people from the acquisition of goods designated for further transactions. I shall follow the Lhomi in grouping all of these under one term, 'barter', using the sub-category 'trade' to mean a series of transactions for profit. Goods can be switched from consumption to trade, or vice versa. This has two implications: firstly that 'trade' is not divided off as some morally distinct sphere separate from the household economy. In inter-ethnic barter many, if not all, things which are traded are still linked by cultural classifications with their original producers or owners. Even several transactions do not completely destroy the link with the original producers, which remains as a shadow of the idea that goods 'stand for people'.

Secondly, barter as a system is open-ended, and therefore cannot be analysed simply as a relation between two transactions. There are conceivably others in most kinds of deal. What I acquire from you is not just useful for me, but can nearly always be viewed in regard to its potential for someone else as well. This, if acted upon, necessarily requires a transformation of value, in that no goods have an absolutely equivalent place in the systems of consumption of different households, let alone those of 'ethnic groups'. Even potatoes or salt, for example, have different places in the diets of Lhomis and their neighbours to the south, the Gurungs. Goods have acknowledged paths, their origins and their destinations, and the communities which form the stopping-points along the way constitute a web of dependencies. The 'rates' at which goods are transacted do absolutely reflect supply and demand, but the point is that these two categories are culturally determined in very particular ways. 'Supply' and 'demand' thereby lose the capacity to act as abstract concepts for a general analysis.

I shall suggest that barter, which incorporates barter in money (rupees) so that the homogenising valuation role of money is denied (see Humphrey, 1985), is an essential and long-term strategy in transforming the 'meaning' of objects as they pass from one culture to another. Because money itself is bartered, i.e. it has different and inconsistent values as transacted against labour, grains, etc. in one village from another, it cannot act as an external measure for all prices as in a market economy. If the Muria (see Introduction) can maintain 'their' cultural values in the flow of many centuries of Indian cash trading, the Lhomi have done the same by the expedient of refusing to admit money as the index of value. We are dealing here not with the transformation of objects as they pass between *economic systems* (as in the case of Scottish lambs auctioned to EC buyers, see Introduction), but with a movement of goods between differentiated cultures within one barter system. Objects are alienated, but they remain recognisable, 'characteristic' of the economic–cultural type in which they originated, i.e. the tribal 'ethnic group' which produced them. This is the case not only because of differences of environment in the vertical regional economy, but also because of deliberately maintained cultural specialisations. This establishes different values for particular goods as they move from culture to culture (Appadurai, 1986, Introduction). The use of money as an index and the introduction of markets would transform such a system, creating uniform values where none exist in the process of production.

In an earlier paper (Humphrey, 1985) I suggested that it is the present-day weakness of integrative structures among the Lhomi, either 'vertical' (for example taxes via local chiefs to the state) or 'horizontal' (for example large-scale and long-distance trading organisations), which allow them to deny the index-of-value function of money and give preference to barter. This would suggest, *contra* Hart (1987), that in this region at least, over-arching political structures are not necessary for barter to function amicably. Hart's argument appears to rest on the old presupposition of the hostile nature of barter relations. In North-East Nepal, where self-interest and morality are not in conflict, barter itself is not perceived as antagonistic, rather the reverse. It is precisely the links created by barter which establish friendly relations and which cross ethnic and political boundaries, as we shall see from a discussion of the strategic position the Lhomi find themselves in.

Lhomi barter in the regional political economy

The Lhomi (Nep. Kar Bhote) are a small group of farmer-traders who live in some fourteen villages on the craggy slopes of the Arun Valley just south of the border with Tibet. They speak a dialect of Tibetan, are Buddhists, and basically share the *rong* (deep valley) variant of Tibetan culture. However, as far as memory goes back, they have not been included in the Tibetan state, but loosely attached to the Himalayan polities which took it in turns to claim control of the region, the Gorkha kingdom, Walong-chung, Sikkim, and now the kingdom of Nepal. One political advantage to the Lhomi of maintaining an essentially non-monetised economy lay in the possibility this gave them of de-linking themselves from monetary taxation, of being 'unable to pay'. It did not free them from dues paid in kind, but put them at a remove from direct monetary domination.

Trade systems in this region run north–south, down the valleys which link Tibet with the plains. To the north of the Lhomi in the Arun valley, on the very border, are Chiawa farmer-livestock herders. Their neighbours to the south are a series of farming tribes, Rais, Limbus, Tamangs, and Gurungs, which occupy ecological niches at lower altitudes. Yet further south are settlements of Hindu farmers, Bahuns (Brahmins) and Chetris.

The Lhomi correlate this complex ethnic situation with three ways of gaining a living: there are the high-altitude nomadic pastoralists of Tibet

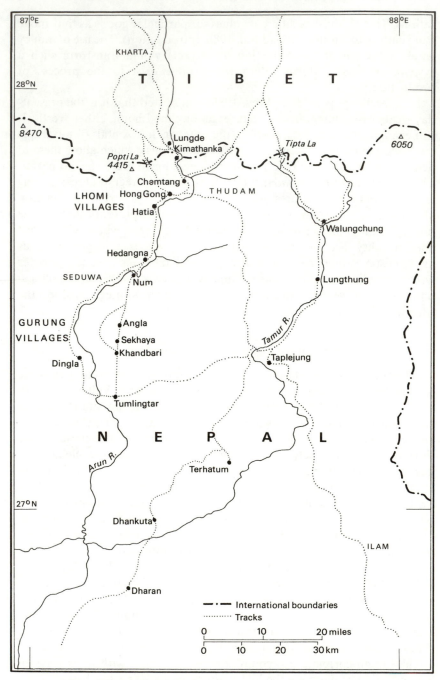

Map of North-East Nepal.

'*ḋog-pa*'[3] (*brog pa*), the semi-settled herder-farmers of the border '*sa-ma ḋog*' (*sa ma̓ brog*), and the village-based farmers '*shing sa-wa*' (*zhing sa pa*), the category which includes both themselves and all the other tribal groups living below them. The products of these three ways of life are different, and exchange between them is expected and integral to the economy. They are like three pools, each with a different eco-system. Since the southern tribes also occupy slightly different niches, they too can be seen as distinct pools within the category of the '*shing saw-wa*' farmers.

ḋog-pa	*sama ḋog*	*shing sa-wa*
Tibetans	Chiawa	Lhomi
	Makalu 'Sherpa'	
		Rai
		Tamang
		Gurung
		Limbu
		+
		Bahun
		Chetri

Within these categories, if we take the Lhomi point of view, there is today a particular pattern of barter dictated by their strategic–ecological position. The important communities for them are: the Tibetan *ḋog-pa* nomads, the Lhomi *shing sa-wa* themselves, and the Gurung farmers of the southern hills. The *ḋog-pas* produce meat, dried fats, butter, woollen goods and yak hair products which are essential to the Lhomi way of life. They also acquire from inside Tibet salt, and various medicinal and religious goods which can be traded by the Lhomi southwards. The Lhomi add to these numerous small items for trade, which they either produce themselves, such as garlic, pig's bristles and potatoes, or gather in the forests, herbs, poisons and antidotes, wax, musk, hartshorn, bear's bile, etc. These are taken south, together with the Tibetan goods, to trade with the Gurungs and other peoples. These lowland farmers produce rice, maize and millet which are essential to the Tibetan diet, and are taken north by the Lhomi to complete the circle.[4] Very little trade takes place between the various Lhomi villages, and still less between them and the various Bhote neighbours with similar economies to the Lhomi. It is complementary economies which trade.

The weak link in the present circuit is the Lhomi to Gurung trade, since from the 1960s the southern hills were flooded with Indian salt which almost eliminated demand among Gurungs for Tibetan salt. Lhomi supplies of herbs, pig's bristles or Chinese gym-shoes cannot make up for what was once a dependency. They were, however, able to bind the Gurung farmers to them by another tie. The Gurungs arrived in this area of Eastern

Nepal as *raikar* farmers, that is, without hereditary communal rights (*kipat*) to land.[5] They needed access to pasture for their flocks of sheep, since the production of woollen goods for trade was one of their most important economic activities. The Lhomi headmen, who did have *kipat* rights to land, seized the opportunity to sell rights of use of their pastures to the Gurungs. These pastures are located in the high mountains to the north and west of Lhomi villages. The result is a complex relationship, whereby Gurung shepherds, attached to farming households in the south, trek up and through the Lhomi villages several times a year. They put their sheep on Lhomi fields for fertiliser, and take Lhomi flocks along with their own, and in return the Lhomi provide food, shelter, storage facilities, and labour to help with herding and shearing. Many Gurungs have secondary wives, whom they send up to live in Lhomi villages half-way to the pastures. In winter Lhomis flock down south to escape the cold and to work in Gurung farms for payments in rice and other grains, hides, and sometimes even cattle, all being items which can be profitably bartered later with the Tibetans. The pastures and support for the shepherds who use them are absolutely necessary for the Gurungs, nearly all of whom keep sheep. It is lucky for the Lhomi that the issue of the legality of *kipat* in relation to usufructuary rights has never been decided, despite Gurung representations to the government. This gives the Lhomi some edge in a relation which otherwise would tend to favour the Gurungs, and it is the background to the many trade friendships between people of the two groups.

Lhomi trade has also been able to withstand, more or less, the other major change to affect the situation, the Chinese invasion of Tibet in 1959. It seems clear from my informants that when the Chinese invaded they also took a sizeable chunk of good summer pasture at Lungde, moving the border south, so that the Tibetan *dog pas* who used to live in the same political realm as the Lhomis are now cut off by a major guarded frontier. The Chiawa *sama dog*s are now on the southern side of the border, at Kimathanka, and find themselves in conflict with the Lhomis over control of the trade down the Arun valley. The construction of a good trail up to Kimathanka to service the Nepali border troops stationed there has enhanced the position of the Chiawas. Being on the spot, they are known personally to the Chinese border guards, who allow them to trade in Tibet and take their yaks to summer pasture there. Other communities from Nepal wanting to trade or use the pastures are forced to pay fees in butter and accept high Chinese official exchange ratios which do not correspond to the rates offered by ordinary Tibetans on the black market. All of this has made the Chiawas a very rich community indeed, and has limited the possibility for a *sama dog* way of life in the Lhomi region.[6] The Lhomis' only recourse is to bypass the Chiawas by maintaining their primary trading links with the Tibetan community at Khada, accessible by a different and more difficult route over the Popti La pass.

Ideas of trade, profit and debt

Transactions between the groups in the Lhomi circuit are seen in terms of what we might call 'balanced recompense'. Barter in the sense of giving one thing and getting another is called '*jeba*' (*brje ba*), while '*jebo*' (*brje bo*), means to compensate, or make up to the other. Barter as a total transaction between two people is '*jelen*' '*len*' (*lan*), meaning 'mutual reply', 'return', or 'retaliation'. The idea of reciprocity is to be expected for barter, but more surprising is its compatibility with the concepts of both trade and debt.

The term '*tsong*' (*tshong*) is the most generally used, and encompasses all of the above and trade outside the village. It simply means a transaction carried out for one's own benefit. Profit can derive from one transaction, which both sides consider fair, each giving away something he wants less for something desired more. It can also derive from trading, i.e. from two (or more) barter exchanges, the first in one place and the second in another, each of them fair in its context. The profit results from the differences in values in the two pools. No distinction is made between the products which are simply bartered on one's own territory and those which are traded on. Potatoes, for example, are at the consumption end of the spectrum, but people do also trade them, i.e. they will barter other products to obtain potatoes in the village, add these to what they have produced themselves, and take the lot down south to trade for grain and make a profit. Or, as in the following diagram, trader B barters his onions for wool in his home village 1 at a rate which is considered fair on both sides, and then travels down to village 2, where he trades the wool against grain. The profit lies in the fact that the amount of grain he receives is worth more in village 1 than the onions first paid out, i.e. x is worth more to the trader than y, despite the travelling time involved.

Location 1	**Location 2**
A trades with B	B trades with C
B receives z amount of wool	B pays z amount of wool
pays y amount of onion	receives x amount of grain

Debt is known as '*bulon*' (*bu lon*), this being exactly debt as we know it, used both for the situation created by delayed barter and for formal loans with interest charged at set rates for the time elapsed before repayment. In practice, however, debts do not have the social connotations of inequality we might expect. Many loans are given to kin or close associates in the village,[7] and Lhomis say that virtually everyone takes them at some time during the year. They are not given out to make a profit. There are no money-lenders in Lhomi villages. What happens is that a person requiring funds discovers that someone has some spare cash or grain, or any tradable item in fact, and begs it as a loan. The giver is reluctant because he or she knows that loans are used mainly for trade and the principal may never be returned, let alone the interest. Giving out a loan means that the creditor will himself probably have to take out a loan in order to do the business he had been planning. On the other hand it is socially difficult to refuse a loan. In these circumstances, the pressure put on the borrower is a moral one in my experience: when a loan is taken a lamp is lit, a ritual scarf offered to the creditor, a vow is made by the borrower, and the lender makes some resigned and magnanimous statement to the effect, 'Pay me back if you can.'

Trade and barter in practice

Here I use the term 'barter' for a single transaction, and 'trade' for a series of linked barter deals. Let us look at trade to the north first. This is carried out with Tibetans not at entrepôts or markets, but individually, frequently with lifetime exchange partners who are known as '*ḍog-po*' (*grogs po*), 'friend'. The 'friends' formerly used to arrive in Lhomi villages with loads on yaks or carrier-sheep, and were received with enormous welcome and civility, with ritual scarves, bowings, speeches, *chang*, and gifts. Such large transports from Tibet now (1979–80) being forbidden, most trade is done by Lhomis who go into Tibet on foot, in *ad hoc* groups of two to three, carrying their goods themselves. It is rare to take porters, and the companions share their profits equally. They stay in caves or in the open on the way, and with their Tibetan friends when they reach their destination. Transactions are subject to changes in rates depending on the local situation. Any kind of item for which there is a demand can be bartered. Even though people sometimes said 'Food should not be exchanged for goods', in practice, in the early 1980s, this was far from true. I could see no evidence of 'spheres of exchange'. From the Tibetan side come wool, butter, cheese, dried meat, yak tails, roast barley flour, livestock, salt, woven aprons, jackets, rugs, sacks, religious objects, antique carpets, musical instruments, musk, hartshorn, herbs, tea, Chinese boots, caps, jackets, and gym-shoes, bowls and knives, vacuum flasks, matches, even a so-called phoenix egg, and so on. These are traded freely with rice, maize, millet, and other grains, chillies, amber, silver coins, hides, watches, tobacco, sugar, biscuits, vegetable dyes, torches, batteries, cotton cloth, bangles, etc. from the south of Nepal. The poverty of the Tibetan commues in the early 1980s put the Lhomis in an advantageous position. 'If you take grains to Khada', they used to say, 'you can ask for *anything* in return.'

Where the barter trade takes place is important. The person arriving to trade is a visitor, the person *in situ* the host, known as the 'owner' (*bdag po*). In return for the protection and hospitality offered by the host, the visitor is supposed to make the greater concession in bargaining, which in effect means, after due negotiation, accepting the going rate in that place. The situation is reversed when the host goes to trade on the visitor's territory.[8]

Accepting the going rate also means using the weights and measures of the locality. The Tibetans use different ones from the Lhomi, and the Lhomi different ones from the people further south. Now the expression 'weights and measures' may convey the wrong impression. It is true that people do talk in terms of rates for barter. People will say: 'This year in our village two *kathi*s (a round wooden pot) of maize exchange for three of potato seed, but last year it was three *kathi*s of maize for two of potato seed, and yes, we give four *doko*s (baskets) of manure for one *kathi* of salt', and so on for many, many different items. The whole thing is quite extraordinarily complicated. What they do not bother to say is that all these *kathi*s and *doko*s are home-made, and that my *doko* may be really much bigger than yours. It is as though the stated rates are just a way of being able to think, 'Well, what we had was a fair deal.' They standardise transactions only in an approximate way. For many goods, of different qualities, like woven aprons, which are exchanged against grain, there are no stated rates. Everything depends on whether you want a warm apron or a beautiful one, or how much you want one at all. The word 'bargaining' also may convey a mistaken impression of Middle Eastern haggling which is a sort of standardised game of wits. Here negotiation is hardly a confrontation at all, but rather a polite petitioning from the visitor.[9] All this means is that for us, as anthropologists, to talk in terms of 'exchange ratios' misses the point. What people are doing is substituting one good for another according to what is, in the last resort, the host's village view of what is fair.

In fact set barter trade rates, where they exist, are not really so much addressed to the incoming traders as they are to other co-villagers. Richer houses with plentiful stocks to dispose of would benefit by bartering at lower rates. I did not think to enquire on this myself while in the field, but Baumgartner's material on the Sherpas shows clearly that the rationale of barter rates, which are collectively established at the beginning of the season, is village solidarity expressed as a means whereby poorer people are not disadvantaged (Baumgartner, 1980: 135). The obligation not to vary widely from the rates is a duty to one's co-villagers, and the benefitting of one's barter opposite may be expressed by little tokens around this.

When people calculate the 'value' of what they are giving up in relation to what they are receiving, this is in relation not to an abstract 'price', but to their own possibilities, both at home and in further transactions in the personalised trade circuit they have created. Such circuits are highly individual. The possibility of trading at all depends on there being sufficient workers in the household to take care of the farm during trade journeys.

Let us look at this question in relation to trade in the south. This is numerically the main direction of trade, since nearly all families can go there during the slack winter months, whereas only the households with many working members can afford to send someone north to Tibet during the summer. Poorer people have to make do with the south. They usually do not have Tibetan goods to trade, but have to rely on what they have produced or gathered locally, and these form 'packages' of great variety. For example, one man from Chemtang took south home-made incense, ropes, *kurki* (a medicinal herb) and bamboo baskets, while another took spices, garlic, wax for seals, and poisons. Some people rely on one large item such as an ox, bought in the south with a loan, to be laboriously urged over the mountains and sold for a profit at home. Such circuits create their own 'prices'. Thus, for example, if someone acquired in the village some Tibetan yak-hair sacks and took them on his circuit, he might have a good idea what he could ask for them from his friend A in Angla, but this would not be identical with what a co-villager might get for them from his friend B in Sekhaya.

Even in the south, where there is more of a market economy, money does not affect this situation much. Not only is it difficult even for lowland villagers to get to market (hours of laborious walking), but the demand for money among their Lhomi partners is very variable. A certain minimum of money is necessary for everyone in order to buy kerosene, iron, and edible oil at the bazaar.[10] Poor Lhomis sell trivial items for money, such as eggs, beer, or homemade artefacts on the fringes of the weekly market in Khandbari, at the annual fair (*mela*) on the Barun River held in honour of a local deity, or door-to-door in the lowland villages. Quite rich Lhomis will take road-mending contracts for money, and it is common to take occasional work as porters for cash. But many people, especially the poor, virtually avoid the money economy – and yet even they will suddenly need money for a marriage or sacrifice – and then do anything they can to get it.[11]

Larger, more valuable items are never brought south without a known destination, a friend strategically situated. The great majority of trade in the south is done with ritual friends called reciprocally *mit* (pl. *miteri*, f.

mitini) in Nepali. A *mit* must help not only the partner, but also his or her entire pool of relatives, must observe ritual avoidance of the wife or husband, and undertake funerary rites when the *mit* dies. This is a serious, life-time commitment to a relationship with someone of the same sex, similar to that with the Tibetan *dog po* friends, but perhaps more ambiguous because of differences in culture. But in both cases mutual trust is the essence of the relationship, since the reciprocation of barter is often delayed and may be intermeshed with other kinds of help.

As far as I could understand, the poorer Lhomi families who go down south in winter to do odd jobs on Gurung farms do not work for their *miteri*. The labouring relationship, the exchange of work for goods, is an unequal one, inappropriate to ritual friends. Nevertheless the tie is a social one, and far from alienated. It is mediated by long-standing links between Lhomi and Gurung villages. These incorporate not only the use by Gurungs of specific Lhomi communally owned pastures, but also religious links, whereby lamas from Lhomi *gompas* (temples) regularly travel down to the appropriate Gurung village for healing, astrology and the averting of hailstorms. These lamas spend several months of every year in the Gurung village at times when weather-controlling abilities are required. They are highly respected and paid in grains, which they also barter when they go north again. The Lhomis who come down for winter work do not always go to the same Gurung family every year, though they do go to 'known people'. But then, in the linked villages, everyone knows everyone else.

The Lhomis quite deliberately make themselves strange and 'other' to the Gurungs during these trips. They live under trees, in caves or barns and take pains to dress badly and appear poverty stricken. With their long tangled hair and wild demeanour they are even somewhat frightening. But the Gurungs treat them well. The expression used is that the Lhomis have 'come on a visit'. Of the garlic and potatoes they commonly bring with them to barter the Gurungs say: 'If we feel pity we give two *pattis* of millet or maize for one *mana* of garlic, otherwise only one *patti*.' In other words, even in the comparatively depersonalised relations of winter labouring, where people are related more as members of villages than as friends, there is a strong element of individual 'moral' action.

Schrader, describing trade in the Walungchung valley which is adjacent to the Arun to the east, uses the expression 'a moral economy of trade' (c.f. Scott, 1976 'the moral economy of the peasant') to explain exchange relations with the Tibetans (1988: 283–4). In his view, this moral economy does not extend to trade with the culturally more dissimilar people of the south.[12] But according to my material from the Arun Valley the extension is bilateral, and from the theoretical point of view this has to be so, as long as the mode of exchange continues to be based on repeated acts of barter along known paths of goods.

Let us now turn to barter between households inside the Lhomi village. It is clear that economic power does play some role here, in that one side may be less likely to want to make a deal than the other and therefore can dictate the terms. As one poor man said to me, 'I need oxen every year for ploughing. If they demand [a deal] in work I must go for that, if they demand in grains, then I must pay 32 *kathi*s of maize or millet. They don't want my potatoes.' This being said, even rich people do not usually overstep village rates. These can be upheld as moral obligations because the most scarce item in the Lhomi economy is labour, not land or livestock. Almost every household needs the help of others at some point in the year. Only a tiny number of families do not have land and live by labouring for others. Yet all households, the rich especially, need extra labour at some point, for harvest, building houses, wedding preparations, terracing, and irrigation. We can see from this the enormous significance of labour exchange (*nga-lak*). A day's work is an item which can be acquired normally only for another day's work.[13] The fact that any adult's labour day has equal value establishes a 'natural' equivalence between the parties to barter.

It is an important fact about this society is that this equality applies to women as well as men. A day of female labour is equivalent to that of a man and there is a relative absence of a sexual division of labour.[14] Most women take part in barter on their own account, though when there is a need to travel they usually send a son to do the trip.[15] Thus, although there may be status differences and economic inequalities between the parties to barter, all adults are enabled to be contractual subjects and thereby moral agents in barter.

To summarise: both to the north (Tibet) and the south (the lower hills villages) the Lhomi trade mainly with ritual friends. This is especially true of more valuable items and delayed barter. What is required here is trust, which is what the ritual friendships provide. The exchange of labour for goods during winter in the low hills villages does not take place with ritual partners, but is nevertheless likely to be repeated with the same village, and therefore both sides have an interest in maintaining their reputations, the Lhomi for neediness, and the Gurungs for generosity. Inside the Lhomi home village there is small-scale barter with neighbours and any strangers who come up for local produce, such as potato-seed. Here, village exchange rates are set for given time periods to attempt to ensure that barter is 'fair' in that situation. Finally, Lhomis barter or sell things for cash at fairs and markets, and sporadically hawk goods around houses in the lowlands. The buyers need not be known at all. The 'fairness' of such transactions depends entirely on each side actually seeing what is offered. With such a wide range of relationships there can be no external social criterion defining what is 'moral' action. But there is, I suggest, a subjective one, based on the actors' mutual assessment of the place of their goods in one another's economic situation. This cannot be equated simply with their agreement to transact, since, as we shall see, people do sometimes cheat and mislead one another.

Cheating

What would be *not* fair in this system? In particular, how does fairness co-exist with self-interest? This question arises in connection with both immediate barter and relations involving debt (delayed barter and internal loans). There are ideas of greater and lesser iniquity in barter. Nancy Levine provided me with some information on this from North-West Nepal which seems similar to the Lhomi practice. Not very serious and relatively common is cheating in immediate barter by supplying products which look, at first sight, all right, but which turn out to be intentionally adulterated, for example grain mixed with the dregs from making beer. In this case, the person might expect to find trading partners doing something comparable, such as providing salt of poor quality or mixed with stones. Such a person would find himself or herself engaged in an escalating battle of deceptive practices, one which produces no greater sanction than grumbling and negative gossip. Such a reputation for lack of fairness would be enough to damage the trade possibilities of most people, but if a trader were able to invest ill-gotten gains in items much needed by neighbours, these people would find themselves taking a risk in trading with him or her again – while making efforts to protect themselves against cheating. The possibility of getting away with it is, in the end, limited by the fact of mutual dependency between neighbours brought about by the scarcity of labour.

Cheating is not identified with exchange rates charged *per se*, because these are tied absolutely to social relationships. People would quote to me escalating rates for a given item with known, distant, and outside people, it being taken for granted that these were 'fair' in the circumstances. A much wider latitude is possible with people who are complete strangers. A Rai assistant of mine was all agog to do a deal involving musk, a highly valuable item. He borrowed money right and left, and went up to the border with China, where he obtained two balls of musk for 2,000 Rs from a Chiawa pastoralist at Kimathanka whom he did not know at all. He gloated that he would be able to sell them in Kathmandu for 5,000 Rs. But when we got back to town he found to his dismay (and all of us who had lent him money) that the going rate was far less than he had paid for them. 'What cheats those Chiawas are!' was my reaction. 'No', my Rai friend replied, 'I accepted.' He maintained, perhaps to save face, that the distant yak-herders could not have known about changes in prices in Kathmandu. The point is that the Chiawas would have expected the Rai, who worked in Kathmandu, to have found out about the prices, to have known what he was doing. In other words, blame is not attached if each side acts in accordance with a reasonable estimation of the economic possibilities of the other.

Far more serious is failing to repay a debt or a delayed barter agreement. The person cheated has no recourse but to hound the malefactor, and may literally sit on his doorstep until he pays up.[16] This is another reason why delayed barter is only practicable on a regular basis with known people. In general terms its theoretical importance is that it establishes the need for trust-maintaining ties, such as the ritual friendships in highland Nepal (see Anderlini and Sabourian, this volume).

The immoral behaviour of traders appears in folk sayings as a serious sin with religious consequences in the afterlife, likened to the sin of killing. Of course people may pay no attention to such precepts, but they do serve as talking points for apportioning blame. It is in using power to take extortionate interest that the misdoing is often identified. In Lhomi villages, although small amounts of common produce circulate beyond barter in sporadic gifts this is demeaning to a regular recipient, and it is more common for poor people to take grain as a loan (*bulon*) at hard times in the year and pay it back after harvest at the common rates plus interest. It is therefore significant that rates of interest and a surcharge to the debtor (*tekki*, Nep.) are fixed. Overcharging would incur serious moral disapproval and I did not hear of any cases during my visit.

The ambiguities of dubious transactions are greater when they take place within long-term relationships. Many years ago a Tibetan refugee, Myagmar, arrived with some yaks. These he sold for a large sum of money to a distant Lhomi relative, Tsering, who, it was rumoured, had exploited Myagmar's total ignorance of the situation and had not paid him enough. That was thought not fair. But on the other hand Myagmar was thought to be rather a fool. The money somehow melted away, he was often seen cross-eyed with drink, and he stayed on as a rather incompetent tailor and singer of Tibetan songs for the nostalgic delight of the Lhomi. He lived with Tsering's brother. 'See how I care for the poor', this man used to say virtuously. Neighbours nevertheless blamed the Tsering family, really along the lines that they had destroyed Myagmar's capacity for operation as an equal person. Barter should reproduce *reciprocal*, not one-sided, dependence. Later Tsering, making great play of his generosity, gave

Myagmar a loan, of coral stones which he could exchange, to enable him to go to Kathmandu to find work.

At the same time the morality of barter enjoins a certain flexibility in relation to the perceived wealth of the counterpart. It is good to 'take pity', but bad to appear to be well-off. Needless to say, if both sides do this, both benefit. Everyone in a Lhomi village lives in the same kind of house, wears the same clothes, and locks up their storage sheds to conceal what is within. There is relatively little display of wealth,[17] unlike the Western Gurungs with their large houses and rows of shining brass pots, and the difference may lie in the fact that these Gurungs are not primarily a trading people. Lhomi represent themselves as simply as possible: me, and you.

The points which incur blame (deception, the exploitation of ignorance of local prices, manipulation of transactions by obtaining much needed goods) co-exist with 'normal' self-interested behaviour (differential rates for unknown people, the disguising of one's wealth) but they indicate that the latter has its limits. I argue that this expected, but limited, self-interest is in fact what is seen as 'fair', and that it involves awareness and intention, an estimation of the possibilities open to the other which is founded on knowledge of the world outside. This expected, limited, self-interest in the long run also serves to reproduce ties of mutuality. How does this work?

Mutuality, competition and ethnicity

The common humanity of the partners to barter is refracted by sharply distinct ethnic representations which occur in almost all of the highland valleys of Nepal. Why should such elaborate distinctions be reproduced in such restricted space? It is suggested here that the operation of barter creates 'stages' in the transit of goods where profit can be taken; or, to put this another way, that a 'community' may define its edges where it can obtain differential rates for important flows of goods. This may have originated with environmental distinctions in the vertical economy, but it has been elaborated by purely cultural boundaries. Marked differences in style and cultural consumption separate the groups in organic solidarity. These ethnic frontiers differ analytically from those much less clear-cut boundaries between culturally *similar* groups which are in competition for the same niche in trade.

In the Arun Valley food is the focus for most obvious 'ethnic' differences,[18] which are correlated with distinct economies, marriage patterns, styles of clothing, houses, ornaments, and of course language. Most manufactured things must be transformed to be acceptable: tailors sew Indian cotton into Lhomi patterns, smiths turn scrap-iron into Lhomi pots and knives, jewellers weld rings onto rupees and melt down silver to make characteristic necklaces and other decorations. It simply never happens that a Lhomi woman wears a Gurung blouse, or a Rai farmer builds his house in the Lhomi style. A Gurung woven rug (*radi*) is as alien in a Lhomi house as a zebra-skin would be in an English sitting-room – in fact more so, as Lhomis have no fashion for the exotic. Even those items which appear to be 'the same' as they pass from community to community, for example, potatoes, are not, if only for the reason that potatoes have a quite different role in the Lhomi diet, where they are a staple, from the Rai or Gurung, where they are a side-dish.

This means that there is a double transformation of value as items A and B are transferred between different ethnic groups X and Y. There is nothing to measure an abstract, non-personal value for A or B, since for group X either A or B is more desired at a particular time, while for group Y the reverse is true, otherwise the barter would not take place. The implication also is that it is impossible for someone in this region to act as a *neutral* individual; the person cannot but be defined as, and act as, a member of a group.

The visual signs of belonging to a particular community symbolise what are seen as essential differences between kinds of people. '*Rik*' (*rigs*) is the word Lhomis use to mean breed, species, culture, or spiritual descent. It was the translation used for the Nepali, and generally north Indian, term *jati* (caste or tribe). In one Lhomi view there are at least six kinds of '*rik*' in their vicinity: Lhomi, Nawa (inhabitants of villages immediately to the north of the Lhomi and including the Chiawa), Sherpa, Po-pa (Tibetan), Gorkha (Nepalese), and Kham-pa (incomers from Kham in the north-east of Tibet). Sometimes they would distinguish among the Gorkhas, the '*riks*' of the Rais, Limbus, Tamangs, Gurungs, etc.

Now in origin these are not such very clear categories. The Nawas, according to Furer-Haimendorf are a clan of the Sherpas (1964: 19) as are the Chiawas, and the Lhomis certainly include amongst themselves clans of people who are by descent Rais, Sherpas, Limbus and Khampas. But the point is that the people of the Limbu clans inside Lhomi villages make themselves look just like other Lhomis, and not a bit like Limbus. As Fürer-Haimendorf (1971) and Levine (1987) have shown, transformations of ethnicity in northern Nepal can be very rapid, and are represented publicly by the changes in economic strategies, food, clothing, etc. mentioned above. In the northern Arun the status of the Nawas, for example, who are in the process of transforming themselves into people like the Lhomi, is unclear.

Nor are the groups on the Nepal side of the border actually very distinct from the ecological–economic point of view. It is true that each group tends to live at an altitude typical for itself, that Rais specialise in rearing pigs, Gurungs in keeping sheep, and Lhomis in forest produce. But they are all farmers whose basic subsistence rests on a wide range of crops and vegetables, maize, millet, rice, buckwheat, lentils, potatoes, barley, soya beans, etc. It is the patterns of consumption and hence 'demand' in the barter trade which vary. In the Lhomi case ecological differences inside their lands are as great as those outside it. In sunny, low-lying nooks there are banana groves, orchids, and monkeys swinging from the trees; in the highest villages people keep yaks. The clear distinctions between the peoples of the Arun Valley are cultural–economic, not ecological–economic.

Ethnic groups are seen by the Hinduised Nepalis in a hierarchical way and the idea easily slips into that of 'caste', but for the Lhomi the important idea is that of difference, not hierarchy. Anthropologists of the Himalayas have tried to represent this in various ways: as concentric circles (Fürer-Haimendorf, 1964), or as a 'four-fold classification' on the lines of a division of labour in a polity (Allen, 1978). In the case of the Lhomi there is certainly no idea of a clear hierarchy.[19] They claim to despise the actually much richer Chiawas and call them 'dirty', while in fact eagerly seeking, though rarely obtaining, their daughters in marriage. For Lhomi only the Tibetans of central Tibet are respected for their great religious institutions, and in the locality it is only the former hereditary chiefs (*goba*s) and Buddhist lamas who stand above other people. This does not prevent either of these categories being seen as equal in other circumstances, notably that of trade.[20]

This egalitarianism should be seen against the background of historical competition for domination of the Himalayan trade routes.[21] As Lhomis often pointed out to me, it is trade, not farming, which makes you rich. The kingdoms south of the mountains (Gorkha, Sikkim, Bhutan, Ladakh, Cooch Behar, etc.) were all established in strategic relations to routes into Tibet and flourished quite largely on the basis of trade (Rhodes, 1980: 264). But much of the border is inaccessible to large-scale traffic, and here the people actually on the frontier and prepared to struggle up the passes have the first whack at the trade. The Lhomi are in this situation, blocked only by the Chiawas at Kimathanka, and their strategic advantage depends on them keeping the lower groups out, sometimes by literally obstructing the trail.[22] This explains not only Chiawa hostility to them, but also Lhomi dislike of later incomers, such as the Nawas, who settled on Lhomi lands as *raikar* farmers some generations ago and are still not fully accepted. Tibetan refugees are not welcome in Lhomi villages, although some maintain a foothold there. I heard even a lama being bawled out for seducing a local girl: 'You dirty *Nawa* dog! Why do you want to leave your bastard here?' village women shouted at the tops of their voices.

The Lhomi have a great reputation for poisoning unwelcome visitors. I do not know if this actually happens, but there were certainly two or three kinds of poison available, made from aconites and datura, and my Rai and Tamang companions insisted on acquiring antidotes before they ventured into Lhomi territory. Lhomis themselves ascribe use of the poisons to the Seduwa Sherpas, who live to the south-west, and are rivals for control of the trail to the town of Khandbari.[23] The similar Khumbo group 'don't talk too good about the Lhomi and call them insulting names behind their backs' (Schickelgruber, personal communication).

So what is very noticeable is that the overt cultural differences between trading *partner* groups (Tibetan nomads, Lhomis, and Gurungs) are far more marked than those between trading *competitors* (Lhomis, Chiawas, Nawas, Khumbo and Seduwa Sherpas). If relations between barter partners, people not like yourself, are friendly, those between potential competitors for trade, people like yourself, are hostile.

The very same pattern, the matrix of friendly/hostile relations works also in the depths of the community, but compressed in the micro-world, so that here groups are frequently both friend and enemy to one another. 'Communities' such as the Lhomi are separated into villages, each of which has a slightly different ecological–economic situation and character. Lhomis are also divided into exogamous clans.[24] Clan members are dispersed in several villages. When you look at them these clans are both heterogeneous and have claims of various cross-cutting kinds. Some arrived earlier, some more recently; some have rights to communal land, others do not; some are original inhabitants, others come from far away; some have 'better mouth' (status) than others. Clan members tend to live together in named sub-sections of villages separated by streams. They have their own deities. Crucially, they have different access to resources, both inside the village, and, because of their various links and partnerships, with the external world. Relations between them can be both friendly and acrimonious. Usually the pretext for quarrels are matrimonial, husband and wife, of course, belonging to different clans. Slanging matches resound in the echoing valleys, knifings are common, and what the Lhomi describe as clan 'wars' are intrinsic to everyone's historical mythology.

Differentiation and sharing

Barter, trade and loans occur within the village as well as outside, so the idea of 'mutual recompense' with someone who is different from you is used to cross internal boundaries too. What is interesting is that this has not led to economic differentiation inside the Lhomi community. Sahlins has pointed out that trade of household surpluses in South-East Asian hinterland societies often leads to an internal ban on sharing rice, to absence of levelling mechanisms, to fragmentation of households, and a high level of self-interest and differentiation, as each family accumulates its produce in order to buy valuables from the cultural centres (1972, 223–5). This pattern has not occurred in the Upper Arun valley. The difference can be attributed to the absence here, because of the difficulty of the trails, of large-scale high-value trade, and to the fact that the Lhomi do not uphold the accumulatory values of metropolitan hierarchical society, whether of central Nepal, Tibet, or India. Their frame of reference is their own society, within which it is at least as honourable to share as to accumulate.

This can be seen in relation to debt. Repayments are often not made in the same item borrowed, but in whatever the borrower has managed to produce or in labour reckoned in days. So the term *nga-lak* is used both for labour repayments of debts and for reciprocal labour at busy times of year. *Nga-lak* is not considered demeaning, but is rather the general form of adjusting labour to the tasks and produce present.[25] Now although creditor households do use grain repayments after harvest as a supply for advantageous external trade, what we do not find is a regular systematisation of this, resulting in internal hierarchy, as was present in Ladakh (Grist, 1985). In other words, there is no grain debt-bondage, no system of patron houses with client grain-suppliers. No household is above giving help in *nga-lak*. The absence of established patronage networks can be seen from the fact that in the 1979 panchayat elections Lhomi contenders personally went round to bribe people to vote for them.[26] When there was a famine a few years back there was no institutionalised safety network, and people had to have recourse to the individual generosity of others. The main benefactor in Pang-Dok village was widely described by other people as 'religious'.

We return here to the subject of morality, or rather the coexistence of various kinds of economic transfer and moralities within this society. I shall briefly discuss these in order to make clear why I see the ethics of *karma* as particularly salient in relation to barter. The Lhomi have a strong notion of collectivism or inclusiveness, which coexists with their recognition of people as different species. This is expressed economically in a proliferation of *sharing* institutions, chiefly the distribution of food at religious festivals. A village has its own mountain guardian god, given propitiatory sacrifices twice a year by the whole community, and clans also have their own deities. *Standardised collections* for the sacrifices are made from each household. Then there are from five to seven Buddhist temples ('*gompa*', '*lhakang*') per village, and each of these have regular monthly rituals of a mainly expiatory kind. The contributions are made by rotas of the households attached to the temple, but anyone can attend to worship and consume the food and beer. Finally, the most important temple in each village holds several big festivals during the year, at the Buddha's birthday,

Dasein, Tihar, the Tibetan New Year, etc. Again, provision is by rota from the wealthier households, everyone is invited (including Gurung friends), and food and drink are ladled out irrespective of contribution or status. People sit on the hillside by the temple in great communal huddles (See Figure 4). The great number and frequency of these occasions for sharing means that almost everyone has occasion to be a donor, even though the clan attached to the major temple can think of itself as *the* donor on behalf of everyone else.

Another type of economic obligation, now in decline (Humphrey,1985) are the dues or tribute which used to be owed to *gobas* (hereditary chiefs) and are still owed to lamas for what they provide the people: good government and religious blessings respectively. Dues took the form of either labour or tithes in grain. The rendering of dues is perhaps similar in rationale to contributions to sacrifices, being fixed in amount and a necessary statement of the petitionary relationship with political leaders, lamas and gods. But it is unlike barter, because dues contain an inherent status difference and have no bargaining element.

Sharing at religious festivals among the Lhomi is still very important, and is not just a source for ideas of commonality, but also a destination for wealth. It is thus essential to the reproduction of the egalitarianism of Lhomi society. However, it may be under threat. We can contrast the Lhomi with groups such as the Khumbu Sherpa, which had easier access to Tibet and whose *tshong-pa* (traders) became very wealthy indeed. Furer-Haimendorf (1975: 294) notes that Khumbu high-level trade was rapidly monetised; traders amassed their wealth by using money in the metro-politan centres of both Tibet and Nepal to buy goods in demand the other side of the frontier, creating great economic differentials inside the Sherpa community. Now Fisher suggests for the Tarangapur Magars of North-West Nepal that money and barter form two incompatible trade circuits, the money one leading to accumulation and the barter one reinforcing communal values (1986: 184–7). But the Lhomi example suggests that the incompatibility between money transactions and barter Fisher observed may be an accident of locality and timing in that particular community. What is important is the distinction between the accumulation and the circulation (sharing) of wealth. When thirst for accumulation takes hold, as Sacherer demonstrates for the Rolwaling Sherpas who have been flooded by tourists with cash, there is a decline in religious traditions and donations (1981: 164). Very few tourists as yet struggle into Lhomiland. But perhaps all we can say here is that these 'old hands' in the world of goods have pretty good defences, but they may not be impermeable in the future.

The present prevalence of barter over 'formalised exchange' (to which

Lhomis at a communal festival.

the salt-grain trade, with set rates, places, times, amounts and ritualised group relations, may have approximated at various periods in the past, Jest (1975)) indicates a flexibility and openness to change necessary in unstable economic conditions. Barter is an agreement to treat an incommensurable mutual transfer *as if* it were of equal benefit, but this does mean that ratios may actually change over time to the detriment of one side or the other. Barter thus seems like a precarious 'holding strategy', which allows an egalitarian ideology to remain in place over the shifting sands of actual transactions.

Relative to twenty years ago, when the Tibetan trade flourished, exchange ratios have declined for the Lhomi. These days, when talking of barter, they do not discuss 'brilliant coups' and what they stand to gain. Rather, they grumble about the difficulty of it all, about their need for things, particularly Tibetan goods, to maintain their own way of life. For them, nothing these days comes up to scratch: their temples are denuded, their children illiterate, their clothes and possessions old and worn. My Gurung, Rai and Tamang assistants commented that the Lhomi are in fact well-off in regional terms, and that even the poorest of them are not really poor. But as the Lhomi seem to see it, barter is not so much a question of 'good deals' cleverly accomplished, as a matter of taking whatever action one can, of self-reliance, of seeking any opening where one may give, in order to get back what one 'needs'. But it is also a way of keeping up the ritual friendships, often by quite trivial transactions, which are important for other reasons too: support in times of trouble, safety when travelling, and simply friendship as such. It is significant that in this 'difficult' situation the Lhomi talk not of exploitation but of religion.

The morality of exchange and religious life

I never heard Lhomi blaming their exchange partners for their decline. Deceit or non-fulfilment of an agreement would be culpable, but for general changes in barter rates they make no distinction between reductions in what they are able to get and what they themselves are able to provide. Both are explained by external events: landslides, hailstorms, the Chinese invasion of Tibet, the flimsy bridges swept into rivers in spate, the invasions of monkeys and other animals and insects which destroy the crops, thieves, corrupt officials and so on. Now there is an apocalyptic religious view which attributes such disasters to the epoch, the decline of the age, but more salient is the attribution of two alternative, and more immediate, causes: 'our sins', on the one hand, and the retribution of the gods on the other.

What 'our sins' might be was never specified exactly rather the idea seemed to be that since there had been so many landslides, etc. there must have been sins. I was present at two extravagant collective rituals to banish sins accumulated through *karma*. Performance of the rituals had been delayed for several years because the lamas had gone on strike, angered by the new panchayat government's decision to charge them tax like lay people. In the lamas' view rituals for the exorcism of sins *were* their service to the community. Many people, but particularly lamas, attributed the disasters causing decline in exchange rates to the build-up of unexorcised sins of the entire community in the period of the strike and absence of expiatory rituals. But in private at night, to the alarming cracks of boulders crashing down the mountainside – any of which might cause a landslide – people also used to blame the lamas, for their sins, which must have weakened their spiritual strength and their defence of the community. Furthermore, it did not go unremarked that the prosperous village of Walungchung in the next valley, formerly home of several extremely wealthy traders said to have been extortionate in their methods, had been virtually destroyed by a landslide a few years ago.

The same *karmic* reasoning was also used to explain individual success. Even as a child, the Lhomi girl or boy is not regarded as a *tabula rasa* on which society inscribes its features; the *karmic* weight of actions in previous lives are brought into this world with the baby, and one might say that their result is represented by the sum of personal characteristics and social 'property' which children inherit. People used to hesitate to say who was rich in the Lhomi villages (which may, of course, have been related to our work for a government-linked development project), but several times people murmured, 'So-and-so is said to be rich. He must have good *karma* from his previous lives.'

We can see two implications of these explanations: first, the time-scale of *karma*, which in theory has results only in subsequent lives, can be shortened to include retribution in this life. Second and more important, just as persons represent their communities in this region (for example as lamas, workers or traders in the Gurung villages), the misdoings of persons or groups were held to incur *karmic* retribution for whole communities. In other words, the Buddhist doctrine of *karma* was moulded to fit the nature of Lhomi social life. Here the self is never simply an individual as in the modern West, but is a composite, including supposed previous selves and the refractions of the person implied by identification with concentric social groupings (the household, village, ethnic group).

But taking action, as opposed to explaining misfortune, serves to specify and unite the sense of self. Good *karma* does not wipe out sins (bad *karma*) but coexists with it. There is a sense in which even for the single person this general *karmic* balance need not be tied to anything as particular and trivial as specific daily actions, if only because no-one knows how their spiritual state stands. And yet it is the accumulation of all these actions, in this and previous lives, which constitutes *karma*. This means that if people actually invoke *karma* in relation to themselves in real life situations attention should be paid to the moral implications of every action. It is in this active sense, as opposed to the general idea that 'being ordinary humans we must have sinned', that I suggest an analogy between the rationale of *karma* and that of *jeba* (balanced recompense, barter). The agency of the self is the same in both cases and both are concerned with actions involving choice and their just reward.

So, as barter is a particular type within the general context of economic transactions, it can perhaps be linked to a specific way of thinking within religious morality. *Karma* is only one of the strands in the complex religious thinking of the Lhomi, and the extent to which it is invoked to explain misfortune is variable. *Karmic* thinking co-exists with a super-naturalism which attributes independent action to spirits and deities: they may attack you just for the hell of it, irrespective of your deeds in this life or any other. I agree with Lichter and Epstein (1983) that, although *karma* theoretically encompasses every activity, it can be analysed as separable from propitiatory sacrifices to unreliable deities. The point I wish to make here is that barter is not afloat somewhere beyond any thinking about ethics, and that its 'self-interest' is closer to the *karmic* way of thinking than to that of the propitiation.

This may seem a perverse argument, in that, like barter, sacrifice to capricious deities has often been seen as a self-interested contract. But in Lhomi culture I would suggest that propitiatory sacrifice should be classified with other forms of propitiation as a rendering of dues. We have seen that in donations to lamas the reward is a blessing, hoped to be immediately auspicious, i.e. to bring luck. Justice does not enter here. The layperson cannot choose to act 'fairly', because he or she is religiously another order of being from the lama, and can do nothing to equal his blessing. The same was true, in terms of political protection, for dues to the *gobas* where payments were a recognition of subordination to the intrinsic power of the *goba* clan. In propitiatory 'sacrifices' to the gods the sense of offering dues is given by the *fixed* nature of the contributions from a *rota* of households which are *obliged* regularly to provide this service. On the other hand, sacrifices for the expiation of sins explicitly invoke a *karmic* explanation. But even here in fact, as we have seen, rituals are held and scapegoats are constructed not when 'a sin' has been committed, but when a disaster threatens or has happened. In other words, sacrifices in general are not seen as actions freely chosen by the self, but as social obligations, or as forced by capricious and fortuitous external events.

As Lichter and Epstein (1983: 240–2) point out, Tibetans have a notion of a person's worldly luck or life-force (*rlung-rta*) which can be contrasted with *bsod-nams*, the stored-up merit of a soul's career (*karma*). Lhomi also have this idea of life-force, symbolised by the 'wind-horse' flags flying in front of every house. In theory, it is this luck or life-force, not the moral *karmic* state, which is improved by propitiatory sacrifices and which is damaged by impending calamities. But in popular religious thought *karma* and *rlung-rta* seem to get mixed up. Lichter and Epstein say that in Tibetan lay people's religion it is thought that high *rlung-rta* can succeed in stalling the consequences of bad *karma* until some other life (1983: 241). The Lhomi, whose Buddhism is even more compromised by a backwoods village life far from the literate monastic tradition, seem to bend the idea of *karma* itself, so that it comes close to *rlung-rta*, and is used as the explanation for worldly success. The two ideas can be distinguished, however, in relation to intention: in *karma* what is important is particular intended acts, which go with faith, and with remorse that can ameliorate the results of sins. Although Lhomi people said in a general way that over the years of the lamas' strike there must have been unknown sins, they acknowledge that *karma* is really about known, intended actions. But intention is unimportant to *rlung-rta*, where the emphasis is all on god-inspired accident or a fated astrological cyclicity beyond human control. These in brief are the religious ideas within which the morality of exchange has taken place.

The term for exchange, *jeba*, itself appears in religious expressions connected with the notion of *karma*.[27] We find it used in a colloquial expression for 'death-and-rebirth' or the 'transmigration of the soul', i.e. with the meaning 'to barter one's life' (*che brje ba*). Too much should not be read into this metaphor, but it does indicate that *jeba* can be used in the context of the idea of transformation and that of just desserts, because this is of course what the Buddhist receives on death. Whether reborn as a mouse or a prince, this result has a cause which is the cumulation of actions. One's actions and the result for one's destiny are not qualitatively the same, but they inevitably imply one another and are linked by the mechanism of *karma* to the idea of abstract and ultimately non-social justice.

This paper does *not* suggest that people when bartering are consciously motivated by the idea of *karma*. But it is proposed that the notion of a fair deal is a moral one related above all to intention, and that we should see this in the context of the religious ideas present in this culture, of which the most relevant in my view is the concept of *karma*.

In Tibetan culture the most common term for *karma* is simply '*le*', work and the fruits of work. Lhomi regard both trade and farming as work. They live in the knowledge of labour in the fields and its products which are bartered. There is no notion of the non-workers, the less than responsible adult person, the moral minor (as women are sometimes designated in other Asian societies). Work and its result are universal for all individuals, and thus determine what is an abstract principle. Transmuted to the notion of the fruits of one's actions, and thereby to the abstract notion of fairness or justice, this central idea becomes integral to barter too, or rather to the whole range of economic activities (barter, trade and credit) which imply conscious reciprocity. It is in the moral, and yet relative and contextualised, meaning that barter is reciprocal. It takes into account what goods mean to people in their particular circumstances. Essential to it is the notion of the morally responsible person, giving one thing and receiving something different, the link created by the two being not measured value but immeasurable justice.

NOTES

1 I use the word 'morality' to mean a system, within, and less inclusive than, 'ethics', which states commonly held ideas about obligation. If ethics is about how one should live, morality states one's specific obligations, usually in terms of a general rule (Williams, 1985).

2 In 1979–80 some Lhomi informants quoted the sum of 61 rupees for the brideprice, while the total cost of a wedding was between 3,000 and 5,000 rupees.

3 Inverted commas indicate approximate pronunciation.

4 Similar trade circuits exist in the region between other ethnic groups with complementary economies, for example the Kulung Rai act as intermediaries transporting grain from lowland farms to the Khumbu Sherpas in return for salt, forest produce and Tibetan goods (McDougal, 1968: 11).

5 For a discussion of this see Lionel Caplan (1970).

6 Currently there are only a few individuals in Lhomi villages who maintain herds of yaks and cross-breeds. These are all fairly recent (two–three generations back) immigrants from Tibet, who use their links to use pastures over the border. They are much envied by the Lhomi *jimi*s, i.e. *kipat* land-owners, who still resent them for their intrusion into the district. In their turn they despise the Lhomi for not having the 'tradition' of yak-breeding, which is profitable because of the high demand for yak products.

7 This is one point on which I should correct information given in my earlier paper on barter (1985) where I stated that most loans are taken outside the village. Looking at my data again, I find that although the Lhomi do also take loans from Gurung farmers, which has different social implications, many loans are also taken out inside the village.

8 Individual Tibetans in 1979–80 did still come to Lhomi villages to trade, but not regularly as before, and in much smaller numbers and with fewer goods.

9 Jest writes on comparable barter in Dolpo, 'Qu'il s'agisse des échanges de Tarap avec le Tibet (grain-sel) ou avec les vallées du Sud, une pratique traditionelle préside à ce troc. Elle est marquée tout d'abord par un attitude de fidélité entre les échangeurs; ... cette fidélité est la base de la vie communautaire,

car seul le respect des taux convenues et l'absence de mise en concurrence des hommes et des marchandises peuvent garantir l'honnêté des transactions' ['Whether it is a matter of Tarap's exchanges with Tibet (grain-salt) or with the valleys to the south, a traditional practice presides over this barter. It is above all marked by an attitude of trust between the exchangers;... this trust is the basis of community life, because only respect for agreed prices and the absence of competition between men and between merchandise can guarantee the honesty of transactions] (1975: 164–5).

10 Virtually all Lhomis also use money to buy subsidised rice at Tumlingtar. This, they say, is necessary for subsistence, but some of it is also used in the Tibet trade.

11 Animals used for sacrifices, such as sheep, goats and chickens, and also other animals such as cattle, have prices quoted in money, which usually rise the more distant the place from the market at Khandbari. This does not prevent the Lhomi from acquiring them by barter or by work if they can. Otherwise, they must buy them (particularly chickens) with money at the Khandbari market.

12 Schrader quotes his informants as saying that this 'moral economy of trade' allows for high profits to be taken from the unsophisticated Tibetans. The Walungchung traders could extract these profits because their own moral code is only binding in their own community. The southern groups, on the other hand, are distrustful of the 'strange' northern people, making high profits in the culturally foreign setting impossible (1988: 283–4). I find this argument unconvincing and illogical, since it annihilates any sense the 'moral economy of trade' might have. In my view the barter traders will attempt to make profits wherever they can, but always bearing in mind the estimation of the economy of the other and the need for repeated transactions.

13 Poor people will sometimes ask to be paid for a day's labour in grains or some other needed product. These rates are agreed within the village, but differ between villages. Adolescent boys are sometimes hired by a rich household on an annual basis to do shepherding and other livestock work. The pay, in kind or in money, is made to their parents. This does not last after adulthood, i.e. after the boy is married in his mid-teens. I never encountered a household with a permanent servant (*hali*, Nep.) except in the case of one or two subnormal men and women not capable of maintaining their own households.

14 Research by Diemberger and Schickelgruber among the Khumbo Sherpas (Nawa) of Seduwa has provided details of the division of labour by sex. In this society, which is essentially similar to that of the Lhomi, the absence of a division of labour by sex is the result of the pasturing system, whereby most households have to split into two parts, one in the village and one with the livestock, and the general shortage of labour requires both sexes to be able to perform all tasks. Both men and women do handiwork and barter their products. Despite the virtual absence of a sexual division of labour the Khumbo do see the male and female genders as complementary and opposite from the ideological point of view (Schickelgruber, personal communication).

15 Lhomi women maintain their own 'accounts' within the household from their transactions. There is severe criticism of people who use relatives' products such as food, even those of close kin within the household, to make themselves out to be generous hosts. Nevertheless, for large transactions involving the

outside world (marriages, sacrifices, ritual dues at festivals) the household pools its resources and acts as an economic unit.

16 Nancy Levine kindly told me of the following instance from North-West Nepal:

There was a man from whom I used to buy much of my wheat. He was a lama and husband of one of my ceremonial friends. Because I lacked storage facilities I could not take delivery at once of all the grain I bought each autumn and chose to take delayed delivery from the people I trusted most. Late in 1983, the year of the famine, this man began showing a certain reluctance to deliver my remaining wheat. What friends advised me to do was to visit his home together with all members of my household to 'remind' him of what he owed us. This obliged him to fix us an elaborate meal. I had to do this several times, and, in the end he paid me only part of the grain owed and used a very tiny measure in so doing. The response of my household was resignation, and we contented ourselves with the fact that we had eaten a good bit of grain at his house, enjoyed the visits, and in future would take immediate delivery of grain from this man. We also told everyone we knew about how he cheated us. People were sympathetic, but the fact of the matter was that he had the most high-quality wheat in the region and there was no choice but to deal with him in future. (personal communication)

17 The major display of wealth is in women's jewellery, but women from the richest families are not necessarily those who wear the most magnificent necklaces in everyday life.

18 Bahuns do not eat any kind of meat, nor take alcoholic drink, but all of the hill peoples do both. Tamangs and Lhomis will eat the cow, but Rais and Gurungs do not, although they will eat buffalo. Yaks are counted the same as cattle, though differentiated from buffalo, and the Lhomi eat them. Rais eat pork of all kinds, but the Gurungs will only eat the meat of white pigs, not black ones, and they will not eat goat. Some groups of Rai also will not eat goat, and hesitate before the innards of the pig. Lhomis eat all kinds of meat, including game, but they do not eat fish.

19 Schrader describes a hierarchy of three distinct named classes among the Walungchung people, based on the date at which these groups arrived in the valley and ideas of purity. He links this to the economic advantages of ownership of the best land and the consequent edge given in trade. Trade down this valley at an earlier period was far larger in scale than along the Arun and resulted in much greater differentials in wealth (1988: 275–7).

20 There are no lama monasteries in the upper Arun. Lamas are people who have some training in religious rituals, but otherwise they marry and maintain farming households like other people.

21 As Fürer-Haimendorf has pointed out, the egalitarianism and absence of food restrictions of the Buddhist trading peoples of the Himalayas can be related to the need to move freely among many different ethnic groups (1975: 289).

22 This situation at the village level is documented also by Jest for Dolpo, who say, for example, 'Aujourd'hui encore, afin de réserver le monopole des échanges, les Tarap-pa interdisent aux habitants de Panzang de franchir le torrent de Do, limite de la vallée de Tarap en direction du Sud' ['Still today, in order to preserve a monopoly over exchanges, the people of Tarap forbid the inhabitants of Panzang to cross the river Do, which is the border of the Tarap valley in the south'] (1975: 158).

23 Formerly, the headman (*goba*) of the southernmost Lhomi village, Syaksila, used to maintain an armed band for the control of the trail. Today, the *goba* having lost power to the Nepali panchayat government, there is still a supernatural threat. Syaksila is distinguished by the presence of a gigantic rock, the size of a large house, which is attached by a mere corner in a most dangerous-looking way to the mountain-side. I was told very seriously that the head lama kept it tied there by spells, and he might at any time release it to cause a landslide and block the road.

24 The idea of the clan '*ru*' (*rus*) meaning 'bone', is continuous with *rik* (species), since it also implies a qualitative and fundamental differentiation (see also Levine, 1981). The clans are patrilineal and exogamous; there are around 10–15 clans in any village.

25 Also common is the exchange of grain, oxen hire, manure, salt, etc. against the use of a spare field for a season, again at rates accepted in a given village.

26 The election in 1979 in Hatiya panchayat nearly ruined the father of the winner, who had to sell most of his cattle to pay for the 'entertainment' of the voters.

27 The latent homology between *karma* and barter has a metaphorical base in language. I am aware of the dangers of attributing too great a significance to 'conventional metaphors' (Keesing, 1985), and in what follows I have no proof that the conceptual associations are made by Lhomi people. Nevertheless, the links may be sufficiently salient to be mentioned here. *Karma* is translated in Tibetan as *rgyu bras*, 'cause-effect'. In everyday language it is known simply as '*le*' (*las*), 'work', the idea being action and the inevitable moral consequences of that action, the reciprocity of the universe. The linguistic link between *karma* and barter is the term '*len*' (*lan*) 'reply', which we noted earlier is one of the words used for barter, in the sense of 'recompense'. '*Len*', whose root meaning is 'a time', as in once, twice, thrice, etc. occurs in several compound terms denoting *karma*, destiny or fate, notably in the common expression 'len-chá' (*lan-chags*) meaning any bad thing which happens to someone which is looked on as retribution for crimes in a former life; '*ien-len*' is the expression of the dependence of one thing on another, recollection, consideration, or kindness.

ACKNOWLEDGEMENTS

I am grateful to Barbara Aziz, Nancy Levine, Geoffrey Samuel, Stephen Hugh-Jones, Christian Schickelgruber, and Nick Thomas for materials and discussions which were helpful in writing this paper.

REFERENCES

Allen, N. J. 1978 'Fourfold classification of society in the Himalayas', in James F. Fisher (ed.) *Himalayan Anthropology: the Indo-Tibetan Interface*, Mouton, The Hague and Paris.

Appadurai, Arjun (ed.) 1986 *The Social Life of Things: Commodities in Cultural Perspective,* Cambridge University Press, Cambridge.

Aris, Michael and Aung, San Sun Kyi (eds.) 1980 *Tibetan Studies in Honour of Hugh Richardson*, Aris and Phillips, Warminster.

Aziz, Barbara, 1977 *Tibetan Frontier Families*, Vikas, New Delhi.
  1978 'Social cohesion and reciprocation in a Tibetan community in Nepal', in J.
    Preston and B. Misra (eds.) *Community, Self and Identity*, Mouton, The
    Hague.
Baumgartner, R. 1980 *Trekking und Entwicklung ins Himalaya: die Rolwaling
    Sherpa in Ost-Nepal*, Rüegger, Diessenhofen.
Caplan, L. 1970 *Land and Social Change in East Nepal: a study of Hindu-tribal
    Relations,* Routledge and Kegan Paul, London; University of California Press,
    Berkeley.
Chapman, Anne 1980 'Barter as a universal mode of exchange', *L'Homme*, 20 (3),
    33–83.
Ekvall, Robert B. 1968 *Fields on the Hoof: Nexus of Tibetan Nomadic Pastoralism*,
    Holt, Rinehart and Winston, New York.
  1978 'Correlation of contradictions: a Tibetan semantic device', in James F.
    Fisher (ed.) *Himalayan Anthropology: the Indo-Tibetan Interface,* Mouton,
    The Hague, pp. 251–62.
Fisher, James F. 1986 *Trans-Himalayan Traders: Economy, Society and Culture in
    Northwest Nepal*, University of California Press, Berkeley.
Fürer-Haimendorf, Christoph von 1964 *The Sherpas of Nepal*, University of
    California Press, Berkeley.
  1971 'Status and interaction among the high castes of Nepal', *The Eastern
    Anthropologist*, 24, 7–24.
  1975 *Trans-Himalayan Traders*, Murray, London.
  1984 *The Sherpas Transformed*, New Delhi.
Gell, Alfred 1986 'Newcomers to the world of goods: consumption among the
    Muria Gonds', in Arjun Appadurai (ed.) *The Social Life of Things*, Cambridge
    University Press, Cambridge, pp. 110–40.
Gray, J. N. 1984 'Lamb auctions on the borders', *European Journal of Sociology*,
    25 (1), 59–82.
Gregory, C. A. 1982 *Gifts and Commodities*, Academic Press, London.
Grist, Nicky 1985 'Ladakh, a trading state', *Acta Biologica Montana*, 1985 (5),
    91–102.
Humphrey, Caroline 1985 'Barter and economic disintegration', *Man* (NS), 20,
    48–72.
Jest, Corneille 1975 *Dolpo: Communautes de Langue Tibetaine du Nepal*, Editions
    du CNRS, Paris.
  1978 'Tibetan communities of the high valleys of Nepal: life in an exceptional
    environment and economy', in James Fisher (ed.) *Himalayan Anthropology*,
    Mouton, The Hague, pp. 359–64.
Keesing, Roger M. 1985 'Conventional metaphors and anthropological meta-
    physics: the problematic of cultural translation', *Journal of Anthropological
    Research*, 41, 201–17.
Levine, Nancy E. 1981 'The Theory of Ru: kinship, descent and status in a Tibetan
    society', in Christoph von Furer-Haimendorf (ed.) *Asian Highland Societies in
    Anthropological Perspective*, Sterling Publishers, New Delhi, pp. 52–78.
  1987 'Caste, state and ethnic boundaries in Nepal', *Journal of Asian Studies*, 46
    (1), 71–88.
Lichter, David and Epstein, Lawrence, 1983 'Irony in Tibetan notions of the good

life', in Charles F. Keyes and E. Valentine Daniel (eds.) *Karma: an Anthropological Enquiry,* University of California Press, Berkeley.

McDougal, Charles 1968 *Village and Household Economy in far western Nepal,* Tribhuvan University, Kirtipur, Nepal.

 1979 *The Kulunge Rai: a study in Kinship and Marriage Exchange,* Ratna Pustak Bhandar, Kathmandu.

Ortner, S. B. 1978 *Sherpas Through their Rituals,* Cambridge University Press, Cambridge.

Parry, J. 1986 'The gift, the Indian gift, and the "Indian gift"', *Man,* 21 (n.s.).

Rhodes, N. 1980 'The development of currency in Tibet', in Aris and Aung (eds.) *Tibetan Studies in Honour of Hugh Richardson,* Aris and Phillips, Warminster, pp. 261–8.

Sacherer, Janice 1981 'The recent social impact and economic impact of tourism on a remote Sherpa community', in Furer-Haimendorf (ed.) *Asian Highland Societies in Anthropological Perspective,* Sterling, New Delhi, pp. 157–67.

Sahlins, Marshall 1972 *Stone Age Economics,* Aldine-Atherton, Chicago.

Schrader, Heiko 1988 *Trading Patterns in the Nepal Himalayas,* Verlag Breitenbach Publishers, Saarbrucken and Fort Lauderdale.

Scott, J. D. 1976 *The Moral Economy of the Peasant,* New Haven, Connecticut.

Strathern, Marilyn 1986 'Kinship and economy: constitutive orders of a provisional kind', *American Ethnologist,* 12, 191–209.

Thomas, Nicholas 1985 'Forms of personification and prestations', *Mankind,* 15 (3), 223–30.

Williams, Bernard 1985 *Ethics and the Limits of Philosophy,* Harvard University Press, Cambridge, Mass.

6 Inter-tribal commodity barter and reproductive gift-exchange in old Melanesia

Alfred Gell

1 Introduction

By and large, 'Maussian' gift institutions have had a favourable press in anthropology, and 'commodities' an unfavourable one (for an extreme case cf. Baudrillard, 1975). 'Gift–reciprocity–Good/market–exchange–Bad' is a simple, easy-to-memorise formula. But perhaps the tide is about to turn. Parry (1986, 1987) has exposed the 'moral ambiguity' of the gift in an Indian context. In what follows I propose a critique of 'gift-exchange' theory in a more familiar context. Melanesia is deservedly famous for the prevalence of 'ceremonial-exchange' institutions there, so much so that it is easy to forget that barter or trade was highly developed in 'old Melanesia' (i.e. Melanesia as it was in pre-colonial times). This fact is often forgotten, witness the paucity of the treatment given to commodity barter in both of the general monographs on Melanesian exchange and economy which have appeared in recent years (Rubel and Rosman, 1979; Gregory, 1982). I intend to demonstrate that this myopic stance concerning the presence of an indigenous commodity barter economy in old Melanesia has resulted in serious deficiencies in the theoretical treatment of 'exchange' in non-commercial contexts as well.

In this essay I propose the evidently rather daring hypothesis that Melanesian ceremonial exchange institutions, particularly the category of prestations which I call 'reproductive gifts' are symbolically derived from a 'template' which is provided by commodity barter. I believe that it is wrong to polarise 'gift' economy as if it were antithetical to commodity exchange, when in fact the relation is one of mutual implication, both materially and symbolically or rhetorically.

Thus, I am led to contest the idea that ceremonial exchange is a 'primordial' transactional form from which all other transactional forms may be conceived as deriving – 'after the Fall' as it were. On the contrary, I will suggest that ceremonial exchange is a hybrid product arising out of the ambiguous confrontation of two other transactional modes which may indeed be considered 'primordial', namely 'sharing' ('generalised reciprocity' in the terminology of Sahlins, 1965) and 'swapping' ('commodity exchange' as defined by Gregory, 1982). The potency of gift exchanges as constitutive features of social reproduction in Melanesian societies arises, not from the fact that 'the gift' expresses some Platonic Essence of sociable conduct, but precisely from the ambiguity of the gift between 'sharing' and 'swapping' – participating in features of both of these, without amounting to either. Neither flesh nor fowl nor good red herring, the gift is admirably calculated to divert attention and conceal motives while certain crucial re-arrangements of social relationships occur.

'Reproductive gift-exchange' in Melanesia arises through the re-casting of social relationships which could be conducted without material transfers of objects-as-gifts, into a relationship-idiom in which these transfers figure centrally. I hold that these transfers of gift-objects mimic the processes of commodity exchange which take place on the edges of 'societies' (units for the purposes of social reproduction) i.e. inter-tribal barter and the like. This re-contextualisation of the 'form' commodity exchange from the periphery to the centre of the social field affects it profoundly, so that the commodity exchange 'form' is not easily recognisable in 'the gift' and may be strenuously denied. But commodity exchange is, nonetheless, the prototype for the regime of 'reproductive gift exchanges' in Melanesian society, and, in its 'internalised' form, it provides a cover for the reformulation of crucial social relationships so as to permit a radical severance between reproduction as natural process and re-productive as a social process.

In order to introduce my argument, there are certain points which need to be established.

(1) I have to show that commodity exchange was an important feature of traditional Melanesian society; i.e. 'gift exchange' was not the *only* transactional mode available.

(2) I have to show that 'sharing' is different from gift exchange (and obviously from commodity exchange) and that 'sharing' was an important transactional mode in its own right.

Having made the case for (1) and (2), I will then go on to discuss the emergence of gift exchange. For present purposes, 'gift exchange' is to be understood as 'reproductive' gift exchange, i.e. prestations explicitly linked to phases in the relations between affinally linked groups (marriage-payments, child-payments, death-payments, and the like). I propose that 'reproductive gift exchange' corresponds to a reconstruction of the relationships involved in marriage and affinity on a 'template' provided by commodity exchange relationship, with the result that these relationships are removed from the sphere of economic relationships dominated by the ethos of 'sharing'. I interpret this shift as motivated by certain tensions inherent in Melanesian societies where commodity-exchange forms are contingently under-developed. I hazard the empirical generalisation that societies, such as Umeda, which have no access to commodity exchange networks, lack a regime of reproductive gift exchange as a direct consequence of this fact.

The 'tensions' which mark non-commodity-exchanging societies in Melanesia (and which motivate the emergence of the regime of re-productive gift exchange in societies elsewhere) have to do with gender politics. In non-commodity-exchanging societies men are placed in disadvantageous and conflictual relationships through their relationships with women, which are obviated, to some extent, once the transactional mode of 'reproductive gift exchange' is established. Having dealt with the impact of the regime of reproductive gift exchange in those societies in which commodity exchange is only a 'peripheral' element in economic organisation, I will conclude this essay by considering the situation in coastal/riverain societies in which commodity exchange is a 'dominant' factor in economic organisation. Some of these societies are dependent on barter for their basic subsistence, and here we note a further shift in the patterning of gender relations resulting from the emergence of women as independent commodity-exchange transactors in their own right.

2 Commodity exchange in old Melanesia

Let me begin by clarifying what I mean by 'commodity exchange' and by 'reproductive gift exchange' where these two terms are used contrastively. 'Commodities' are items which are alienated in exchange during at least one 'phase' of their existence (cf. Appadurai, 1986). Following Gregory, I define commodity exchange as the exchange of alienable objects between transactors in a state of mutual independence, and the exchange as one which establishes a qualitative relationship between exchange objects. When 'a given quantity' of X moves against 'an equivalent quantity' of Y, a commodity swap has occurred, and the transactors involved in the swap are 'quits' with respect to that transaction, whatever state their relationship towards one another may assume with respect to other transactions and other social contexts.

Gregory goes on to contrast commodity exchange with gift exchange, which he defines as the exchange of inalienable objects between transactors in a condition of reciprocal dependence, which establishes a qualitative relationship between the transactors rather than a quantitative relationship between the objects transacted. Here I differ from Gregory, because I believe that gift exchange is much more like commodity exchange than he is prepared to recognise.

My objections to Gregory's neat definition of gift exchange by simple inversion of the definitional properties of commodity exchange can be briefly outlined as follows.

(1) Objects *are* alienated in gift exchanges. In making a prestation, the donor loses access to the exchange-object, which passes to another, and with it the power to donate that object to a different recipient, whereas the recipient gains both of these. In making a prestation, an object of value is 'sacrificed', and the prestige, power, etc. conferred by the act of giving are proportional to the consensual evaluation of the onerousness of the sacrifice involved. What is not 'alienated' in gift-giving is not the gift-object itself, but that which *cannot* be alienated, namely, the social identity of the donor, which still attaches to the object after it has been given away. But there would be no increment of glory to the 'name' which clings to the object after it has been given away, unless the giving-away of the object were a genuine sacrifice or 'loss' to the giver, expressible as a series of opportunity costs incurred in not holding onto the object (for consumption or for disposition in some alternative, and possibly more advantageous, way).

(2) Gift-exchange partners who are in a debtor–creditor relationship, or who are 'mutually indebted' with respect to a multitude of incomplete transactions, are, as Gregory suggests, in a relation of dependency which extends over time. However, this feature cannot discriminate between commodity exchanges and gift exchanges for the following reasons. (1) This situation is just as prevalent in the sphere of relationships based on commodity exchanges, where debt, credit, and 'trust' between mutually dependent parties to a trading relationship may be all-important, and (2) even if it is true, *de facto*, that gift exchangers are indeed 'mutually dependent' this is not the objective which is actively sought, which is precisely the opposite, i.e. to be able to 'call it quits' after a long series of socially salient, high-prestige, transactions. If the objective actually were, as Gregory implies, to maximise outgoings so as to maximise 'indebtedness', the strategy of the 'big man' would be to seek out the 'rubbish man' and ply him with immense prestations, confident of never seeing them return. But nothing of the kind occurs; gifts are given to financial equals, individuals who can be trusted to return them, possibly with increment. The aim is to demonstrate autonomy, the ability to not get into debt or to waste substance on 'bad risks' in the gift/debt economy, while still maintaining a high volume of transactions. 'Dependency' of any kind is contrary both to the spirit and the practice of the economy of reproductive gifts, which is the means available to transactors to demonstrate 'equivalence' with exchange partners through a matching series of reciprocal prestations. And this 'matching' of powers in the sequence of gift exchanges is 'quantitative'. Gifts are accounted for and

precisely enumerated, just as they would be if they were commodities moving against commodities.

What distinguishes 'gifts' and 'commodities' is the *social context* of a particular transaction, not the character of relationship between people and things (alienable/inalienable) or between people and people (independent/dependent). For our purposes, 'gifts' are transactions in objects which occur in the contextual setting of social reproduction through marriage, affinity, and alliance. 'Commodity' transactions are transactions in objects in a setting definable as 'trade', 'barter' and the like. The objective is to understand the linkage between transactions in these two contextual settings.

Let me return to the first of the two points mentioned above. I promised to show, first of all, that commodity exchange was an important feature of traditional Melanesian society and that 'gift exchange' was not the *only* transactional mode to be encountered there, despite the absence (in general) of money, markets and the state. I could save space by simply asserting this, in the confidence that nobody at all familiar with the literature would be rash enough to gainsay such an elementary observation. However, it is necessary to emphasise the point, because, although well-supported in both the older and more modern ethnographies, it has been lost sight of in some of the more recent theoretical literature, notably the important synthesising contributions of Rubel and Rosman (1979) and Gregory (1982). In a recent article on Maring trade Healey writes:

[Gregory] gives insufficient attention to the importance of trade as a stimulus for production, and as a means for acquiring goods for circulation in prestations. The effect is to deconstitute the economy and results in a failure to examine the interconnections between forms and objectives of production, distribution and consumption. The indigenous economy is then effectively reduced to production for subsistence and gift exchange, and the circulation of valuables in prestations alone. (Healey 1986: 129).

These strictures are applied to Gregory, but they are of wider application. In fact, hinterland inhabited areas of old Melanesia were usually, though not universally, criss-crossed by inter-tribal trade routes in pre-contact times, and for the New Guinea highlands a comprehensive survey of inter-tribal trade has been published by Hughes (1977, cf. Brookfield and Hart, 1971) detailing both the routes used and the objects which moved along them. Objects characteristically moved between five and fifty miles, though occasionally much further. In this traffic 'markets' were exceptional (Epstein, 1968; Salisbury, 1970; Gewertz, 1978, 1983). In the hinterland, trade was conducted through individualised trade partnerships between men, who met periodically, in person, to exchange trade items. At these meetings information would be relayed about 'demand' for items up and

down the exchange road, since traders were involved in trade relationships with a variety of partners located in different places.

Inland, traders were sometimes, but not necessarily, specialised producers of one or more trade commodity, otherwise acting as middlemen
between producers and end-users. Here – but not on the coast – there are
no recorded instances of communities which could be said to be trade
dependent for basic subsistence (vegetable food). Hinterland trade was
'peripheral' barter between men belonging to distinct social groups, not
mutually implicated (by marriage) in 'reproducing' each other. Hughes
states that trade in pre-contact days was recalled with a good deal of
nostalgia by old men who had been involved in it, as an exciting,
prestigious, and profitable male pursuit.

But there is no suggestion that the objects distributed through trade
channels among hinterland societies were of overwhelming utilitarian
significance; the hinterlands could have 'got by' without inter-tribal trade,
and the fact that they did not do so must be attributed to factors other than
stringent material requirements.

In coastal/riverain Melanesia the situation is different, since here we
find a number of communities which are dependent on trade for their
continued existence. Trade-dependent communities maintain 'ecological'
adaptations which necessitate ongoing trade in vegetable staples as well as
'valuables' (Hogbin, 1951 (Busama); Schwartz, 1963 (Manus); Harding,
1970 (Siassi); Malinowski, 1915 (Mailu) cf. Irwin 1983). More recent
studies by Gewertz, 1983 (Chambri); Lipset, 1985; and Barlow, 1985
(Murik lakes) have greatly increased our knowledge of such communities
and further investigations are in progress (Macintyre on Tubetube, 1983).
Such trade-dependent communities are located sporadically all around the
coast of New Guinea (except the south-west coast of Papua) and off the
main islands of the Bismark archipelago. Trade-dependent, or partly
trade-dependent communities are also to be found along the lower and
middle Sepik, whose cultures are in many ways 'coastal' in character,
despite being situated inland.

What can one say about the general characteristics of inter-tribal barter
trade in old Melanesia? I cannot attempt to provide a summary of the main
items involved in the coastal or hinterland trades (for details, see references
cited above), but there is one point which emerges from archaeological
work in the area which deserves notice. It seems clear that the emergence,
particularly along the coast, of trade 'centres' where specialised production
for trade is undertaken, and which exercise local monopolies in certain
trades, supported by restrictive practices governing the export of technology and 'trade secrets', has been a progressive development in the
course of Melanesian pre-history (Irwin, 1983). In earlier epochs it would
appear, for instance, that pottery production took place at a larger number

of sites along the coast (and in consequence, pottery was traded over shorter distances) than was found to be the case at contact. The pottery production centres in operation at the time of contact were, moreover, often dependent on other communities for their raw material (clay) from whom it was obtained by barter, yet the clay-providing communities made no pots themselves. The underlying 'specialisation' of the pot-making communities was not in pot manufacture by itself, so much as in the physical and social technologies of trade and distribution. Outside these specialised trade centres, pot-making had become a 'lost art'.

These interesting observations point toward a more general conclusion. 'Barter trade' as an economic phenomenon is often interpreted as a reflection of ecological discontinuities (the inherently uneven distribution of particular resources needed for the production of commodities in general demand throughout a trade region). But, even admitting that the resource-base of particular communities in old Melanesia was of uneven composition, there seems to be a 'drive' towards local specialisation in production for barter trade which emanates not from ecological disconti- nuities *per se*, but from the mechanism (trade) which seeks to redress these discontinuities.

But such a drive towards trade specialisation can only be explained on the basis of a cultural mechanism which predisposes communities to participate eagerly in commodity exchange even when local production could provide substitutes for commodities obtainable through trade. It seems clear that commodities obtained by trade are often at a premium simply because they are obtained through these channels, i.e. commodity exchange, as a transactional form, confers value on product which they would not otherwise possess. One can see this occurring in connection with the widespread trade in salt in the highlands. The basic know-how for producing 'salt', by burning leaves etc. or wood steeped in natural brine, is known to most highlands groups, but only a few of them (for example the Baruya) have become specialised salt-producers, and these tribes produce quantities for trade. Once a 'brand' of salt is established, local substitutes are no longer acceptable, despite the existence of the technical means to produce them. The exotic import is at a premium because it is bound up with a transactional mode (commodity exchange) which is positively valued and which confers value on commodities.

But if, as I have suggested, commodity exchange is a favoured transactional mode, gratifying to participants independently of the use- value of the items passing to and fro, does this mean that commodity exchange, in its Melanesian form is really 'Maussian' gift exchange – i.e. a 'non-commercial' 'prestige' transaction dominated by political, rather than 'economising' or utility-maximising motives?

One can certainly discount the existence throughout most of the region, of a 'market' economy in pre-modern times; trade was carried on, and value-ratios between commodities were set, in the absence of the 'market' situation of generalised competition between sellers to find buyers, and among buyers to find sellers. Rates of exchange between trade partners were not arrived at by haggling, but by convention, and were altered only in response to change in overall circumstances (political circumstances as much as economic ones) and had little sensitivity to short-term fluctuation in supply and demand. Ratios were 'lagged' to a very marked degree, or completely immobilised (for an excellent discussion, cf. Modjeska, 1985).

The question we have therefore to face is whether 'avidity for trade' (Sahlins, 1972) and relative indifference to 'costs' in energy/labour/time terms gives us grounds for asserting that 'trade' in old Melanesia was motivated by 'social' considerations, so that barter was indeed gift reciprocity oriented towards 'Maussian' objectives. The general argument of this essay depends on giving partial – but only partial – assent to this proposition. The basic format of a 'partnership' sustained by the passage of valuables between partners is indeed common to both gift exchange (reproductive and ceremonial) and barter exchange. But commodity exchange is, nevertheless, distinct, and perceived to be distinct, from the kinds of exchanges which enter into the process of social reproduction.

There can be no suggestion, for instance, that 'big-men' are 'big' traders. An Iatmul big-man, for instance, has two possible sources of shell rings; he can obtain them by participating in internal exchange, or he can trade for them, by offering stone axes (obtained via Chambri from the Sepik hills) to Sawos trade partners. The literature contains nothing to suggest that the 'trade' strategy has a significance, in the careers of known Iatmul big-men, which is comparable to the significance of 'internal' exchange. Yet the Iatmul continued to trade with the Sawos and fought wars with one another over access to Sawos villages. Trade relationships are valuable and politically important, but are not directly articulated to the internal exchange processes which determine internal political standing. The emphasis in the literature is on trade as a source of excitement and social enjoyment, rather than as a basis for power. (For comparison, in the context of Indian 'tribal' society, cf. Gell, 1982, 1986.)

Nonetheless, it would be mistaken to suppose that because commodity exchange is gratifying to participants, it is 'ceremonial' or 'ritual', not oriented towards obtaining commodities. It would be no less true to say of a Baniya at an Indian Bazaar, a commodity exchanger to his very bones, that he found in the activity of trading a deep source of pleasure and excitement. Indeed, there is a sense in which trading, as an activity, must, almost by definition, be a source of subjective gratification, since to trade is to accept a more-valued commodity in exchange for a less-valued one. That is happiness.

3 The indigenous service economy

It may be said, therefore, that in hinterland areas of old Melanesia low volume inter-group barter trade was pervasive as a valued masculine activity, and that in coastal and some riverain areas 'trade-dependent' societies existed, and trading activity was quite intense. My argument is that this pervasive network of commodity exchange inflected internal processes of social reproduction in most old Melanesian societies in a specific direction. In order to demonstrate this point, it is necessary that I should sketch in the pattern of social reproduction in old Melanesia in the absence of this influencing factor, so as to show the 'baseline' state of affairs, before the commodity exchange template takes hold. It is possible to do this, because there are a few Melanesian societies in which, for historically contingent reasons, inter-group commodity exchange is not practised; and I am prepared to generalise empirically by saying that in these societies 'reproductive' exchange is not practised either.

One such non-commodity exchanging society is Umeda, where I did my own fieldwork (Gell, 1975). In Umeda, there are no imported shells, valuables, axes, etc., and virtually no domesticated pigs – and there are no marriage-payments, child-payments, death-payments, and the like; i.e. no 'ceremonial' or 'Maussian' exchanges of any importance. I believe that these facts are linked together.

At this point I intend to make certain suggestions about Umeda society which are, from a Melanesian standpoint, rather heterodox, and at variance (interpretatively speaking) with the account of Umeda which I published in 1975. I am now persuaded, shocking as this may seem, that 'exchange' – any kind of exchange – plays no significant part in Umeda social reproduction. It is difficult to make this assertion for two reasons. Firstly, there is the weight of opinion from Mauss, Lévi-Strauss, etc. which holds that social communication, the exchange of women, gifts, commodities, messages, and so on, are essential to the constitution of any social order whatsoever, and Umeda cannot possibly be an exception to this universal rule. Secondly there is the 'received version' of the trend in Melanesian social evolution, which is expounded in both of the recent general monographs on the subject, by Rubel and Rosman (1979) and Gregory (1982) and which is referred to in more general terms by other writers, such as Godelier (1986). This received version holds that even where exchange of valuables, such as pigs and shells, is poorly developed, 'exchange' is still fundamental because social reproduction is based on the exchange of women between exogamous clans or lineages i.e. on affinal reproductive 'gifts'.

The foundation of the social order is the exchange of women, described by Gregory (echoing Williams) as 'the supreme gift'. Gregory and Rosman and Rubel both suggest that the most 'elementary' forms of social organisation in Melanesia are manifested by societies which practise direct woman-exchange, i.e. 'sister-exchange'. Marriage-payments and the like come in subsequently as a means of obviating direct woman-exchange, replacing a ceded sister not with a sister, but with an array of valuables, so as to expand the scope and complexity of social organisation beyond an exogamous moiety structure. These authors propose what one could call a 'from the bottom up' interpretation of reproductive gift exchanges; these exchanges 'were once' (at the bottom of the scale) woman-for-woman exchanges, and have been transformed and expanded into exchanges of women against valuables, and latterly, in response to intensification of production, into exchanges of valuables against valuables, as in ceremonial exchange systems of the Moka/Tee type.

My interpretation can be contrasted to this one as a 'from the top down' interpretation; reproductive gift exchange results from the extension of 'external' commodity exchange type relations into the domain of affinal relations between groups interested in each other's reproduction.In order to substantiate the 'from the top down' interpretation, I have to show that 'reproduction' can be carried on *without* exchange, and that is what I will now attempt to show.

It is conceivable, to me at least, that all socially necessary activity can be carried out by individuals as a result of moral obligation, not because these individuals stand in relations of reciprocal 'exchange' with other individuals. Thus, to cite the most fundamental instance, the sexual division of labour is not sustained by reciprocity between the sexes (a pact to make mutual sacrifices for the benefit of the other) but is sustained by role expectations applying to men and women respectively, as duly socialised persons. Women behave as women, and perform the duties appertaining to the roles of daughters, wives, sisters, mothers, etc. not because the services they perform are reciprocated, but because they are obliged to do so, and are morally responsible for their behaviour. Services are performed according to role-definitions, and, although there is 'harmony' (more or less) in the patterning of interlocking role-relationships, so that they form a coherent system for practical purposes, this systematicity is not sustained by an ethos of the mutual exchange of equivalent sacrifices, i.e. 'reciprocity'. The prescribed role-definitions oblige each and every person to perform services towards prescribed others in accordance with the division of labour by sex and age, and the recognition of kinship statuses. Moral obligation dictated by role-definitions provides a basis for a political economy and social–reproductive regime, which I will name 'the indigenous service economy'. In such an economy, material transfers between individuals (food changing hands between one person and another, for instance) occur as a function of the existence of a moral obligation, incumbent on the transferring party, to 'provision' the transferred-to party to the transaction in some respect. For instance, the provisioning of children by parents involves material transfers which flow directly from the moral definition of role-relationships between parents and children, and are not 'prestations' which produce, or repay, 'debts'. In the Indigenous Service Economy material transfers are the physical embodiment of 'service' obligations.

The Indigenous Service Economy corresponds, partly, to what Sahlins calls 'generalised reciprocity' in his (all too) well-known paper on the 'Sociology of Primitive Exchange' (1965). But to call 'sharing' (and domestic provisioning) 'reciprocity' is most misleading, because in households reciprocal relations are just what one doesn't find. Asymmetrical role-relationships are the order of the day (Hu/Wi, Pa/Chi, EBr/Ybr, Br/Si etc.). One cannot discuss, under the rubric of 'reciprocity', transfers of objects and performance of services in a transactional context, which is specifically designed as the one in which role-relationships are asymmetrical and incommensurable, accounts are not kept, and in which recompense for sacrifices made cannot be demanded, and need never be forthcoming.

It is therefore quite wrong to imply, as Sahlins does, that gift exchange (balanced reciprocity) is emergent in the transactional context of intra-household generalised reciprocity. Gift exchange – in which accounts are kept, and recompense must be forthcoming – is defined in *contrast* to what goes on inside households, or, more generally, in the Indigenous Service Economy. 'Generalised' and 'balanced' are not two alternative forms of reciprocity; balanced reciprocity is reciprocity, because 'balance' (comparability of mutual sacrifices) is built into the notion of reciprocity as such: 'generalised' reciprocity is the absence of reciprocity, i.e. non-reciprocity.

My general point, in all this, is that the exchange economy (the reproductive gift exchange) is to be understood as the means for the reformulation of the basis of human relationships in terms *other* than those set by the Indigenous Service Economy. 'Exchange' provides an escape route from a social order in which objects are transferred, and services performed, out of moral obligation, substituting for it one in which transfers and services can be conceptualised in terms of the schema of the mutually advantageous exchange of sacrifices.

I introduce Umeda, at this point, in order to exemplify social reproduction in a regime in which the Indigenous Service Economy is dominant. But societies of this kind have been given another, and more perspicuous name: 'bride-service' societies. It is under this rubric that they have been described by Collier and Rosaldo (1981) in an article which has decisively altered my understanding of Umeda society and affinal relations, as will become very apparent as I proceed.

'Bride-service' societies are simple societies in which the main expression of affinal relations is the imposition of service obligations on married persons *vis-à-vis* their in-laws, rather than the institutionalisation of marriage payments or other reproductive exchanges. What most distinguishes bride-service societies, especially from the standpoint of the argument currently being advanced, is the onerous and 'marked' character of the son-in-law *vis-à-vis* the wife's parents. Sons-in-law become, to a greater or lesser degree, appendages of their wife's parents, obliged to serve and provision them while they live, and these obligations descend to the junior generation as obligations to serve and provision the mother's brother. Collier and Rosaldo point out that in bride-service societies, women are not seen as group 'reproducers' but as bait for sons-in-law and the focus of male sexual rivalry. As points-of-attachment for client-like sons-in-law, they have room for manoeuvre, and enjoy a degree of premarital sexual freedom as well as having scope for adulterous liaisons subsequently. Their position with respect to male peers is relatively advantageous. On the other hand, the position of young men is relatively disadvantageous, since, though they all desire to get married (eventually), to do so is to come under the sway of their wives' relatives.

Umeda is a 'bride-service society' on Collier and Rosaldo lines. Unfortunately, I did not understand this fully when I was in the field, or immediately afterwards, because at that time I was still under the sway of the 'exchange/reciprocity' model of Melanesian society, and was determined to see 'sister-exchange' as the primordial transaction in Umeda social reproduction. If (anachronistically) Collier and Rosaldo's essay could have been brought to my attention at the relevant time, I might have been less scornful of the emphatic testimony of my informants, who were mostly young men belonging precisely to the category for whom the downside of marriage, for males in a bride-service society, loomed most ominously. Vain regret! Misled myself, I have been all too successful in misleading others, notably my colleague Chris Gregory.

4 Umeda affinity: bride-service and sister-exchange

Umeda is situated in unfavourable terrain in the Border Mountains of the West Sepik Province, PNG. Umeda was excluded from significant intertribal barter trade by a number of factors. To the north, there is a trade route which runs along the relatively densely occupied Wasengla valley, which articulates with trade routes along the north coast of New Guinea and West Irian. But informants' accounts suggested that relations with

Wasengla valley tribes were unremittingly hostile in pre-pacification times, and the Umedas did not dare venture into the no-man's land lying between themselves and the Wasengla valley (the *Aw-sis*, the limit of their world) across which Wasengla raiding parties would periodically make forays. I found no artefacts of Wasengla manufacture in Umeda, suggestive of active trade; the Umedas having nothing to offer that was coveted by the Wasenglas except their hunting territory. To the south, Umeda had social relations, but not trade relations, with Punda, and Punda with Yafar etc., but these inter-village relations did not involve trade, and were tenuous at best. The Sepik, with its abundance of trade routes, was inaccessible to all of these communities, which were exceptionally small, scattered, and basically nomadic. Umeda was entirely self-sufficient in items which, elsewhere, are typically exported and imported. Umedas manufactured their own salt, lime, and paint; created their own dog- and pig-teeth ornaments, decorative net-bags, purses, hair-ribbons; and obtained their plumes, furs, etc. by hunting. Umedas also made all their own stone tools, sago-pounders (still manufactured and in universal use in 1979–80) and small axes, which were obsolescent by the time I arrived.

Umedas were nomadic for most of the year, working in family groups at isolated sago-stands, hunting, gathering, and engaged in desultory gardening. They were, in fact, hunter–gatherer-like in many respects. They possessed the 'sharing' ethos to a marked degree, and the corresponding lack of interest in amassing personal property. Umeda women had the 'sexy', rather than 'reproductive', image so well-described by Collier and Rosaldo. The basic theme in Umeda society was male sexual rivalry, fired up by the capriciousness and sexual manipulativeness of women.

The essential point about Umeda in terms of this discussion, is that sons-in-law were obliged to live and work in the bush with their in-laws for extended periods. In the bush, men practised shifting residence between camps located in their own clan-territory, their wife's clan-territory, and the clan-territory of their matrikin. While residing with affines, husbands undertook two main kinds of work, viz. hunting and pounding sago. Umeda is rather unusual in that the heavy work of pounding up the pith of the sago log, preparatory to washing the starch out of it (which is done by women) is exclusively a male task. This pounding work is done by sons-in-law while residing with affines, and they eat and live as members of their affines' sago-working camp. They also hunt, collect wild food, and assist in gardening. This account of Umeda bride-service obligations is duplicated among the neighbouring Yafar described by Juillerat (1986) except that, among the Yafar, men leave pounding sago to women.

Umeda youths with whom I discussed these matters were most demonstrative about the disadvantages of marriage, of which the outstanding one was the 'shame' (*loweh*: the word for brother-in-law) of having to live intimately with in-laws in a subservient and patronisable condition. Only after many years of marriage and the demise of the wife's parents did these obligations disappear, at which time sons assumed obligations towards their fathers' affines (as sisters' sons) and, through having daughters, men might begin to patronise sons-in-law of their own.

But Umeda youths were most unwilling to step onto this treadmill, and dreamed of escaping to the coast and to a condition of permanent bachelorhood (and access to prostitutes, since, in their eyes, sex on a 'strictly cash' basis was as enticing as it was unobtainable locally). At the same time, however, they did everything within their power to attract the favourable attention of potential wives and fathers-in-law. They hunted assiduously, beautified themselves, and would, in earlier times have sought occasions to demonstrate their bravery in war.

Bride-service institutions give rise to a basic tension because men as hunters, fighters, and lovers are encouraged to become equal and independent, but hunting, fighting, and love-making inexorably lead to affinal servitude, a condition of subservience from which only increasing age offers any escape, and that a very uncertain one. One finds a pervasive contradiction between the 'autonomous' values of the 'male republic' (male–male solidarity, hunting, 'sporting' warfare between traditional enemies and so on) and the 'shameful' inequality which comes from marriage, domesticity, and affinal servitude.

But if this is a correct interpretation of Umeda marriage, why did I not perceive this originally? Why did I find it so easy to represent Umeda (as on the whole I did) as one dominated by an 'exchange' mentality?

There are two features of Umeda society which seem, at first glance, to support an 'exchange' interpretation of Umeda marriage and affinity. They are (i) the systematic transfer of meat (of wild game, notably wild pigs) from wife-receivers to wife-givers, and (ii) the common and recognised practice of 'sister-exchange' in this society.

Let me deal briefly with (i). As in many hunting–gathering societies, Umeda hunters were strictly forbidden to eat any part of game which they had killed themselves. Meat was given, as a matter of stringent obligation, to those individuals to whom the hunter was connected via a female tie, i.e. wife's parents, matrikin, sister and sister's husband, and so on. Of these gifts, the largest and most important went to the wife's parents. Once the affinal and maternal portions had been packed and distributed, the remainder of the animal was shared generally in the camp.

Now it could be argued that these portions of killed game sent to affines are 'prestations' which reflect the presence of woman-debt incurred by wife-receivers with respect to wife-givers, and that is indeed how I originally interpreted them. But this is not correct. The affinal portions are not 'presents' which are 'given' – they are 'shares' which are 'sent' (*asmhui-*

piav). No debt is repaid, instead, it is an obligatory service which is being carried out, i.e. the son-in-law's obligation to hunt for his parents-in-law. The meat is not an exchange-object at all, but a by-product of a service obligation dictated by the Indigenous Service Economy. It is in this respect comparable to the pounded sago pith, or gathered wild foods, with which the son-in-law is likewise obliged to furnish his parents-in-law. On the other hand, meat differs from these in being associated with 'prestige' male values, and this is a point I will return to later.

Next let me take up point (ii) above, i.e. 'sister-exchange'. Quite a high proportion of the marriages I recorded were between sets of siblings and could be counted as 'sister-exchanges'. However, there was absolutely no question that sister-exchange marriages were more legitimate or approved than any other kind of marriage. What 'legitimated' marriage was the recognition of affinal service obligations, not recompense of a woman for a woman. In fact, when I asked about sister-exchange, Umeda informants claimed that it was an innovation of the recent past, having been imposed on them by the first Dutch patrols in the area, as a device to lessen fighting. Umedas went on to say that it was much better, in their eyes, to seduce a woman or obtain one by violence, and that exchanging sisters was an unappealing strategy which would procure only unappealing girls (too young or too old, or with skin rashes) but that they were obliged to follow it because to do otherwise was to run the risk of being imprisoned on charges of fighting or rape by the colonial authorities.

I discounted all this and went on doggedly totting up 'exchange' marriages so that I could represent it as a 'rule' of marriage, despite the fact that I never discovered an Umeda term which specifically distinguished 'exchange' from 'non-exchange' marriages. And of course I could do this, since there were many marriages of this kind, and a clear awareness, on the part of informants, that certain movements of girls in marriage had been precipitated by the need to square accounts between sets of siblings united by previous marriages. 'Sister-exchange', as a practice, is not at all mythical; but the question is – does sister-exchange really count as 'exchange' in the commonly understood sense?

In a sense, the whole notion of 'sister-exchange' is nonsensical, because if A and B were really to 'exchange sisters', A's sister would become B's sister, and B's sister A's sister, and neither would be any nearer obtaining a wife for himself. Given that *by definition* A's sister is unmarriageable for A, and B's sister is unmarriageable for B, which we may assume, then in permitting their sisters to marry elsewhere they are 'giving up' nothing for which reciprocation might reasonably be demanded. In fact, when B marries A's sister, she continues to be A's sister, just as she was before, and B's sister, now married to A, is B's sister still; A and B's sisters are A and B's *married* sisters, which is what, in the nature of things, they must become. There is no logical reason for supposing that marriage interferes in any way with descent or siblingship. It can be represented as doing so, but it certainly does not do so by necessity. If A getting married to B's sister is not an infringement of any right or power that B, as her sibling, has over her (which certainly does not include the right to expect wifely services from her) then her marriage to A is in no sense a sacrifice, made by B for the benefit of A. And if this marriage, considered in isolation, is not a sacrifice made by B for the benefit of A, it follows that the reciprocal marriage of B to A's sister is not the means of requiting this never-outstanding sacrifice. Since neither has made any sacrifice, sacrifices cannot be mutually exchanged.

The rationale for sister-exchange is quite different, as the Umedas made clear, had I been prepared to listen. In bride-service societies, males compete for women, and gaining a wife is a mark of social approval with respect to prowess in hunting, fighting, and the art of making one's self sexually attractive. The 'losers' with respect to any marriage, are not the girl's male kin, but the eligible competitor males, who might have got to marry the girl, but in the end did not prevail. Sister-exchange does two things: (i) it establishes parity of social esteem between men in relationships of symmetrical affinity, and (ii) it reduces conflict between men who are not affines and who might otherwise come into damagingly competitive struggles over a restricted number of available marriageable women.

Despite the existence of sister-exchange as a means of moderating male conflict over the distribution of brides, social reproduction in societies such as Umeda is not founded on reproductive 'gifts' taking the form of women. In fact social reproduction is carried out via the institution of marriage, and the accompanying obligations of services and provisioning, i.e. by the Indigenous Service Economy.

In the absence of 'exchange' as a primordial institution in this 'simple' Melanesian society there seems no reason to posit the 'elaboration' of exchange institutions (sister-exchange → marriage payments → ceremonial exchange) as the trajectory of social evolution in Melanesia, as envisaged by the 'from the bottom up' interpretation mentioned above. In the simplest Melanesian societies, the ones cut off from the commodity exchange nexus, there is no 'exchange' to be elaborated. There is no 'gift' economy, no gifts either in object-form or in the form of persons.

But there is, so to speak, 'space' for exchange, a space which, in Umeda, for contingent ethnohistorical reasons, remains unfilled. This space lies within the confines of the masculine republic, within which men can exchange blows or caresses, insults or compliments, but not *objects*, unless they have objects to dispose of, which in Umeda they do not. But, even in Umeda, they almost dispose of gift-able objects, in two senses. Firstly, men are, by virtue of their hunting specialisation, associated with transfers of high-prestige, high-value, low-volume food (meat), which, as a comestible, can be focalised and quantified in a way which bulk staples (cooperatively produced by both sexes) cannot be. These meat transfers are, so to speak, precursors of gifts within the Indigenous Service Economy. Secondly, the seductive notion of 'sister-exchange' as an exchange of women – false though this is – exercises its enchantment not only on misguided anthropologists, but equally on many of the practitioners of this strategy. Sister-exchange is not exchange, but, given the conceptual possibility of construing affinity in general as an exchange process, it can readily be made to appear so. It is a rhetorical trope ripe for strategic misuse. Thus a society like Umeda can be considered 'pre-adapted' for the emergence of a regime of reproductive gifts, while remaining itself within the confines of the Indigenous Service Economy.

The next step in the argument must be to attempt to isolate the mechanisms for the transformation (in structural, rather than historical, terms) of systems of social reproduction conducted on the basis of the Indigenous Service Economy into systems of social reproduction conducted on the basis of reproductive gift exchange. My claim is that commodity exchange plays a crucial role in this transformation.

5 The obviation of bride-service: Maring trade and marriage-payments

Commodity barter, as Marx pointed out, arises at the boundaries of social systems. These boundaries are a male preserve, physically and symbolically, because men are specialists in hunting and violence. In the hinterland, barter trading is masculine and disarticulated from social reproduction – in particular from the processes of the Indigenous Service Economy, and the inequalities inherent in affinity. At the margins of the world, men encounter other men in war and trade, but not as parties interested in reproducing one another. In this mutual disinterestedness there is exhilaration, danger (violence is never far from the surface) but also solace. Solidary relationships, no longer fateful, no longer charged with the inescapable burdens of moral conflict, assume a sharply positive diacritical weighing against the background condition of generalised suspicion and hostility. They assume the form, not of role-complementarities or the uneasy rivalry of social peers obliged to support one another yet always pitted against one another, but of 'partnerships' – alliances maintained against all the world, peers and enemies alike. Trade partnerships are in a sense subversive, in the way that Simmel claimed that our love relationships are subversive.

At these social boundaries, it would be vain to look for a 'market' because there is no hegemonic power to exert the peace of the market-place. The 'trade partnership' in which each partner guarantees, as far as possible, the safety of the other in their mutual trading activities is the absolutely necessary condition for the existence of commodity exchange. As such, it stands as a primordial form of social relationship, antithetical in every respect to the moral basis of relationships dictated by the Indigenous Service Economy.

Traders do not meet to exchange compliments, but to exchange commodities; the voluntaristic amoralism of a partnership 'against all the world' can only be sustained through the transactional schema of object-exchange, because, lacking 'personal' referents, the relationship can only be established with reference to things, which are all that the parties to it have in common. In exchange, objects are focalised, quantified, valued, and so on; and there is recognition of debt, credit, and reciprocity. It is the transaction of these objects, now commodities, which sustains the partnership, and, because the partnership-relation is valued as an end in itself, the objects involved carry a symbolic charge stemming from this source; they are over-valued because their presence evokes a valued relationship and a privileged kind of social interaction. Where there could be enmity and danger, lo! – there is this shell, the axe...

Let this suffice as a sketch of the ideological associations of commodity exchange in the hinterland. I turn now to a more detailed consideration of commodity exchange, marriage, and reproductive gifts in a New Guinea Highlands society which is no longer dominated by the Indigenous Service Economy. The example I have chosen is the Maring (Healey, 1978, 1984, 1986). What is the relation between commodity exchange and reproductive gift exchange in a medium-intensity highlands society of this type?

The first point which needs to be made is that among the Maring the physical inputs into reproductive exchanges are originally derived from barter sources. Maring society is not trade-dependent, yet the Maring have contrived to make themselves 'artificially' trade-dependent in that the volume of their reproductive and ceremonial exchanges, both in valuables and pigs, could not be sustained without inter-tribal barter trade. This is indeed the almost invariable state of affairs among comparable societies in Melanesia having significant levels of reproductive exchange. Not physi-cally dependent on enemies and trade partners for subsistence, they are dependent on them for essential contributions to the internal circulation of symbolically essential items; for which they must pay with their exports.

In recent times Maring have participated in two major trading complexes; the trade in salt against axes (in which they acted as middle-men, producing neither themselves) and the trade in shells and pigs against fur and feathers in which they acted both as middle-men and as producers (of fur and feathers). Axes were a component of marriage-payments, as were shells. Nowadays, money functions as a 'valuable' in exchanges of this kind, replacing shells. This is not to be interpreted as 'commercial-isation' of exchange, just because a modern medium of exchange, which has been partially inflation-proofed, is preferred to shells, which have been in excess supply. The availability of money enables Maring to conduct transactions in 'sound money' which is what shells used to be, but are no longer. Money is what has saved the 'traditional' exchange system from total eclipse, here and elsewhere in the highlands, and is by no means the factor tending to subvert it.

Healey has provided a detailed account of Maring trade (1978, 1984). The theoretical issue raised by his work is that, whereas it is clear that Maring traders regarded their trade partners as 'exchange partners' in the usual Melanesian fashion, nevertheless these men are indisputably engaged in commodity barter, and their relationship is terminologically distin-guished by the Maring themselves, from the relationship existing between parties, to 'internal' exchanges.

Partners are constrained to trade with one another and to keep the relation alive with a flow of valuables; laggard performance may invite retribution in the form of sorcery. The objective of trade is the transaction of valuable objects, but the accumulation of wealth is not the aim in view; once acquired, trade items must be passed on or fed into internal exchanges. Maring trade, according to Healey, has a strongly 'sociable' character. 'In practice [trade] is a mode of expressing social relationships via a balanced exchange of valuables' (1986:141). But, if barter is an 'expression of social relationships', does it not collapse into Maussian exchange, the Maring rhetorical distinction between gift- and trade-transactions notwith-standing?

Current orthodoxy might favour this very conclusion, but consider:

(1) Social reproduction without gift or commodity exchange is possible, as the Umeda example shows.
(2) Maring gift exchange is physically dependent on inputs which are commodities (i.e. alienated).

In other words, the question is not whether Maring commodity exchange equates with gift exchange, but the other way about; i.e., whether gift exchange equates with commodity exchange. It seems more logical to suppose that commodity exchange is 'primordial' in that (i) commodity exchange is logically separable from the processes of social reproduction *per se*, and (ii) social reproduction can occur without exchange, either of commodities or gifts. Hence 'reproductive gift exchange' is logically a dependent variable of social reproduction and commodity exchange, which are independent variables (not dependent on each other or on

reproductive gift exchange). Whereas reproductive gift exchange is
dependent on both.

Let me pass on to an examination of the constituents of the Maring
regime of reproductive gift exchanges. Here, I think, one is better able to
grasp the essentially artificial character of gift exchange – mimicry of
commodity exchange in an internal, reproductive, context – and the way in
which the Indigenous Service Economy continues to exist in a disguised
and modified form under a veneer of reciprocal exchange of sacrifices in
'gift' form.

Marriage-payments are made to the bride's father and brothers after a
number of years of marriage and usually the birth of one or more children.
Payments are made in two media (pork and shells/valuables) and is
divided into two components comprising both media of exchange. The first
component is assembled by the groom himself and is transferred to the
bride's father and brothers. This component is never reciprocated in kind.
The second, and much larger component (2 or 3 times larger) is contributed
by members of the groom's clan and political support-group, is passed by
him to the bride's father and brothers, who distribute it to their clan and
supporters. This component has to be reciprocated subsequently by the
recipients. The assembling, re-distribution, and eventual reciprocation of
the second component of the marriage payment articulates both intra- and
extra-clan male–male relationships in an idiom of the reciprocal exchange
of valuables. But it also serves as a 'cover' for the actually unreciprocated
component paid by the groom himself to his wife's agnates.

In this way Maring achieve two contradictory objectives simultaneously.
The second component and its reciprocation serve to locate marriage in a
transactional setting dominated by equivalent and reciprocal male–male
exchange relationships, as if, so to speak, marriage were little more than a
pretext for the serious business of life, which concerns men exclusively and
which places them, as exchangers, in the centre stage in the process of social
reproduction. At the same time, this screen of 'diversionary' transactions
serves to cover the really crucial, but relatively covert, unreciprocated
payment of the 'real' bride price. But what does this payment represent?

It seems to me that what this payment does is to permit the groom to get
on equal terms with his affines, i.e. to obviate the direct expression of
obligation through the performance of bride-service by means of a payment
in lieu. It is the means of converting a potential 'patron' into a 'partner'.
Reproductive exchanges do not abolish social distance, they create it; and
in so doing they liberate Maring husbands from the intimacies which so
terrify an Umeda youth contemplating his matrimonial future.

Through the reformulation of affinity in the idiom of exchange, the
peripheral is made central, and relations between men, mediated by
valuables (which they control) replace relations between men mediated by

women (whom they do not control). The peripheral barter-exchange schema provides an idiom for an all-male social universe, weakening the position of women accordingly. Moreover, as this transactionalisation and musculinsation of the processes of social reproduction takes place, the Indigenous Service Economy becomes an almost all-female affair, in which male participation becomes more and more marginal.

One can see this most clearly if one takes a closer look at the 'pork' constituent of the groom's component of the marriage payment (the meat of three or four pigs from the groom's herd slaughtered for the occasion). An Umeda son-in-law sends quantities of meat to his father-in-law; a Maring son-in-law gives quantities of pork to his father-in-law as part of his marriage payment. On the surface, this looks like precisely the same institution. But it is not so by any means. The source of an Umeda son-in-law's contributions in the form of meat is himself (i.e. a pig hunted and killed by him personally and actually identified with him) whereas the source of a Maring son-in-law's pork gifts is his wife, since she is the 'mother' who has raised the pigs from the produce of her own gardens during the lifetime of the marriage. In this way Maring women contribute heavily to their own marriage-payments.

But these are, nonetheless, said to be made to 'compensate' her agnates for the 'loss' of their sister/daughter. An instant's reflection is all that is required to ascertain that no such 'loss' has actually been sustained by them; and that it is, in fact, only as a married woman, contributing to her own marriage payments, that male agnates are able to derive benefit from her productive activities. But this fact is obscured by the idiom of object-exchange between male transactors. The Maring wife ends up not only performing wifely services for her husband, but also performing the services an Umeda son-in-law performs for his father-in-law.

The conclusion, which seems to me inescapable, that the regime of reproductive gifts in societies such as the Maring rests on a special kind of bad faith, is further supported if one considers another important element in the conventional (local) justification of marriage-payments. These payments are considered to be compensation for the (fictitious) 'loss' of a sister/daughter as a productive/reproductive group member, and secondly to be compensation for the loss of 'substance', i.e. agnatic essence derived from ingesting the produce of agnatic land. Marriage-payments 'replace' lost physical substance imbued with agnatic essence. Pork-gifts symbolise this return of lost substance. But, as we have seen, the source of the pork-gifts is the woman herself, who is obliged to replace herself in porcine form. As a 'mother' of pigs her progeny are reclaimed by her agnates, just as, later on, her female offspring will be reclaimed by them according to the local preference for delayed bilateral cross-cousin marriage (known as 'the return of the planting material').

The superficial appearance of marriage-payments suggests that affinally linked groups are independent 'units' which engage in exchange. The flow of gifts and personnel following from the mutual exchange of sacrifices, the 'loss' of a woman over here, the corresponding 'loss' of pigs, shells, etc. over there. But the underlying situation is quite different. Women are not 'lost' to their natal group in marriage; they remain 'female agnates' charged with a three-fold reproductive task; to reproduce their own group as 'mothers' of pigs and as mothers of 'returnable' daughters, and to reproduce their husband's group in the ordinary way. Affinal prestations are not therefore a 'buying-out' of agnation (compensation, say, for a rupture in the relation between an agnatically linked brother and sister). They are actually the expression of an agnatic monopoly on agnates of both sexes; the onerousness of exchange obligations *vis-à-vis* affines and matrikin increases as a positive rather than a negative function of the perdurable nature of the tie between cross-sex siblings. The 'exchange' idiom creates the appearance of a rupture between affinally linked groups which does not actually exist, at least for married women.

In short, Maring reproductive gifts achieve two things: they establish a male domain, internal to the society, in which relationships of 'equivalence' between 'partners' can be represented as crucial to social reproduction through attaching 'reproductive' meanings to transactions in valuables and pork. Meanwhile, these transactions provide an ideological cover for the fact that 'women' are not being 'transferred' between groups at all, but are simply being charged with reproducing, according to service obligations incumbent on them as married women, both their natal and affinal group.

6 Women and commodity exchange

Oversimplifying somewhat, one might say that in the Melanesian hinterland, reproductive exchange arises out of a strategic reformulation of the Indigenous Service Economy, such that women remain within its orbit (as producers and reproducers) while men escape from it, as transactors (i.e. as commodity exchangers and through the mimicry of commodity exchange in reproductive gifts). But the situation changes radically once one brings into consideration those coastal and riverain Melanesian societies among whom commodity exchange has penetrated deeply into society, so that it is no longer a matter of the 'periphery' of society, but, so to speak, its inner core. At this point the association between masculinity and commodity exchange breaks down, because the commodity exchanging activities of women become as fundamental to social reproduction as their productive and reproductive activities, indeed, they are one and the same.

It has often been noted that in coastal Melanesia, and along the Sepik, women enjoy a greater degree of social prestige than is commonly the case in hinterland societies such as the Maring. Few would dispute that there is a causal link between this somewhat elevated status and the role of women in commodity barter, and in the manufacture of barterable commodities. The classic instance of this from the older literature is Mead's (1963 (1935)) account of female 'dominance' among the Tchambuli (Chambri), and although Mead's account has been qualified and historically contextualised by Gewertz (1981) basic elements of the picture remain intact. Chambri women enjoyed social advantages because they were the manufacturers of mosquito-bags in great demand along the Sepik before the introduction of mosquito netting, and they also maintained a fish-for-sago trade which was essential to the provisioning of Chambri society.

In societies such as Chambri (Gewertz, 1983) and Murik, which I will describe in more detail shortly (Lipset, 1985; Barlow, 1985) both sexes are involved in commodity exchange, and subsistence depends on the import of food (sago starch). Under these circumstances two things can be observed to happen. The status of women is altered, and inequality reappears in affinal relations. Whereas, in the highlands, wife-givers rank equal to wife-receivers (or even below them, where the marriage payments are 'officially' valued more highly than the woman herself, because they represent the value to the group of the 'opening of an exchange road') – in the coastal/river setting wife-givers always rank above wife-receivers.

The Murik lakes provide us with an example in terms of which we can explore the relationship between social reproduction and commodity exchange in a trade-dependent society (Barlow, 1985; Lipset, 1985). The Murik are an (agriculturally speaking) 'landless' people living at the mouth of the Sepik river, whose continued existence depends on trading links with neighbouring inland sago-suppliers, and who trade up and down the coast. They are specialists in sailing-canoe transport, trading as middle-men, and as producers/manufacturers of various high-value foods, valuables, and 'immaterial' valuables such as songs, cults, designs, etc. Myths of the foundation of Murik society do not recount a cosmogony, but a series of migrations from an ancestral site in Chambri lake, to their current location, involving numerous sojourns at various places along the coast and up the river, where they now maintain trading links. These trade partnerships are personal and hereditary, descending cognatically within families.

The Murik are involved in three distinct nexuses of trade. For basic starch, the Murik women barter fish for sago with trade partners in neighbouring sago-producing 'bush' villages. This trade is exclusively female and sago-suppliers are called 'mothers'. Exchange rates are fixed, but are strikingly unfavourable to the Murik, who appear to get only 1/8th the quantity of sago per fish as the Chambri women, engaged in exactly the same trade with their neighbours in the Sepik hills, did for theirs. This reflects the fact that in their hey-day the Chambri were under the military protection of the Iatmul, whom they supplied with mosquito-bags, axes, etc. and who were prepared to back up 'stand-over' tactics in the fish-for-sago barter market (Gewertz, 1983; Modjeska, 1985). No such outside protection is afforded to the Murik whose indigence in sago obliges them to accept very stingy treatment from their 'mothers'. But the fact that this difficult-to-obtain starch is traded for, and dispensed, by women, contributes materially to the 'moral superiority' of women in Murik society (Meeker, Barlow and Lipset, 1986).

The second trade nexus in which the Murik are concerned is coastal canoe trade in low-volume, high-value items, pigs, decorations, shellfish, pots, and, above all, high-quality decorated baskets, in whose manufacture the Murik women are specialised. Women travel in canoes with their menfolk on expeditions along the coast, and maintain their own personal trading partnerships, which they have inherited. On these expeditions, it was the tradition that women would conduct affairs with lovers in their partner's village, in which they were supposed to take the initiative (rather reinforcing the point made above regarding the 'subversive' element in both trading partnerships and love relationships).

The social position of a man in Murik society was dependent on the contributions made by women to trading ventures, both as transactors and as manufacturers of 'copyright' baskets. A Murik man married to a notorious termagent, who frequently harangued him in public, declared to Barlow that he remained married to her because his reputation in trade depended on it:

[my trading partners] can all come at once and try to overwhelm me. But I always win. Everything goes to them. Not one debt stays with me. I always pay back every one. This is the way of my wife, which is why I hold on to her. Her way is to make baskets very quickly. Like a machine she makes baskets. (1985: 108)

The third nexus of trade is long-distance inter-island trade in large sailing canoes, handled by all-male crews. But even here women are crucially involved. Inter-island trade partnerships are inherited, and women inherit such partnerships as well as men. Women depute their husbands, brothers, etc. to trade for them with their overseas partners. Moreover, much of the merchandise is of female manufacture and, so to speak, emblematic of the powerful women who have created and patented much sought-after basket designs.

But perhaps more important to inter-island trade is the role of women as 'negatively' responsible for the success of the expedition through restraint in sexual and other behaviour while the canoe is at sea. Chastity and elaborate taboos are imposed on women during this period; a woman's skirts must not blow in the wind or the canoe will be swept away, she must not remove the plug from a water jar lest the canoe start to leak, and so on. These precautions do not just reflect the Malinowskian dictum that hazardous and uncertain enterprises are hedged about with magic and taboos. They correspond, rather, to the reassertion of an element of gender-exclusiveness in this kind of commodity exchange, as opposed to the lack of any such exclusiveness in the coastal trade. The open sea plays the same role in this as the 'frontier area' between tribes plays in the hinterland trade, i.e. it is given over to the masculinity and female influences must be shunned there (though attacks by flying witches are an ever-present possibility). Long-distance seaborne trade is the last bastion of the masculine republic, and the sea itself comes to be a sort of nature-reserve for men, when all else has been lost through the active presence, or even predominance, of women in commodity exchange. No wonder overseas trade is elaborated even when, as in the Kula, there is no commercial rationale for it, so that it becomes a purely 'ceremonial' traffic. The Kula is mimicry of commodity exchange, just as I have suggested that marriage payments are; which is not to say that it actually is commodity exchange. Its purpose is to sustain, and expand, a transactional relationship between men, originally associated with external commodity exchange, in circumstances in which commodity exchange as such is no longer a male monopoly.

Among societies such as the Murik (and Chambri, Iatmul, etc.) we find paradoxically both a heavy emphasis on onerous and unreciprocated reproductive gifts (passing from wife-receivers to wife givers) and a re-emergence of bride-service, i.e. specific work obligations incumbent on sons-in-law to contribute to projects undertaken by their wife's kin. However, these bride-service obligations do not stem from a recrudescence of the Indigenous Service Economy, but from the final triumph of exchange, as a principle of social relationship. Sepik marriage-payments are conceptually, and really, 'payments' for the effective alienation of women from their natal groups; payments for women who are, however, regarded as being 'without price' by their status-conscious agents. Return gifts are never sufficient to cover the debt incurred by the wife-receiving group, who remain permanent (indebted) inferiors. Sepik bride-service is not a matter of moral obligation, but a matter of working off an unrepayable debt. At this point, one can certainly agree that social reproduction is carried on according to a regime of reproductive gifts and the universal transactionalisation of relationships. But it must be stressed that this development does not take place *against* the development of pervasive commodity exchange, but precisely because of it, because it is only in this context that women become so pre-eminently valuable.

In this essay I have tried to show that 'barter' was much more than a sideshow in old Melanesia, since it provided both the physical resources and the ideological template for the elaboration of the kinds of Maussian 'reproductive gift' institutions for which the region has become so well known. I hope that I do not need to reiterate that reproductive gifts, though derived from a commodity exchange 'template', never amount to commodity exchanges in themselves. There is a density of metaphor in Melanesian life-cycle prestations which is *sui generis*, not to be reduced to 'mere' commercial transactions. Brides are not really 'bartered'. But I hope that I have also argued convincingly that there is a basic conceptual mistake underlying our willingness to collocate words like 'mere' with words like 'barter'. Commodity barter transactions do not take place in a social vacuum, nor do they occur without provoking powerful symbolic associations, not least under the conditions prevailing in old Melanesian societies. These conditions necessitate the development of so-called 'trade partnerships' – an innocuous-sounding label for what is, in effect, a momentous symbolic precedent. Under the 'sign' of barter, social relationships come into existence which are no longer pre-empted by the morality of reproduction and its service obligations. At the social margins, a constructed world comes into being, mediated by flows of objects along transactional pathways, which increasingly infiltrate the reproductive sphere from which it was originally excluded, but not without itself undergoing a sea-change. I have traced certain of these transformations in the course of this essay, but there is clearly much more that might be done in this direction, which might lead to a general revision of current ideas about the evolution of 'exchange' in Melanesian society.

REFERENCES

Barlow, K. 1985. The role of women in intertribal trade among the Murik. *Research in Economic Anthropology*, 7: 95–122.

Baudrillard, J. 1975. *The Mirror of Production*. Telos Press, Indianapolis.

Brookfield, A. and D. Hart, 1971. *Melanesia: a Geographical Interpretation*. Methuen, London.

Collier, J. and M. Rosaldo. 1981. The politics of gender in simple societies. In S. Ortner and H. Whitehead (eds.) *Sexual Meanings*. Cambridge University Press, Cambridge.

Epstein, T. 1968. *Capitalism Primitive and Modern*. ANU Press, Canberra.

Gell, A. 1975. *Metamorphosis of the Cassowaries*. Athlone Press, London.

1982. The market wheel: symbolic aspects of an Indian tribal market. *Man* (n.s.) 17: 470–91.

1986. Newcomers to the world of goods: consumption amongst the Muria Gonds. In A. Appadurai (ed.) *The Social Life of Things*. Cambridge University Press, Cambridge.

Gewertz, D. 1978. Tit for tat: barter markets on the middle Sepik. *Anthropological Quarterly*, 51: 36–44.

1981. An historical reconstruction of female dominance among the Chambri. *American Ethnologist*, 8: 94–106.

1983. *Sepik River Societies*. Yale University Press, New Haven.

Gregory, C. 1982. *Gifts and Commodities*. Academic Press, London.

Godelier, M. 1977. 'Salt money' and the circulation of commodities among the Baruya in perspectives. In *Marxist Anthropology*. Cambridge University Press, Cambridge.

1986. *The Making of Great Men among the Baruya*. Cambridge University Press, Cambridge.

Harding, T. 1970. Voyagers of the Vitiaz Strait. American Ethnological Society monograph no. 44. University of Washington Press, Seattle.

Healey, C. 1978. The adaptive significance of trade in the New Guinea Highlands. *Mankind*, 11: 198–207.

1984. Trade and sociability: balanced reciprocity as generosity in the New Guinea Highlands. *American Ethnologist*, 11: 42–59.

1986. New Guinea inland trade. *Mankind*, 15: 2. Special issue on recent studies in the political economy of PNG societies, (ed.) N. Modjeska and D. Gardiner, 146–63.

Hogbin, H. 1951. *Transformation Scene*. RKP, London.

Hughes, I. 1977. *New Guinea Stone Age Trade. Terra Australia 3*. ANU Press, Canberra.

Juillerat, B. 1986. *Les Enfants du Sang*. Maison des sciences de l'homme, Paris.

Lipset, D. 1985. Seafaring Sepiks. *Research in Economic Anthropology*, 7: 67–94.

Irwin, G. 1983. Chieftainship, Kula and trade in the Massim. In J. Leach and E. Leach (eds.) *The Kula*. Cambridge University Press, Cambridge.

Mackintyre, M. 1983. Kune on Tubetube. In J. Leach and E. Leach (eds.) *The Kula*. Cambridge University Press, Cambridge.

Malinowski, B. 1915. The natives of Mailu. *Transactions of the Royal Society of South Australia*, 39: 494–706.

Mead, M. 1963 (1935). *Sex and Temperament*. Morrow, New York.

Meeker, M., K. Barlow and D. Lipset. 1986. Culture, exchange and gender: lessons from the Murik. *Cultural Anthropology*, 1: 6–74.

Modjeska, N. 1985. Exchange value and Melanesian trade reconsidered. *Mankind*, 15: 2. Special issue on recent studies in the political economy of PNG societies, (ed.) N. Modjeska and D. Gardiner, 145–63.

Parry, J. 1986. The gift, the Indian gift, and the 'Indian Gift'. *Man* (n.s.) 21: 453–73.

1987. On the moral perils of exchange. Unpublished Ms.

Rubel, P. and A. Rosman. 1979. *Your own Pigs you may not Eat*. Chicago University Press, Chicago.

Sahlins, M. 1965. The sociology of primitive exchange. In M. Banton (ed.) *The Relevance of Models in Social Anthropology*. ASA1. Tavistock, London.

1972. Exchange value and the diplomacy of primitive trade. In *Stone Age Economics*. Aldine, Chicago.

Salisbury, R. 1970. *Vunamami*. University of California Press, Berkeley.

Schwartz, T. 1963. Systems of areal integration in the Admiralty Isles. *Anthropological Forum*, 1: 56–97.

7   Qualified value: the perspective of gift exchange

Marilyn Strathern

A thing by itself cannot properly be counted

(Strauss, 1962: 15, an early ethnographer of the Hagen area, quoted in Lancy and Strathern, 1981: 784)

It is a curiosity that anthropological attempts to describe non-monetary transactions may well end up concentrating on their monetary aspects. This can happen in specifying how persons measure the relative worth of the things they transact. It has become conventional to admit a range of 'social' factors in the computation of relative worths, and the long-standing debate about the embeddedness of transactions in relationships is now taken for granted. Nevertheless, the principles by which comparability is established between the things themselves invariably remains the analytical focus, whether these things are material or metaphysical in nature, and whether the transactions are balanced or unequal. The procedure incorporates what one could call a barter model of value.

Barter has always been a somewhat mixed analytical concept. Anthropological theories of exchange systems have tended to take barter, as indeed they have taken trade, as a self-evident activity. For barter appeared to 'provide the imagined preconditions for the emergence of money' (see Introduction and Humphrey, 1985: 48). It was regarded as a strategy through which people obtained things that they needed, that is, doing in the absence of money what people with money also do. In short, it was understood in 'monetary' terms. The discovery of the gift, however, was the discovery of people exchanging things which they did not need, and unpacking that paradox has dominated anthropological theorising on exchange ever since. For here the challenge was to uncover the principles by which people 'needed' to exchange at all – and the answer has invariably been that people need society, viz. to lead a socially integrated life and interact with those around them, the transactions expediting such integration. This provided a powerful model for thinking about the exchange not just of things, but also of persons – the computation of

169

people's relative worth. Interest in teasing out the implications of this discovery quite eclipsed the analysis of barter itself.

The curiosity is the extent to which that view of gift exchange in fact continues to deploy the barter model of value. For it locates social interest in terms of the respective values that persons exchange with one another, measured through the worth of what they transfer, in the same way as bartered items are measured against one another. The relationship is thus conceived as an *exchange ratio*. But there are some questions to raise against assumptions that commonly attend this conceptualisation.

First, if the essence of barter is the exchange of unlike items (Gregory, 1982: 47), then the exchange appears motivated by the respective interests of the parties in the items themselves. It is thus seen to establish a ratio between the items by which the transactors compute gains and losses. Gift transactions highlight the opposite case – the possibility of people exchanging like items, as in the ceremonial exchange systems of Melanesia, shells for pigs or pigs for pigs, from which it is deduced that the crucial ratio must be the respective social standing of the transactors. However, the analysis remains the same. Donors and recipients are regarded as measuring one another, 'bartering' prestige (say), insofar as the transaction rests on establishing equivalences. The assumption of equivalence became a point of debate in transactional analysis, and has dogged accounts of reciprocity ever since: is the equivalence of the goods a precondition for or an outcome of their being exchanged?

Second, that question itself derives from the assumption that there is necessarily an enumerative basis to transactions, a measurement of respective worths in the manner items are counted. The only computation of value to be derived from such an assumption must be functionalist: in gift exchange, the ratio between the items exchanged will integrate the value of the items with the standing of the parties and the kind of relationship they wish to sustain. But the question that was asked of equivalence must also be asked of enumeration itself. Is the capacity to express things in terms of unit worth a precondition for, or an outcome of, the transaction?

Third, an enumerative basis for transactions hides a further assumption about substitutability. The barter model of value supplies a simple reason for substitution in terms of the parties' needs. There is no problem about establishing the substitutability of the items in question since each party is defined as supplying what the other wants. All the problems are seen to lie with computing equivalence. I wish to suggest to the contrary, however, that there arise situations in which the chief focus of negotiation is the substitutability of items, that such a situation is intrinsic to what we know as 'gift exchange' in Melanesia, and that it consequently problematises the barter model of value. In short, where unit equivalence turns out to be as much an outcome as a precondition of a transaction, the unit worth of items becomes a metaphor for their substitutability.

At least as far as Melanesia is concerned, I suspect we have been dazzled by local rhetoric: by the precision of the counting, by the quantitative displays, by the close records kept of transactions. We look at the counting, and overlook what the counting is for – not to establish a ratio based on the aggregation of individual items, but to create an analogy between them, and thus their one-to-one substitutability. Equivalence will always (can only) appear as a matching of units.

Magic and romance

We might initially ask what is at the basis of a concern with ratios, and what the barter model of value implies.

Commenting on the conventional distinctions between barter, gift and commodity exchanges, Appadurai properly suggests that we should desist from a romantic exaggeration of these contrasts. We should thus look at 'the commodity potential of all thing rather than searching fruitlessly for the magic distinction between commodities and other sorts of things' (1986: 13). The commodity potential of things lies in the extent to which 'the social life of any "thing" [can] be defined as...its exchangeability (past, present or future) *for some other thing*' (1986: 13, my emphasis). While one is bound to acknowledge that magic and romance has interfered with the analysis of economic life, this definition of a commodity prompts the further question about what it is that makes one item exchangeable with, or substitutable for, another.

Written into Appadurai's definition is the proposition that what is exchanged against one thing is invariably another thing. Now he is certainly not arguing that exchange has no social referent; on the contrary, he specifically delineates the social nature of the commodity by drawing attention to its exchangeable potential. Thus he refers to the 'tournaments of value' by which participation in exchange measures the strategic skill and standing of the actors. The *kula*, for instance, constitutes a 'complex system for the intercalibration of the biographies of persons and thing' (1986: 22). The value of objects (after Simmel) is determined reciprocally by the interest which the transacting parties have in them. '[E]conomic value is not just value in general, but a definite sum of value, which results from the *commensuration of two intensities of demand*. The form this commensuration takes is the exchange of sacrifice and gain' (1986: 4, my emphasis). While the mutuality of the actors' interests is obviously important, this is still a version of the barter model of value insofar as it is taken for granted that, whatever is measured, the measurement is done through the comparison of the component things. The exchange simply provides the occasion for the comparison.

I do not wish to argue that we should ignore the comparison of things. What is interesting about barter is precisely the way indigenous models of the relationships involved focus on what is being exchanged. They invite the computation of numerical values: the comparison of entities yields a ratio, the one expressed as a proportion of the other, though Humphrey (1985) notes that the comparison may be short term and discontinuous with other transactions.

Whether the social standing of the parties or the utility of the items are in question, it is the moment of exchange – concretised in the image of a 'flow' of things – at which, in this view, value is made visible. X travels in the opposite direction from Y. Yet the image of *things* moving 'against' each other contains its own magic and romance. It depends on those metaphors by which we are led into computing values as though all items were discrete entities (units), or could be apprehended as multipliers or fractions of discrete entities. The magic in the idea that the quantity of one thing can be enumerated in respect of that of another is the magic of reification. Relations evoke the intrinsic character or identity of things (so much coal as a proportion of so much iron; so much sago as a fraction of so much fish), and things are thereby presumed to present a unitary quality. A bridewealth of so many items is counted as X pigs, Y shells, and pigs and shells have their own identity. The total value of things exchanged in turn appears computable as a measurement of their component units of quality. The identity of the units already exist 'in nature', so to speak, and the 'cultural' activity of exchange determines their value. Such units are consequently taken as antecedent to the exchange itself – whether they are units of time, labour or useful or beautiful objects.

As we have seen, the barter model of value applied to gift exchange simply transposes that logic from things to persons. Since the things exchanged are often identical, then what must be measured are the relative value of persons for one another. In the case of the exchange of women, a whole generation of anthropological theory has proceeded on the premise that women are identical in their reproductive capacities, so that what must be measured in marriage transactions is the respective pulling power of wife-givers and wife-takers. By concentrating on the comparison of things against things or persons against persons, the barter model makes 'exchange' simply an arbiter of the rate at which the units literally exchange hands. The discreteness of 'things' such as pigs or shells, and 'persons' such as sisters or wives, seem evident enough. Yet their abstraction as units belongs to a particular cultural practice which assumes the priority of individual identity (Thomas, 1985). We can call it empiricist or bourgeois (Modjeska, 1985: 145) or a derivative of commodity logic; I take it here as constitutive of the barter model. It contains the idea that numerical operations can be done with units, and that value rests on the fact that things can be counted.

Rather than apply the barter model of value to gift exchange, I conjure gift exchange in Melanesia[1] to provide a perspective from which the barter model looks magical. Indeed, it does not even apply very well to what we might otherwise identify as barter or trade in the region.

'Barter' in Melanesia

Apparently straightforward studies of both barter and trade in Melanesia have thrown up their own problems.

An intriguing example is the trading of foodstuffs on the Sepik river of Papua New Guinea, where populations exchange produce from the river and lakes with produce grown inland. I refer here to the fish for sago trade between Iatmul and Sawos women as described by Gewertz (1983). Iatmul villages established barter markets on Sawos territory, and every three or four days Iatmul women take fish to the markets to trade for blocks of sago from the Sawos. On average, it is reported, a woman gives 2 kg sago for one unit of fish. Depending on the species, the unit may be a half or a whole of a single specimen.

Gewertz quotes Schindelbeck (1980: 552) on this point, in order to dispute his claim that the exchange is balanced in labour terms. She herself (1983: 21–2) comments on the apparent unfairness of the transaction. According to her computation of how hard the work is, she argues that Sawos women labour at least three times as hard to produce the sago as Iatmul women do to catch the fish. Since this imbalance is not to be explained by the respective needs of the parties (Iatmul need sago more than Sawos need fish), it is to be explained by the political imbalance between the populations. Sawos are forced to accept Iatmul protection and their own inferiority, and the author places much weight on the respective haughtiness (Iatmul) and obsequiousness (Sawos) of the two parties. An imbalance in the value of the goods is thus related to a social imbalance between the parties.

Modjeska, who considers the case at length, comments that in fact there is 'no unequivocal testimony that the women on either side regard the exchange as unequal' (1985: 154). At the same time, he queries the general ethnographic evidence for equating customary rates with equilibrium prices in Sahlin's (1972) terms, offering a general criticism of the analytical basis upon which exchange ratios are commonly computed. Patterns of supply and demand raise the question of the factors that prompt traders to over-supply, in the Sawos case the factors that compel women to bring the extra sago to market that enable Iatmul to gain a better 'price'.

Striking in the Sawos–Iatmul exchange is the manner in which an equivalence is set up between one piece of sago and one unit of fish. To achieve this, fish are classified into types, as we have seen, of which a half or a whole specimen may be regarded as a unit, and large blocks of sago are cut into small pieces. However many fish are exchanged against sago, the whole transaction is based on a replication of units: a sago-sized piece of fish, as it were, against a fish-sized piece of sago.

A similar one-for-one evaluation is found in the Highlands, where men talk of how in the past the rate for one axe was one pig or the rate for one pig was one shell. Healey (1985) notes that in trade-stores Maring tend to pay for each item they buy separately – rather than adding them up and paying in a lump sum. This complements Epstein's (1982) study of urban markets in Papua New Guinea, also re-analysed by Modjeska. Here, vendors expect to sell their product in certain sized bundles. They do not lower prices or increase bundle sizes to meet flagging demand. On the contrary, women may prefer to take the produce home or return the following day to clear their stock. Yet their operating on a basis of one bundle of food for one denomination of money does not mean that the market rate is standardised. The size of the bundles may well fluctuate from day to day, in the same way as the quality of the Sawos sago exchanged for fish varieties. (Similar blocks may be cut into nine or twelve pieces: each piece is still exchanged against one unit of fish.) In the Highlands trade of axes, pigs and shells, much attention was always paid to the quality of the items.

We might then join with Modjeska and query the usefulness of talking of an exchange ratio at all (1985: 158). People discriminate, judge, weigh up the size and appearance of items, take into account this or that characteristic, and may refuse to enter into transactions at all. But they do not do so on an enumerative basis. 'Urban Melanesians do not ordinarily evaluate transactions on the basis of a quantity for quantity ratio (for example, weight for price) but rather by comparing qualities per unit offered at unit prices' (Modjeska, 1985: 158, original emphasis). Healey refers to the fact that in Maring there is no haggling in trade transactions involving money or other commodities and that banknotes pass in standard amounts.

These examples suggest that the ethnographic dichotomy between such trade and barter on the one hand, and gift exchange on the other, conceals similarities. Healey sums up the received view that whereas trade transactions focus on the material goods being exchanged, in gift exchange focus is on the social relationships of the transactors. However, as is also the received view, he instantly qualifies the dichotomy by suggesting that they are simply ends of a continuum. Trade was often an adjunct of gift prestations, or the traded items were needed for gift exchange (cf. Godelier, 1977). The usual conclusion is that either (a) exchange sustained the friendly relations under whose cover the desired items could be obtained; or (b) the trade goods were incorporated into prestations. Indeed, Healey explains the resilience of indigenous trade in Maring and, despite the increasing use of money, its resistance to monetisation, by the resilience of traditional gift exchange. Money is absorbed into Maring exchanges as a valuable rather than a currency.

Healey distinguishes trade from gift by commenting that when Maring trade – and they have a distinct term for the activity – they exchange single items against each other, one plume for one salt pack or whatever. But when they exchange gifts, they will be dealing with collections of items – assembled wealth – that they exchange against some other multiple collection. I suggest that this difference is not what it appears. The singular transaction is in an important sense no different from the exchange of a collection against a collection, nor indeed from that of a collection (for example bridewealth) against a single unit (for example a bride).

Now however much the focus of trade may be on 'the goods' rather than on 'the relationship', the goods *still have to be extracted* from the vendor. The simple presentation of other goods or the need to buy or sell is not sufficient to stimulate a transaction, as the market examples show; a substitution must be effected. Modjeska observes that in Melanesian markets the seller customarily sets the terms of the trade. But, he adds, who then is the seller in a barter situation? Rather than both sides being sellers/buyers in the Sawos–Iatmul exchanges, 'Iatmul fishwives certainly had little doubt that they were in the seller's role' (1985: 158). If the seller's control of the terms of exchange leads one to a 'primitive theory of exchange' (Modjeska, 1985: 157), then it incorporates an indigenous view of the respective activity and passivity of the transactors. Prior to exchange is the issue of exchangeability, and in these systems that rests on the asserted ability of one side to extract items from the other. Who is active and who is passive in this manoeuvre depends on the perspective one takes. And, to follow Gewertz at this point, the relative magnitude of what can be extracted becomes a measure of respective power. But the possibility of exchange rests on a *distinction* between the comparison of quality and the matching of units.

Things and persons will have to be considered as multiple or composite, not unitary in their qualities. Otherwise, we might be puzzled how people so skilled in counting and calculation could overlook obvious quality differences in the objects of exchange when (as the people of Hagen did) they talked of 'one axe' as equivalent to 'one pig' or 'one shell'. As long as one regards a unit as denoting a quality or identity prior to the transaction, the Melanesian notation seems inexplicable. But suppose the matching one-for-one basis for exchange were regarded as after the event. Two points would follow. First, enumeration can be regarded as the finalising outcome of the transaction rather than the basis on which it proceeds. Second, only one number is in fact involved, viz. one.

In the Iatmul/Sawos exchanges several items may be finally handed over as a single entity, and a unit is created in the affirmation of their comparability or exchangeability. By the same token, the component amounts of labour time or the respective utility (the 'quality') that the parties see in the transaction cannot be computable in themselves. If the unit-status of 'one piece of fish' for 'one piece of sago' emerges as a consequence of the exchange itself, it is not a basis through which 'quality' can be counted. People certainly count, as Godelier makes clear, in Baruya exchanges of pigs and salt bars (1977: 140). At issue is how we calculate their calculations. What appears to us as a ratio pig/salt, may appear to them as a one-for-one exchange (1 pig = 6 salt bars (= 1)). If in turn the unit thus appears as a metaphor for substitutability, it indicates an analogy between two items. The question thus becomes how the analogy is established.

In what follows, I am concerned less with the ideology of reciprocity that has, as Parry (1986) complains, dominated the analysis of gift exchange, than with the prior coercion which renders items exchangeable. Although my remarks apply chiefly to ceremonial and reproductive exchanges of the kinds found in the central Highlands of Papua New Guinea, they may also bear on the 'barter' and 'trade' already mentioned. For they comprise a general reflection on the conduct of Melanesian transactions, as though one could describe them from their own unique perspective, and thus mobilise a different set of assumptions from those that underlie the barter model of value. I do not argue through a specific case, but offer a composite of inferences from a range of practices. Some of the evidence may be found in M. Strathern (1988). The reflection is not to be imagined as a simple indigenous view: my intention is to create a perspective on the resources of a specific analytic language (projected as a barter model) from which to apprehend the limiting features of that language. I thus offer a counter projection, a perspective imagined as a gift model.

Gift exchange

In the way in which he deploys a contrast between gifts and commodities, Gregory (1982: 47–8) distinguishes commodity exchange based on an exchange-value, an equation between items expressed as a quantitative exchange ratio, from gift exchange which is based on what he calls the exchange-order of the items, whose rank demonstrates the equal or unequal rank between donor and recipient. His immediate exemplar here is the significant difference between low-ranking and high-ranking valuables on Rossell Island, and on the widespread classification of goods into spheres of exchange. Items have an exchange order, and donor and recipient measure one another through the respective ranking of the gifts. The principle of like for like, where it applies, can be understood as rank for rank (1982: 50). He thus upturns Western commodity concepts, to reveal gift exchange as creating a relationship between the subjects, as he calls them, rather than, in his terms, the objects of exchange.

However, in equating a subject–object relation with that between persons and things, Gregory stops his turn there. I extend my interest into an area where he hesitates to apply the word value, namely the 'equation' set up between things and persons, such as bride and bridewealth (Gregory: pers. comm.). These so-called symbolic equations do not fit into Gregory's scheme, I suggest, because they cut across his subject/object divide. As we have seen, in his scheme, things are measured by quantitative ratio, persons are measured by a qualitative ratio (rank), and the difference between his two forms of exchange is the respective emphasis given in commodity and gift transactions to each. Yet any approach to the notion of value in those societies where gift exchange flourishes must take into account the equivalences between what we would otherwise separate as persons and things (cf. Modjeska, 1985; Godelier, 1986). This is not because the equation between persons and things is a metaphysical key, as one might interpret Mauss' (1954) emphasis, but because of the opposite reason, the very fact that the dichotomy, so patent to Western observers, is in one respect irrelevant in terms of Melanesian cultural constructions.

It is the stark alternatives of the barter model of value, which assumes the intrinsic and separate qualities of persons and things. I prefer to imagine Melanesian gift exchange as based on the capacity for actors (agents, subjects) to extract or elicit from others items that then become the object of their relationship. And, after Gregory (1982: 41), where things and persons assume the social form of persons, persons are necessarily understood as the objects of such relationships.[2] Whether a relationship has any time dimension to it (whether we call it trade or ceremonial exchange) does not affect, I think, the consequent cultural attention paid to the process of extraction itself.

Coercion is essential to the manner in which the 'gift' is created. People must compel others to enter into debt:[3] an object in the regard of one actor must be made to become an object in the regard of another. The magic of the gift economy, then, lies in successful persuasion. It is the separate interest of the partners in the exchange that creates their relationship, and this mutual interest cannot be reduced to a value in reference to one party only, as though there had been an exchange of sacrifices or as though their needs were antecedent to the relationship. In both ceremonial exchanges and marriage, the recipients' 'needs' are forced upon them by the donors: their own 'demand' for the gift is their experience of this coercion. For without the recipient, the donor would have no objects at his/her disposal.[4] The value of an object is not simply determined reciprocally (Appadurai, citing Simmel, 1986: 3); it also involves a contrived asymmetry between the transactors (Gregory, 1982: 47; cf. Modjeska, 1985: 157–61 and Munn, 1983: 302). The donor only has objects at his or her disposal because he/she can anticipate the extractive perspective of the recipient.

Out of everything that a person thus has to dispose – knowledge, children, artefacts, produce – an object is created at the moment when an asset becomes the attention of another. If the use-value of a commodity is realised as a value only in the context of its production for exchange (cf. Ollman, 1976: 182 ff.; Appadurai, 1986: 9), then, by contrast, what is crucial here is production for another, and (from the agents' point of view) a specific, person. The interest of the recipient objectifies the assets at the donor's disposal. Indeed, that interest, in the form of a debt, may anticipate the item as already belonging to the recipient. It is thus construed as detachable from the donor. But what may have to be engineered is that very interest itself. If the recipient is necessary to the donor for the definition of the objects at his/her disposal (realising them as extractable), the recipient is a cause of the donor's actions. Hence the meek (passive) Sawos women can be regarded as the 'cause' of the (active) Iatmul women having to travel to the market with their fish, and (in the manner of *kula* prestations) their haughtily waiting for the sago offerings which they accept with a show of contempt (Gewertz, 1983: 19). Sago is essential to Iatmul subsistence, and the corresponding Sawos perspective is that they are like mothers feeding their Iatmul children (1983: 27).

Exchange objectifies or defines (Wagner, 1967). In formal terms we may say that objects do not exist prior to exchange any more than persons exist prior to relationships; indeed, the partition of persons is the form that all partibility takes. As Munn (1986) exemplifies in detail for Gawa, partibility is constructed through two related manoeuvres, external and internal. When an object is made detachable through the interest of another party, its value is determined by that external interest. It is elicited thereby. But there is an internal evaluation that operates as a necessary concomitant to this, namely the capacity of an agent to objectify parts of him or herself in his or her own regard. These two sources of comparison or evaluation work together.

As a microcosm of social relationships, a Melanesian person is a composite, multiple entity, constituted by the acts of others, internally differentiated in the various origins of his or her being. These diverse internal qualities are made visible (given 'value') in dealings with others. For instance, from his vantage point as a clan agnate, a Highlands man values certain components of his make-up insofar as he owes them to his maternal kin: they become objectified in his own regard. Put more generally: *entities are compared with their origins*, that is, they stand in a potentially homologous relationship to them. Thus persons are construed as much with reference to the social relations which produced them (their 'origins') as in reference to the extent to which they are detachable from those relations. The exogamic rule, which defines both a clan's identity and its partibility, ensures that the clan will detach from itself an out-marrying category of persons who carry its identity – the quality of its being – into other places.

But identity – this or that actor's clan origin, say – is really a shorthand for all the actions that others took to establish the marriage, give birth and nurture the clan person. To say that people are compared with their origins is also to compare their potential acts with these other acts – how the person becomes an agent by taking (further) action in reference to all those past acts of others that so constituted him or her. Have the correct payments been made to this person's maternal kin; does that person accept liability for a brother's offence; are these people loyal to their clan? In other words, an agent's position can be thought of as originating in the acts of others in a way that his or her own acts substantiate. At the same time, an agent's acts can be compared on a particular basis to those which compelled him or her to act. *One entity is elicited by another*. The mother's brother, expectant of a gift owed, sends a soliciting gift which becomes the 'cause' of the main gift. A specific act thus has value in respect of the specific act which caused it and which may be thought of as a counterpart or as analogous to it.

For Melanesian theories of causation suppose a split between the cause of an action and the doer of it, and prestations between kin are predicated on this split. This is, of course, a temporal or perspectival phenomenon. Thus a Highlands clan which divides itself, despatching its sisters off in marriage, becomes an agent with transactable items at its disposal. Seen from the point of view of the sister's husband's clan, however, who add the woman's productivity to themselves, the maternal clan becomes both origin and cause of the resultant child, and a creditor. It is those who discharge the debt, rather than those to whom the debt is owed, who are 'active'. Maternal kin become passive causes of the wealth which flows towards them. They may reassert agency at any juncture – soliciting a gift – but, insofar as they are the recipients of the compensatory actions of others, they are in that perspective inert. What holds true between kind holds also between exchange partners. The cause of an exchange lies in the (inert) recipient to whom a debt is owed. Here the agent is the exchange partner who raises the wealth to pay off his debt. Political life consists in men forcing others to be the cause of their own actions.

A consequence of these premises is that agents constantly have to create their own visibility. This contributes to the significance of extraction: in extracting something from a donor, the recipient anticipates the counter-part agency by which he or she will be able to act as a donor. While forcing others to act is to take a passive part in relation to that act, it can also be constituted for oneself as an exercise of one's own agency. But it cannot be constituted *by* oneself: an other is necessary for its elicitation. Let me spell this out.

Persons are construed as the outcome of relationships between others, who stand to them as either 'cause' or 'origin', and thereby as the object of these relationships. Thus conceptualised as a completed end result of the activity of others, the person (or a collectivity of persons) is simply a composite of the relationships which produced him or her. To be active him or herself, he or she must be made incomplete. Persons have to de-compose or disaggregate themselves. They become agents by *turning themselves into units* (Mosko, 1983). A clan composed of male and female elements thus becomes a 'male' clan with 'females' to bestow on others.

To be rendered incomplete, the social person may despatch a part of him or herself, or be detached from a nexus of relationships. Definitively, an agent's transactable attribute is at once both part of, and separable from, him or her. No longer a composite (person), the agent acquires a unitary identity through releasing what have become extraneous objects defined by external relations (cf. Gillison, 1980). The clan that disposes of its sisters or the mother who gives birth to a child are both agents in this sense. As a detached part, neither sister nor child alone is productive. Yet they are not without value. The 'value' of the sister of the child is constructed in respect to its origin – the bestowing clan, the maternal body or whatever – and is so constructed in the eyes of another, the cause of the transaction, those on whom the sister is bestowed or the husband for whom the woman bears the child. The creation of an object of social identity implies a specificity of connections between persons. Thus in agnatic systems a sister has transactable value because she is seen to go from this particular clan to that. She creates a body of maternal kin who will (say) bless and nurture the child she produces. The all-important necessity for that body of kin to take specific responsibility is evinced in bridewealth – forced to receive it, they are also forced to acknowledge the donor's perspective of themselves at once as the woman's origin and cause (cf. Errington and Gewertz, 1987). Similarly, what is being compared in the giving or receiving of valuables on occasions such as a Massim *kula* expedition or Hagen *moka* is the respective capacity of the actors to detach and attach parts of their own, and thus the other's, identities.

Indeed, any instigation of action will involve a partitioning of identity, as true of marriage transactions which endorse the exogamic rule, as of initiation ceremonies and political exchanges. Detachment is to be distinguished from alienation, in that detachment creates an object whose value exists *both* in respect of its origin *and* in being caused or elicited by another. Detachable parts have no intrinsic value, for they exist in respect of the specific relations between the transactors. A clan bestows a sister who will come to another as a wife. The sister/wife cannot embody abstract value; the sister was detach*able* because of the interest of the affinal clan in acquiring a wife. And she is of value in the perspective of the acquiring clan because they have extracted her from a specific other clan, maternal kin to her children, for whom she also has value. The same holds for wealth: a valuable is detachable because of the claims that a specific other has on its release. It is already owed to him because it is in turn the possession of a specific partner.

One premise of these transactions is that an entity can reproduce itself only through the eliciting intervention of a social other – in being caused to act. This means that it is not itself that an agent reproduces but its relationship with these social others. The new generation of agnates reproduces a different set of dependencies on external clans than were objectified in the persons of their fathers. They draw these interests towards themselves. Yet the paradox is that an interest is known only by what it elicits, in the same way as agency is known only by its effects. There is no guarantee that an agent's actions will make him or her visible as a person except through the evidence of his or her effects on others. There is no guarantee that what he or she produces will elicit a response from her or his partner. We have seen that a significant axis of comparison in gift exchange is between the accomplished deed and the cause of it – leading to evaluations of the agents' success or failure. But there is only ever one thing that can be elicited, namely, another's perspective.

Objects created in the elicitory regard of others ('causes') become a metaphor for that regard. At the moment of exchange, an analogy is created between the kind of regard that two parties have for each other; they exchange perspectives. One view is compared with another, a totalising moment. To adapt Wagner's aphorism, one cannot have half a view. There can in this sense be no ratio or proportioned estimation between perspectives, only the displacement of 'one' by another 'one'. The kinds of computations that turn on amount and quality – how many sago lumps for how many fish, how large a pig in return for how large a pig –

signify how the person appears in the other's eyes. Relative magnitude is not an independent enumerative dimension prior to the point of comparison.

Enumeration

Nonetheless, surely the numbers matter. No one need be reminded of the passion Melanesians have for counting. Pospisil's amusement at Kapauku appreciation of a pin-up, in terms of the number of teeth that shone at them, is legend. Yet what better way to talk about beauty than through metaphors of magnitude. It is not just because they are elaborate about it that one might say Kapauku have a developed aesthetic of number (based on a sexagesimal numerical system, acted out in the way they plan activities months ahead and keep a constant track of enumerated items of all kinds (Pospisil, 1963)). In these Melanesian systems, number *is* an aesthetic. Objects have a numerical form, in the way they have colour, glossiness or gender. It makes a substantial difference to people's responses to what they receive back in relation to the items that they give away, where quantity is (as it were) a matter of quality. When persons are counted – the numbers of men who dance together, the pairing of marriage exchanges – they are made visible through tropes of magnitude, of collectivity or of pairing. For objects (persons) have to be singular or composite or one of a pair: they cannot appear without this quantitative dimension, any more than they can appear without gender, because they cannot appear without taking a form. Enumeration is an aspect of quality.

Now the barter model of value represents things as units in themselves, thereby subsuming quality as an aspect of enumeration. The individuality of an item is taken as given, and thus as the basis of counting, so that one can add or subtract units. By contrast, the achievement of the Highlands clan that collects its men together in a line, or accumulates wealth staked out in a row, is that the individual units are created momentarily, in the process of collectivisation. As persons, people are not units. As we have seen, they are composite in their identity, in the same way as wealth is composite, owed to specific sources. Only in bounding off certain aspects of their personal identity (under the rubric say of 'agnatic brotherhood' and 'male-ness') can the collectivity define its members as agents, in terms of a single order of magnitude – this number of clansmen, that number of males. Hence, a collectivity is created in the first place not by adding these individuals as units to one another, but by submerging their heterogeneous sources of identity. Thus individuals are created in the course of their coming together for a single reason. An agent's singularity is thus elicited within a (social) context; it is not given, if that were imaginable, in nature.

Furthermore, a collectivity, such as a clan, is only so conceptualised in relation to a specific other, another clan, say, or a heterogeneous range of persons defined as peripheral to the clan's centrality. For instance, among several Highlands societies, clans are capable of estimating the number of wives who return to them against the number of sisters married out in a particular direction. Rules against the repetition of close marriages (Strathern, A. and M., 1969) or deliberate arrangements within the component groups of a clan (Wagner, 1969) usually mean that comp-lementary lower-level groups are involved in the receiving and giving of brides and wealth in any pair of exchanges (clans X and Y may be seen as 'exchanging' women; on X's side subclan A will receive a bride, subclan B send a bride, from and to the 'same' external clan). Bride(wealth) is matched by bride(wealth). For the external relationship unifies the internal lower-level groups in respect of one another. It is not necessary for people to agree how to add up the total flow in one direction or another.

At the base of both operations is an assumption about number: namely that there are occasions on which many 'is the same as' one. A collectivity or multiplicity of units can always be represented as a single unit, insofar *as its unity is elicited* in turn by other social identities. Thus, the line of dancers (or component groups within a clan) acts as one in confrontation with their exchange partners/audience. They evince magnitude. Yet they are not being added together.

That latter computation applies, I think, only to a relationship of a particular kind, of neither homology nor analogy. I refer to attachment between items which are regarded as a different order or kind, perhaps with different social origins. Thus, extra wealth may be put 'on top' of a return gift; thus a non-agnate may 'add' himself to a clan's activities. However, a clansman cannot add himself to another clansman, though he may form one of a pair with him. There is thus a distinction between the comparing (pairing) of units of the same order, and the operation of addition and subtraction (attachment and detachment) which involve entities of different orders and which consequently cannot be applied to units as such.

The crucial numerical differentiation between units of the same order, then, is between a unity (or collectivity) and that unity split or doubled. Units are not 'added' to one another – they are divided, or juxtaposed as pairs. This applies both to the summary unit of a set and to the component individual members of it. Indeed, many Melanesian counting systems present both a constant doubling of elements and a constant reduction of multiplicity to unity. Elaborate calculations have been recorded, on a base 8 or a base 20, or via body parts. I touch on one general feature of certain Melanesian systems, drawing on suggestions from Mimica's (1988) analysis of Iqwaye mathematics.[5] This is the computation which discrimi-nates between a unity and a unity replicated dually (split, doubled or paired). Or, we might say, where 'one' has two forms, as a unit or as a pair. ('Two' is not a plurality, but one in another form, viz. the joining of halves or moieties or the alliance of mutualities.)

The concept of unity may be sustained through metaphors of part–whole relations of the kind which Mimica has explicated for Iqwaye. The relations in question are homologous – as in the equation between one man = one clan. Thus when they count, Iqwaye display a 'hand' as 5 fingers. Four sets of fingers and toes (two hands, two feet) compose a 'person' (20). Each finger may in turn stand for 20, for each finger can also be conceptualised as an entire 'person', so a 'hand' of 5 fingers is also 100. In the unity of the entire digit, or the entire person, Mimica argues that 20 thus has the numerical value of one. 400 is similarly expressible as one: as many 'persons' (20) as one person's digits (20).

Operations elsewhere may follow a similar pattern. In Hagen, for instance, a 'hand' has 4 fingers. Here a pair of hands make a set ('eight'), in turn reconceptualised as unity, 'one hand'. 'In counting on the fingers a single hand is considered only a half, it is only a proper hand when it is brought together with the other hand as an eight' (Strauss, 1962: 16; quoted in Lancy and Strathern, 1981: 784). For succeeding enumerations, each finger may thus stand for 8, a substitution which also allows for the demonstration of a superior or prestigeful form of an eight, namely an eight with two extra and qualitatively different components (the thumbs 'added') or what we would call ten (A. Strathern, 1977).

The pairing of the Hagen hands in rendering the eight digits as a unit, 'one hand', takes one term, so to speak, to stand for both.[6] In other contexts, pairing may be made visible as the specific splitting or doubling of units, which sustains a relationship between them. The units are related as two of a kind (for example Lancy and Strathern, 1981). A Hagen pair composes a partnership between entities at once like and unlike.[7] An equivalence or analogy is asserted between otherwise dissimilar persons, as between two brothers, say, or between husband and wife, coupled like night and day or bird and marsupial. We may call this pairing juxtaposition or conjunction, but we cannot call it addition. The pair consists in the relation between the two, not in their summation, although, as we have seen, the pairing itself can be expressed as a unit in juxtaposition with (elicited by) another unit. Mimica demonstrates this for Iqwaye counting of digits, each digit creating its predecessor as a one or a two (pair). Thus the fingers of a hand go one, two, two-one, two-two, one (hand). Five is not the addition of 5 ones, but the point ('one') beyond 2 twos.

These counting systems, then, are not to be set against, but rather evince, the same sequences as described for the computation of value. Numbers tend to take the form of a unity or a pair. This does not mean that

Melanesians are uninterested in multiple enumeration. On the contrary, many of their systems seem to encourage the computation of high numbers and facilitate the precise reckoning of large sums. However, there is a further observation to be made about computation.

Now 20 (in Iqwaye the digits of two hands and two feet) might be the same as one ('person') as a homologous totality or unity, such that one (digit) can stand for 20. However, it is not invariably the same, for a juxtaposition or comparison of 20 and 1 does not always produce a pair. Reciprocity is a question of matching or eliciting one number by a counterpart: my 20 (1) for your 1 (20). If they do not match, and cannot be conceptualised as a pair, then there is no analogy between them, and thus no analogy between the perspectives of the transactors. Only units of the same (analogic) order can be exchanged. Unit worth is consequently the product of pairing, and the outcome of that relationship.

Exchangeability turns, then, not on a ratio between things – so much coal or sago expressed as a percentage of so much iron or fish – but on the substitution of units – a shell for a shell, a bride for bridewealth, fish for sago – conceived, to follow Mimica's argument, as body parts, from bodies (persons) which, to follow my own argument, must first be construed as partible.

Substitution

I have referred both to acts and to perspectives. The substitution at issue is equally conceivable as the displacement of one set of relationships or persons by another.

A unit is created in a dual manner. It may be detached from a whole for which it stands as homologue (the numerical value of 'one' standing for 'many'). In being singled out, severed, handed over or otherwise made transactable, it carries value by reference to its origins in the acts of others and thus to relationships that lie beyond the immediate transaction. A gift indicating the wealth of the donor clan also indicates the clan's capacity to have attracted this wealth to themselves from elsewhere. At the same time, a unit is elicited by the presence of another unit. In this sense a gift also indicates the causative power of the relationship between the immediate exchange partners: power is measured in the success with which the gift does, or does not, elicit an analogy in a pairing or matching counterpart. These operations double on themselves in the Hagen *moka*. Every gift is a whole set divisible into two. (a) The major component repays or literally matches ('marries') a previous debt (the counterpart that is also the origin of the relationship between the partners). (b) The second part 'on top'/'on the back' is conceptualised as the *moka* component proper – it has value in relation to the whole gift, for its incremental status is established by the size of the previous debt, but is simultaneously a test of elicitory power. It is the 'match' of further expectations, and here its value will lie in what the partner will eventually match it with. The point is that the gift realises two sets of relationships, namely a past origin and a present cause, or what makes it part of a person and what makes it detachable.

A similar dualism is seen in reproductive kin exchanges, and even, perhaps, in the market strategies of vegetable sellers, who would throw away produce or take it home at the end of the day rather than sell at a price that would diminish its value through an inappropriate match (Modjeska, 1985: 156–6). The vendor's produce is to be extracted from her by the buyer, who is the cause of her selling, but as long as it is in her possession, its origin in other relationships remains.

Where origins and causes rest in different social identities, to substitute one item for another is to substitute causes for origins, and thus displace one set of relationships by another. In the case of gift exchange, a valuable seen to be the outcome of one set of relations (a previous partnership or household labour) is redefined as the outcome of another set (the currently eliciting partner). A sister as the product of the wealth exchanged between her senior kin becomes a wife as a result of exchanges between affines: the groom's wealth displaces the bridewealth that was given for her mother. The daughter was, we might say, that original wealth in another form, the bridewealth given for her its outcome in further form. A comparison of an entity with its origin (the daughter and the relationships which constitute her) becomes converted into a fresh set of relationships (the wife extracted by her husband's clan). The comparability between them is established at the point at which the transfer takes place.

In respect of people's ability to extract objects from one another, it follows that no formal difference hinges on items being similar or dissimilar in themselves. In this sense it is immaterial whether they are like or unlike. Objects invariably have a unique reference to social relations, are inevitably particularised by their origins, on the one hand, and by the intent with which they are elicited ('objectified') on the other. To extract a shell from an exchange partner, to cause him to yield, is the same process whether the mechanism for so extracting it is another shell or a traded axe. Insofar as value lies in what things reveal about people's acts, what is compared are people's capacities (cf. Munn, 1986: 8).

Extraction depends on perceived parity between the transactors such that the perspectives and expectations of each are focused on the one object, as for example between bride givers and bride takers. Each replicates the interest of the other in the transaction, but by the same token are differentiated from each other by virtue of the relationship. Each is also put into a position of yielding a part of him or herself. The capacity of the person to so detach a part is the capacity to see oneself in another form: to see clan sisters in terms of bridewealth, to see an axe as a pack of salt. Thus substitutability is elicited in the presentation of an item from another origin (the part of another person). To force a situation in which a part that is attached to one is reconceptualised as belonging to another may lead to much juggling of respective claims to power in the calculation over what is, or is not, a fit match. But the final reckoning can only appear as a match.

Each act (or relationship) can be compared only to another specific act (relationship): these child payments for that conception and childbirth; these fish for that sago. This childbirth (fish) does not guarantee that child payment (sago). Rather, the value of one item is necessarily made visible through the other: child payments are childbirth in the form of wealth, sago is a form of fish. It is that substitution which turns an item into an 'object', and does so through visibly presenting its counterpart in a specific shape. The same conceptual process occurs whether a relationship (as between the parents of a child) is given concrete form in exchange items (childbirth payments) or one item (fish) matched by another (sago). The difference to us is that in the former case an immaterial relationship is realised in the payments, a 'symbolic' matching of two orders of things, whereas in the latter one material item simply substitutes for another. But there is no more or less magic to the idea that sago is the form that fish takes for the Sawos and Iatmul traders, than there is to the idea, frequently enough imagined in anthropological discourse, that a relationship may be symbolised by an artefact.

Items in themselves, then, carry no guarantee of equivalence, not even two identical looking pigs. For in terms of particular social relations, in reference to cause and origin, no two things are qualitatively equivalent. This pig was reared by that partner, that by another. Rather, they are made equivalent units in the process of the substitution of relations. We might think of this unity as a reification, the aesthetic form which comparison takes.

Consequently units are always particular analogues and the outcome of particular coercions. No generalised equation is posited, any more than a clan's collective display on the ceremonial ground as 'one man' implies some regular computation, that there must be a required number of men to make up the homology. In fact, any number of men may compose one man; the question is not how many ones make up 20 or 30 or whatever, but how many ones make up (the right) one.[8] And any quantity, size, condition of transacted items may be agreed upon as satisfying the requirement of 'one bridewealth' or 'one pig'. What the oneness reifies is the capacity of the clan to bring outside its internal strength or, in the case of the transacted item, the coercive ability of the partner to elicit and detach the item he can match with his own.

The agreement to exchange (one gift for one gift) is an agreement to compare, through their respective displacement, the powers and capacities of persons, what each party has within and what their other relationships are composed of. There are recognised strategies for keeping back items to produce at the right moment, for claiming to have wiped oneself clean, for what it will take to persuade someone – or get away with extortion. For no social equality is implied in the agreement: only the formal equivalence of each partner as an agent about to act.[9] Uncertainty is reinforced at every stage. Far from exchange relations providing some secure integrative framework, they problematise interactions by challenging persons to decompose themselves, to make internal capacities external.

This returns us to the proposition of the barter model, that the focus of interest in gift exchange is the respective standing of the transactors. Yet what people exchange is always a totality: one perspective for another; your view of my assets for my view of yours. Thus are persons and objects created. And thus the only possible quantity at issue is one. We may speak of a ratio, but if so it is one of an otherwise unquantifiable magnitude – the act of another agent as a measure of oneself as an agent.[10] The difference is qualitative.

One's own acts are returned, then, *in another form* – my bringing fish to market for the sago you laboured to prepare. What is at issue is how the act will reappear, the form its objectification will take. For the return item is never a simple reflection of the original. It always comes back to oneself from another social source, and in that sense qualitatively enlarged or diminished in the process.

NOTES

Pnina Werbner challenged me to produce a non-functionalist analysis of value in gift exchange; Nancy Munn's *The Fame of Gawa* would actually have saved me the trouble if I had read it earlier! I appreciate the stimulus of Arjun Appadurai's chapter, of Deborah Gewertz's account and her subsequent criticism of my argument, Alfred Gell's letting me read his draft paper, and of correspondence with Christopher Gregory, Yadran Mimica and Daniel Miller. Discussions following presentations at the Departments of Anthropology in Cambridge, Durham and Edinburgh were very helpful, and I am particularly grateful to Jane Fajans and Terence Turner. I thank Andrew Strathern for his extensive comments on a previous draft. Finally, I could not have read Robert Foster's paper, *Value Without Equivalence: Exchange and Replacement in Melanesian Society* earlier, but it caps (and refines) this chapter nicely.

  1 Gell (this volume) disputes gift exchange as a universal feature of Melanesian cultures. His argument underlines radical internal differences between different Melanesian societies of the kind Godelier (1986) has also adumbrated. Indeed, I find provocative his suggestion that kinship arrangements such as practised by

Umeda have closer affinities to those systems described by Collier and Rosaldo (1981) as brideservice regimes than to those bridewealth regimes which I have taken as indicative of gift economies (cf. M. Strathern, 1985). One difference turns on the extent to which items symbolise human values – whether or not wealth can move against persons (Umeda perform services for one another, Gell argues, but do not commute obligations into payments). However, I find the self-evident value he accords commodities a puzzle. I do not see how the mere appearance of 'commodities' on people's horizons can account for them becoming a model for the creation of objects. Only a barter model of value would give priority to the idea of things as patent models for representing persons which could dispense with any concomitant idea of persons (or parts of persons) as potentially substitutable for one another. To my mind, there would have to be an enabling condition in the constitution of persons that allowed the commodity to be captured as a metaphor for reproductive exchange.

2 In my terminology, the 'personification' of things in a gift economy is tantamount to objectification, that is, to making visible people's relationships with one another and thus themselves as persons (objects) in the regard of others. We may call 'reification' the aesthetic constraints – the forms and implicit conventions – through which such an appearance of objects (persons) is accomplished. I regard this as more satisfactory than earlier formulations (for example M. Strathern, 1984).

3 My Highlands-centric reading gains some support from Munn's account of Gawan *kula* in the Massim. 'The control embedded in possession of a shell includes not simply Ego's ability to get others to act in ways that carry out his own will, but also his capacity for becoming the focus of the attempts of others to get him to act as *they* wish' (1983: 278, original emphasis).

4 *Apropos* the *kula*, Munn (1983: 283) writes: 'Although men appear to be the agents in defining shell value, in fact, without shells, men cannot define their own value; in this respect, shells and men are reciprocally agents of each other's value definition.'

5 My examples are highly selective. Other Melanesian systems are based on the location of body parts in serial progression, the route from the fingers, to the wrist, arms, chest, and down the other side, culminating in a total set or 'person' or cycle.

6 Lancy and Strathern (1981: 784) give a Pidgin example: K50 may be summated as 'one bicycle' or a *wil-wil*, a unity (50) made up of two parts (wheels, or K25). (K = *Kina*, at that time roughly equivalent to the Australian dollar).

7 A point which holds even for a pair of same-sex siblings, nevertheless differentiated by their names (and minds) (Lancy and Strathern, 1981: 783).

8 Thus in Baruya salt–pig transactions, we are told that 1 male pig = 2–3 salt bars, and 1 female pig = 3–6 salt bars (Godelier, 1977: 140). That is, it takes 3 salt bars *to make a 'one'* in order to elicit one (male) pig, as it takes a pig of a particular size and health to make 'one' in order to elicit salt.

9 It is unfortunate that in English the notion of an exchange has positive implications. Relative magnitude may be evinced in coercion and domination. Deborah Gewertz writes (pers. comm.) 'A calculation of ratio in the exchange of fish to sago is only a way of attempting to demonstrate which side has more power, more efficacy as agent.' She then adds in commentary on the above

argument: 'Any statement of relative magnitude – of augmentation or dim-
inution, of more or less – carries with it, I think, an implication of the
calculation and specification of ratio.'

10 It will be appreciated that my argument is very close to Munn's (for example
1986: 272: value production and creation is the 'rendering of the self in terms
of the favourable attitude of a significant other'; it has to be one or the other
– there is no neutral reflection).

REFERENCES

Appadurai, Arjun, 1986, Introduction: commodities and the politics of value. In
   The Social Life of Things: Commodities in Cultural Perspective, (ed.) A.
   Appadurai, Cambridge: Cambridge University Press.
Collier, J. F. and Rosaldo, M. Z., 1981, Politics and gender in simple societies. In
   Sexual Meanings, (eds.) S. B. Ortner and H. Whitehead, New York: Cam-
   bridge University Press.
Epstein, T. Scarlett, 1982, *Urban Food Markets and Third World Development: the
   Structure of Producer–Seller Markets*, London: Croom Helm.
Errington, Frederick and Gewertz, Deborah, 1987, The remarriage of Yebiwali: a
   study of dominance and false consciousness in a non-western society. In
   Dealing with Inequality, (ed.) M. Strathern, Cambridge: Cambridge Uni-
   versity Press.
Gewertz, D. B., 1983, *Sepik River Societies. A Historical Ethnography of the
   Chambri and their Neighbors*, New Haven: Yale University Press.
Gillison, G., 1980, Images of nature in Gimi thought. In *Nature, Culture and
   Gender*, (eds.) C. MacCormack and M. Strathern, Cambridge: Cambridge
   University Press.
Godelier, M., 1977 (1970), 'Salt money' and the circulation of commodities among
   the Baruya of New Guinea. In *Perspectives in Marxist Anthropology*,
   Cambridge: Cambridge University Press.
   1986 (1982), *The Making of Great Men. Male Domination and Power among the
   New Guinea Baruya*, Cambridge: Cambridge University Press.
Gregory, C. A., 1982, *Gifts and Commodities*, London: Academic Press.
Healey, Christopher J., 1985, New Guinea inland trade: transformation and
   resilience in the context of capitalist penetration. In *Recent Studies in the
   Political Economy of Papua New Guinea Societies*, (eds.) D. Gardner and N.
   Modjeska, *Mankind*, 15, spec. issue.
Humphrey, Caroline, 1985, Barter and economic disintegration. *Man* (NS), 20,
   48–72.
Lancy, D. F. and Strathern, A., 1981, 'Making twos': pairing as an alternative to
   the taxonomic mode of representation. *American Anthropologist*, 83, 773–95.
Mauss, Marcel, 1954 (1925), *The Gift: Forms and Functions of Exchange in Archaic
   Societies*, London: Cohen and West.
Mimica, Yadran, 1988, *Intimations of Infinity. The Cultural Meanings of the Iqwaye
   Counting System and Number*, Oxford: Berg.
Modjeska, C., 1985, Exchange value and Melanesian trade reconsidered. In *Recent
   Studies in the Political Economy of Papua New Guinea Societies*, (eds.) D.
   Gardner and N. Modjeska, *Mankind*, 15, spec. issue.
Mosko, M., 1983, Conception, de-conception and social structure in Bush Mekeo

culture. In *Concepts of Conception*, (ed.) D. Jorgensen, *Mankind*, 14, spec. issue.

Munn, Nancy D., 1983, Gawan *kula*: spatiotemporal control and the symbolism of influence. In *New Perspectives on the Kula*, (eds.) E. and J. Leach, Cambridge: Cambridge University Press.

1986, *The Fame of Gawa. A Symbolic Study of Value Transformation in a Massim (Papua New Guinea) Society*, Cambridge: Cambridge University Press.

Ollman, B., 1976 (1971), *Alienation. Marx's Conception of Man in Capitalist Society*, Cambridge: Cambridge University Press.

Parry, Jonathan, 1986, *The gift*, the Indian gift and the 'Indian gift'. *Man* (NS), 21, 453–73.

Pospisil, Leonard, 1963, *Kapauku Papuan Economy*, New Haven: Yale University Publications in Anthropology, 67.

Sahlins, Marshall, 1972, *Stone Age Economics*, Chicago: Aldine.

Schindelbeck, Markus, 1980, *Sago bei den Sawos*, Basel: Museum für Volkerkunde.

Strathern, Andrew, 1977, Mathematics in the *Moka, Papua New Guinea Journal of Education*, 13, 16–20.

Strathern, Andrew and Strathern, Marilyn, 1969, Marriage in Melpa. In *Pigs, Pearlshells and Women*, (eds.) R. M. Glasse and M. J. Meggitt, Englewood Cliffs: Prentice Hall.

Strathern, Marilyn, 1984, Subject or object? Women and the circulation of valuables in Highlands New Guinea. In *Women and Property, Women as Property*, (ed.) R. Hirschon, London: Croom Helm.

1985, Kinship and economy: constitutive orders of a provisional kind. *American Ethnologist*, 12, 191–209.

1988, *The Gender of the Gift*, Los Angeles and Berkeley: California University Press.

Strauss, Hermann (and M. Tischner), 1962, *Die Mi-kultur der Hagenberg Stämme*, Hamburg: Cram. de Gruyter.

Thomas, Nicholas, 1985, Forms of personification and prestations, *Mankind*, 15, 223–230.

Wagner, Roy, 1967, *The Curse of Souw*, Chicago: Chicago University Press.

1969, Marriage among the Daribi. In *Pigs, Pearlshells and Women*, (eds.) R. M. Glasse and M. J. Meggitt, Englewood Cliffs: Prentice-Hall.

Index